Policy Choices in Internal Conflicts

Governing Systems and Outcomes

Policy Choices in Internal Conflicts

Governing Systems and Outcomes

Editor

V.R. Raghavan

Published for

Centre for Security Analysis
Chennai, India

Vij Books India Pvt Ltd
New Delhi (India)

Published by

Vij Books India Pvt Ltd

2/19, Ansari Road, Darya Ganj
New Delhi - 110002
Phones: 91-11-65449971, 91-11- 43596460
Fax: 91-11-47340674
e-mail : vijbooks@rediffmail.com
web : www.vijbooks.com

Centre for Security Analysis
"9-B" Ninth Floor,
Chesney Nilgiri, 71, Ethiraj Salai,
Egmore, Chennai-600008
Tamil Nadu, India
+91-44-65291889
office@csa-chennai.org
www.csa-chennai.org

First Published : 2013

Paperback Edition 2015

Acknowledgement

The Centre for Security Analysis (CSA) has undertaken a three year research project **Internal Conflicts and Transnational Consequences** supported by the John D and Catherine T MacArthur Foundation. This volume is part of the ongoing project and its publication has been possible by the project grant.

Table of Contents

Foreword

The Project on Internal Conflicts & Transnational Consequences was conceptualised as an innovative exploration of the situation in four different states, each with its long history of internal conflicts. The four states of India, Nepal, Myanmar and Sri Lanka had over decades faced a situation in which ethnic groups seeking a different political disposition had challenged the state with armed uprisings. The decade's long conflicts had led to creating stake holders in the conflicts who were driven more by the consequences of the conflicts than by the original causes of the conflicts. This reversal of the cause – conflict – outcome model to conflict – consequences – continuing conflict offered a new, potentially rich and policy relevant area for analysis. The four states chosen faced the same kind of challenge – armed rebellion – but were governed by different governing systems. India is a democracy, Nepal was a monarchy, Myanmar was governed by a military Junta and Sri Lanka's democracy was a democracy substantially skewed in favour of and dominated by a Buddhist polity.

The project was conducted over three years in four countries. It involved -about 100 scholars with political, social, economic, and military backgrounds. During the process, CSA collaborated with seven think tanks from the four countries thus enriching the study with their expertise. The project produced eleven books which were reviewed in many newspapers and journals. The list of books is in the Appendix.

The conflict management or conflict resolution approaches used by the four states reveal insights into how such challenges can be met in future. Internal conflicts are endemic in most newly independent and developing states. Dealing with them not only requires an understanding of the major causes of conflicts but also anticipating the problems which can lead to the conflict continuing after it is formally ended. India, Nepal, Myanmar and

Sri Lanka have all experienced conflicts which continue in one form or another even after the peaceful or military termination of conflicts.

Post conflict scenarios depend in great measure on the approaches used by the state during the conflict. Generally there are four approaches used by all states. The first is the security approach in which police or armed police are used to contain conflict. Second is the military approach in which the military might is utilised under, either with legal backing or without to eliminate or defeat the insurgents. Third, economic or development plans are used to offset the grievance of parties who have taken up arms. Last, a political accommodation of the demands of conflicting groups is sought. Quite often states have used multiple approaches simultaneously in varying intensity to find an end to the conflict. Given the reality of such conflicts mostly based on identity related causes, states need to address the challenge through accommodation with and amidst multicultural, multi-ethnic and multi-religious contexts.

Long running internal conflicts also impact on the economy and foreign relations of the states which are unable to find an end to internal conflicts. In other words, internal conflicts have serious external consequences. A state's legitimacy to rule, its accountability to international regimes, and its image as stable or weak entity comes under review, which in turn places the state and its leaders under pressures which contribute to the continuance of conflict. The use of military force to subdue or defeat the internal conflict is often seen as a quick solution to the problem. However, the continued use of military force over long periods creates its own dynamic of international opprobrium, human rights excesses, permanent alienation of population with the state, and the long term collateral damage of pitting the military against the population.

Involving the military in dealing with internal conflicts places immense pressures on the military hierarchy. The military in internal conflicts faces the 'trilemma' never being able to simultaneously achieve force protection, of being able to distinguish clearly between combatants and non combatants in the populace and the physical elimination of insurgents. The paradox of sub optimal operational choices creates adverse consequences for both the military and the political leadership.

A state must deal with internal conflicts within a legal frame work of its constitution. The legal dimensions of such measures and experience of the four states made in this volume provides a significant study. Maritime aspects of internal security in states with coastal geographies are another facet which has been examined in this collection of papers.

This volume, the last in the range of perceptive volumes, brings together the lessons, policy choices and options available to states dealing with internal conflicts. It also lists strategic and operational errors of judgments made by states. This volume will offer many insights based on the strategies adopted by the four conflict ridden states over decades. The readers in political, military, economic, foreign policy domains as well as the academia will find this volume of considerable value.

V. R. Raghavan
Lt. Gen. (Retd)
President
Centre for Security Analysis

Overview

K Srinivasan

There had not been many inter-state wars after World War II, a few exceptions being Arab-Israeli wars, Indo-Pakistan wars, Indo-China war, China-Vietnam war, the Korean war and the Falkland war. This is a comparative statement. While this study confines itself to internal conflicts in India, Myanmar, Nepal and Sri Lanka, there have been and are many internal wars going on in Afghanistan, Bangladesh, Pakistan and elsewhere in Southeast Asia, Africa and South America. The inter-state wars have been short. Of course they have caused immense harm to the economy and well-being of the concerned states. Nonetheless, such wars have also acted as catalyst to better internal cohesion and enhanced the national fervour and in some cases have contributed to the development in subsequent phases of respective nation's life. What have done more damage to the developing countries are the internal conflicts generally known as small wars. These small wars have been endemic to the developing countries and have become long drawn out wars. They have divided the societies, caused untold damage to the economy, institutions, governance and polity. Their consequences have been far reaching.

There have been many studies to understand the causes of such conflicts. The causes have been religious differences, ethnic divide, ideological differences, socio-economic and political aspirations. Linguistic issue has also played a role.[1] Often states have failed to understand the potential of such social ills to take timely action. Once the conflict gets intensified, the states rush to address the same, often in ad-hoc manner starting with the use of force. What drives any section of the population

---

[1] V R Raghavan, "Strategic Overview" in V R Raghavan ed., *Internal Conflicts: Military Perspective*, (New Delhi: Vij Books India Pvt Ltd, 2012), p. 20

within a country to develop a feeling of alienation and ill feeling towards the state and what accounts for the state's failure to respond with needed sensitivity and empathy? — Is there something lacking in the way 'the state' deals with its own people that makes them feel left out — People in crucial posts in the government can be fallible and vengeful.[2]

Many a time, the states in their over enthusiasm for nation building attempt to homogenise languages, religion, ethnicities, tradition and customs thus sowing seeds for conflict. Their inability to deal with pluralistic and multi-ethnic and multi-cultural societies have become the causes of the conflicts. India has recognised some of these issues well in time. It created states based on language. It has also created ethnicity based states in the Northeast with good intentions but resulting in newer problems. Amongst various causes, ethnicity or its extended version of identity politics is a major cause and many of the other grievances tend to be expressed through the ethnic prism. Such ethnic/identity politics is basically due to struggle for political and economic power which the state often denies even through the process of conflict management. In the Sri Lankan context, Jayadeva Uyangoda crystallises the cause of the conflict as contest for state power. He further adds that the non-negotiability of the question of state power in Sri Lanka was a consequence of the conflict.[3] This analysis of cause and consequence might as well hold good for almost all internal conflicts. This theory gives pointers to the policy makers as to why negotiations and peace talks get prolonged and internal conflicts go on for years. While many approaches like use of force, peace talks and developmental activities are adopted, the situation does not return to normalcy unless power sharing issues are addressed.

On 23 March 2013, the topics covered in this volume were presented to a select expert audience at Chennai. Very useful and meaningful comments were received during the discussions, followed by valuable comments through mail from the participants. The lack of economic development and employment was one major issue. This aspect was not part of the issues covered in the presentation and is not a subject to be analysed in this volume.

---

[2] B.S. Raghavan, *The Hindu Business Line*, Op-Ed Page, 25 March 2013

[3] Jayadeva Uyangoda, " Sri Lanka's Ethnic Conflict: Role of the State", in V R Raghavan ed., *Internal Conflicts: A Four State Analysis*, (New Delhi: Vij Books India Pvt Ltd, 2012), p. 241

However, while studying the internal conflicts, it is an important issue to be addressed. It is therefore pertinent here to mention a few points. During the course of the project, eminent experts were selected and tasked to study as to how far the lack of economic development was a cause and a consequence in each of the conflicts studied. These studies have been included in the volumes devoted to each of the six conflicts studied. It is interesting to note that lack of development and economic deprivation did not emerge as the main cause in any of the conflicts. In the case of Nepal, the deprivation and poverty by itself did not result in the conflict, but was fully used by the Maoists to get it expressed through prism of ethnicity by offering them ethnic based states/provinces in the proposed federal set up. In the case of Naxalism in India, it was brought to fore by the Naxals to project their ideology.

However, it is interesting to note that this aspect emerged as a major consequence of the conflicts, almost in every conflict. It is also interesting to note that economic aid packages seldom achieved the purpose fully while addressing the conflicts. In the Northeast India, it increased corruption. In Jammu & Kashmir, people became richer because of the conflict, not necessarily with the aid package but for other reasons. It was seen that extremist elements in Jammu & Kashmir and Northeast spurned such economic packages. The level of money being spent in the state by invisible sources including remittances by Kashmiri diaspora and subversive agencies, could be anybody's guess. If mounting expenditure on all these accounts is added, it is bound to be reflected in the incomes of the people. One such outlet of incomes is of the rich class which is reflected in an increase of vehicular traffic. Increasing liquidity is being used to land speculation and higher bank deposits. J&K bank is the fastest growing bank in the country. Its share value crossed Rs.1000 on Jan 1, 2011. The J&K Bank registered 36 percent growth in its deposits in September 2010, to Rs.16,329 crores from 12,041 crores a year ago. Credit deposit ratio of the banks in the State was 49.19 percent as against 70.26 percent observed in the whole country. Whatever, credit is released, most of it is outside the State. Thus J&K is perhaps the only state of the country which is exporting its capital.[4]

---

[4] Balraj Puri, "Politics and Inter-Regional Relation" in V.R. Raghavan ed, *"Conflict in Jammu & Kashmir: Impact on Polity, Society and Economy"*, (New Delhi: Vij Books India Pvt. Ltd., 2012), p.71

These conflicts linger on for years resulting in unforeseen consequences having long term adversarial effect. They destroy the economy, infrastructure and the environment. States are forced to step up expenditure in raising and maintaining police and armed forces. Development gets stalled. Societies get militarised and human rights affected. Achievement of millennium development goals (MDGs) remain a dream. Generations are born and brought up in conflict conditions that have not seen peace and thus are unable to visualise peaceful and cooperative societies. The life and routine in the conflict environment gets embedded into the collective psyche. Entrepreneurial groups and individuals tend to thrive in the given conditions. Even bureaucrats and politicians get used to the system and the status quo mentality takes over. This is a consequence which is very difficult to understand the depth to address. To address the conflict situations, nations tend to bring new laws with their own negative fallouts. The process of addressing the consequences thus creates new problems and become the drivers for the conflict to continue. Emergence of warlords in some areas and corruption are also part of the consequences. Many heads have also rolled due to such conflicts, e.g., removal of Monarchy in Nepal and arrest of the Army Commander in Sri Lanka.

The leftwing extremism in India is a unique one unlike the conflicts in Northeast India, Jammu & Kashmir or even the conflicts in Sri Lanka and Myanmar. Feudalism, lack of socio-economic development, unemployment and ideology angle of the Naxal movement makes it unique. As the problem extends across many states and districts, galvanising the efforts at the Centre, State and district levels is of paramount importance. The entrenched elements tend to perpetuate the status quo since they get a free run in collecting taxes, protection money and commissions from traders, transporters and contractors.

There is no ideal way of addressing the conflicts even if the causes are alike. In each case, the socio-political and cultural environment and geography demands innovative approaches to address the causes and consequences of internal conflicts. The State has to find a balanced way of addressing the causes and consequences.

The UN and the international communities have been working for poverty alleviation and associated problems. A good percentage of the population living in under-developed and developing countries have been affected by internal conflicts. These conflicts seriously affect the states' capacity to improve socio-economic conditions and achieve MDGs. While the UN has been working towards attaining MDGs, the developing countries by and large have been experiencing these serious human problems. Major developing nations though have expressed their concern for resolving the internal conflicts but have not contributed to resolving such conflicts affecting development. The fact, that one should not interfere in internal conflicts because of the issue of "Sovereignty" does not inspire a positive attitude by the international community. In South Asia, one exception is, Norway which tried to help Sri Lanka but failed not because of good intentions but because of the inability to gather international community support and the warring parties, the State and the LTTE. Major donor countries to Sri Lanka like Japan have remained mute. India, though being affected by similar problems has tried to help Nepal in reconciliation and resolving political differences of affected parties to go forward. The major powers who have supported UN efforts on attaining MDGs, have not tried in any way towards resolving the internal conflicts in a meaningful manner which would have helped the developing countries to attain MDGs. However, they have taken keen interest in resolving the conflict in the Balkans. Sri Lanka, Nepal and Myanmar have been left out. While these countries could have been helped by the international community, India did not need such help. One could see that what matters most for themselves is important but are not concerned by the countries suffering from poverty and unable to develop to achieve MDGs. Consequences of internal conflicts also have an impact across the borders to the neighbouring countries. India has helped Nepal to resolve their internal problems because internal conflict in Nepal directly affects India. Problems in other developing countries under study do not have a bearing on the developed nations. The conflicting parties in these countries must be anxious to express their rancour towards the powerful and developed nations for their apathy towards the unfortunate ones.

The CSA has done extensive studies of these conflicts and has published eleven volumes. These studies, apart from identifying the root causes, have emphasised on analysing the consequences since their adverse effect on nations are far more serious because of long drawn out nature. This volume attempts to identify and analyse the policy options, particularly of conflicts generated by the ethnic divide and political management of such conflicts. Legal regimes in four different governance systems have also been examined. The maritime security and the conflicts is another new dimension which has been studied.

In pluralistic, multi-ethnic and multi-cultural societies, nation building is a challenging exercise wherein due importance is to be given for individual and group identities and also to get them work together towards a common national identity. The solution lies in accommodating and not in assimilation – easier said than done.

Essential issues covered by the contributors in the chapters that follow are summarised in succeeding paragraphs.

Sudha Ramachandran in her paper examines the ethno-political conflicts in Sri Lanka, India's Northeast, Myanmar and Nepal. She draws from research studies conducted by CSA. She attempts to draw commonalities in these conflicts. She begins the paper with an overview of ethno-political conflicts in the four countries, providing a summary of various aspects of these conflicts, such as the role of the state in triggering conflicts, the evolution of the conflicts and their dynamics, the state's approach to dealing with conflict, etc. She then goes on to draw attention to similarities in these conflicts and finally makes some recommendations for the future course of action.

She describes these conflicts as ethno-political. By doing so she acknowledges political component of the conflict in addition to the ethnic dimension. The four countries under study are essentially pluralistic societies and have witnessed a surge in identity politics. The political elite in these countries have viewed this diversity a source for unrest which could result in disintegration of the nation state. It prompted them to set out on a process of nation-building that was often contentious as it raised in these plural societies difficult questions regarding the definition of the nation and its constituents, the relationship between state and religion, language etc. The political elites consolidated the nation-state through homogenization of the society through some variant of majoritarianism and centralization of power. They were willing to use coercion to homogenize the society.

Myanmar, Nepal and Sri Lanka constitutionally privileged one religion, language and ethnicity, that of the majority. The so called 'national integration' was unitary in its connotation to the effect the political elites reject federalism and embrace centralization of power to varying degrees. Among the four countries, India is the least centralized. In Sri Lanka and Myanmar, federalism is seen as the first step towards secession thereby denying devolution of meaningful power to excluded ethnic groups. As political elites in the four countries turned to homogenization and centralization to hold their diverse societies together, this approach triggered ethno-political conflict, with ethnic groups that are excluded from the political and economic power structure engaging in struggles against their respective states for recognition of their cultural, social and political rights, rights over land, and so on. The response of the states to these demands has in turn spurred groups to escalate demands and methods, sometimes resulting in armed struggles for separate states. Sudha underscores the centrality of the state in triggering and escalating the conflicts.

She observes that organizations and movements that emerged to protest the exclusion of ethnic groups were exclusionist themselves. If the state responded to ethnic diversity through homogenizing the population, the ethnic organizations sought to forge a unified identity by denying diversity within the group. The ethnic and nationalist organizations often become mirror images of the state - coercive, hegemonic and centralized – and this has severely weakened their struggle.

She noted a relationship between democracy and ethno-political conflicts. Electoral politics which encouraged mobilization, competition and conflict along ethnic lines triggered heightened ethnic activism and rise in ethno-political organizations as evident in Nepal. It gave a new lease of life to ethnic identities. However, authoritarian rule gave an impetus to violent eruption of ethnic activism as democratic and political channels for articulation of demands and grievances are blocked. This led the aggrieved groups to pick up arms to press their demands.

Ethno-political conflicts in these countries are protracted in nature with many lasting for decades. Myanmar and India are home to some of the world's longest running ethnic insurgencies. She points out that the governments avoided addressing the underlying causes of the conflict and the issues that fuelled them subsequently. They also failed to tackle the conflict in all its complexities, respond and recognize its changing dynamics as well as tackle consequences, which often fuel escalation of violence. The state plays in the emergence of ethno-political conflicts and in their proliferation, protraction, intensification and often violent manifestation. Government response to these conflicts has been a 'carrot and stick approach' – use of coercive with extension of economic development packages to the restive region. They have been willing to use extreme force, including deployment of the armed forces, special legislations and giving police and army with extraordinary powers to stamp out secessionist aspirations and insurgencies but also, against non-violent articulation of demands. Governments have also sought to develop the economies of conflict affected regions by extending aid packages, building infrastructure and taking steps to jump-start the economy. She points out that enhancing employment opportunities and development play an important role in blunting grievances; it breeds dependency instead of building local capacity. This is largely because development encouraged in conflict zones is a private sector-led business model which accentuates poverty, destroying local environment through aggressive resource extraction and deepening the existing economic divide. Besides, the economic development initiated in conflict zones is rarely owned and led by locals.

India has pursued political solutions with some seriousness. However, the way it has carried out negotiations or reached settlements has generated new conflicts and paved the way for a return to violence. Sri Lanka, Nepal and Myanmar are reluctant to concede even minimum political demands. Myanmar's 'talks' with ethnic groups has been more in the nature of striking business deals with leaders rather than sustained dialogue towards resolution.

She recommends that states should adopt an approach that allows an individual to define and articulate his/her identity in any way he/she chooses so long as he/she carries out his/her obligations and duties of being a citizen of India or Sri Lanka or Myanmar, he/ she should be able to define and articulate his/her identity as she chooses. Instead of homogenizing the society states must become inclusive and more open to power-sharing arrangements. They must be open to considering a repertoire of responses to ethno-political conflicts, including non-territorial arrangements that could, for instance, meet self-governance demands of scattered ethnic groups. She emphasizes on the need for meaningful dialogue which is inclusive and involves civil society, women's groups, trade unions, religious leaders, etc. A sustainable peace predicates a bottom-up process and the building of peace constituencies among the people. South Asia's experience shows that peace accords that follow inclusive peace processes are more likely to succeed. She adds that preventing ethno-political conflicts from turning violent is not the responsibility of the state alone. Civil society can play an important role in preventing clashes between various ethnic groups.

Sahadevan in his paper analyses the strategies of managing ethnic conflicts in four countries—India, Nepal, Sri Lanka and Myanmar—and assesses their outcomes in a comparative perspective. Such a comparative analysis provides insights into the behaviour of state and non – state actors in the conflict situation. They are useful for theory-building and peace policy-making in divided societies which in turn help in formulating a set of broad policy recommendations on internal conflict management. He provides a conceptual analysis by defining 'internal conflict' and 'conflict management' and identifying the strategies and process of peacemaking. The internal conflicts are categorised on the basis of nature, parties involved, goals and dimensions. Each of these categories is dealt in depth. Based on this categorisation certain characteristics of internal conflicts are highlighted. First, state is a principal actor in internal conflicts with an objective to maintaining institutional structures or preserving its ideology or promoting the interests of a particular community with which the state identifies itself. Secondly, internal conflicts involve groups with strong ethnic, political and communal interests as parties, which support or oppose the state. Thirdly, greed and grievance form a major factor in determining the process of conflict. Lastly, internationalization is a dynamic feature of an internal conflict process.

He points out that internal conflicts have a predictable trends when it comes to initial and intermediate (escalation) phase, but often the final phase (termination/end) is very obscure. It may either get settled by means of negotiations/peacemaking or continue under different leadership who were excluded from the peace process. In this context, a need for all inclusive peacemaking approach is highlighted. However, in reality, such an approach has limitations and constraints as interests of each and every group cannot be accommodated. Moreover, groups very often fail to reach a common framework of solution. Under such situations, conflicts tend to continue in one form or the other till a solution based on mutual consent/compromise is agreed upon. On the other hand, when the use of coercion dominates the state policy, peacebuilding efforts are relegated. This often leads to intractability of conflicts. The analysis of the management of internal conflicts in the four countries under study corroborates this argument.

Different strategies in conflict management adopted by the government are discussed at length. In conventional conflict management strategy, political negotiations between government and warring groups are often adopted. But in many internal conflicts the support of external parties who form a critical component of dissidents power structure play a vital role in initiation, sustenance and termination of conflicts. This makes negotiation a very complex process. Measures to erode rebel's support base also assume importance in the strategies adopted by governments. Politico-economic measures undertaken by government involves economic development work in conflict afflicted areas, relief, rehabilitation and reconstruction measures for conflict affected population, protection of human rights, maintaining good civil – military relation and initiation of peace process.

Negotiating peace is far more difficult than waging a conflict due to some structural and functional attributes of a conflict. The process of negotiations are analysed in detail and the conditions under which these negotiations become successful/unsuccessful are also explained. Sahadevan maintains that negotiated peace is better achieved when the function of the given conflict structure changes with the changing fortunes of the conflict and a third party controlled effective negotiation process leads to radical change in the objectives of the conflict.

While mapping the conflicts in South Asia, they have been categorised as ethnic and centralist conflicts. Ethnic conflicts chosen for the analysis are Naga and Assam conflicts (India), Sinhalese-Sri Lankan Tamil conflict (Sri Lanka), and ethnic insurgencies (including the Shan and Kachin ethnic groups) in Myanmar. The centralist conflicts chosen for the analysis here are: the Maoist insurgencies in Nepal and India, and the movement for democracy in Myanmar. Historical background and causes of the ethnic and centralist conflicts are covered extensively. Unlike the ethnic conflicts, the centralist conflicts have different sets of sources rooted or linked to the governance structure or system. He terms such conflicts as 'systemic conflicts'. All three centralist or systemic conflicts dealt here have originated essentially from one or more of such structural factors as deformity, lop-sidedness, malfunctioning, inefficiency, exclusion, etc. Based on the mapping exercise, a number of characteristics and dynamics of conflicts are deduced– power asymmetry, multiple warring groups in case of ethnic conflicts and except for Myanmar, all other conflicts have attained an internal war dimensions. He then goes on to give the conceptual delineation of internal wars and civil wars.

An assessment of strength and weakness of strategies of conflict management exercised by the governments of India, Nepal, Myanmar and Sri Lanka is made. The strategies used by these governments are coercion, ceasefire, ending/seeking of external support, development work, political negotiations, divide and engage and unilateral political measures in case of Sri Lanka and Myanmar are extensively discussed. Many of these strategies are adopted simultaneously or one after the other depending on the conflict situation. A government desirous of achieving a negotiated settlement has always used coercion in conjunction with other strategies. Coercion invariably remains the first and foremost strategy of all governments. It is a common government strategy; the difference being some governments used it at a moderate level to push the rebels to accept a negotiated deal. Others have applied it excessively to achieve a military victory. From the time a government uses coercion till it is able to start negotiations, a shift in strategies is always possible. The purpose of each strategy is largely determined by the concerned government's conflict goals, response and strategies of rebel groups and power relations between the adversaries. If the use of military coercion and other non-military strategies work to strengthen the governmental position vis-à-vis rebels, reflecting in the increase in power asymmetry in favour of the former, it can either try to take advantage of the ground reality to achieve an honourable settlement or suspend a negotiation process and deny negotiated peace or impose a settlement virtually from a position of strength.

The analysis of conflict management strategies highlights a few interesting points. First, there are two main clusters of strategies, which the governments have adopted. One cluster includes multiple strategies that are much common to most of the governments. The strategies forming this cluster are military coercion, ceasefire agreement, ending or seeking external role, development work, divide and engage rebels and, finally, political negotiations. Successive Indian governments have pursued the strategies in this cluster invariably in all the conflicts except in the Maoist insurgency. In spite of the enormous strategic gains made from the consistent use of military and non-military strategies over the years, India has developed a greater commitment to negotiated settlement than to military victory. Nepal and Sri Lanka have pursued the strategies from the same cluster, but the difference between the two and also in comparison with India is that Sri Lanka pursued all the strategies without committing itself to a negotiated settlement. Thus, its main objective has been to gain relative strategic advantage so that, in a situation marked by greater asymmetry of power relations between the government and the rebels, a negotiated settlement is considered as irrelevant or unnecessary. In Nepal, the government could not take a similar approach; it had to pursue political negotiations seriously as a preferred strategy mainly because the Maoists had denied it strategic advantages in the internal war. The other cluster includes strategies such as coercion, ceasefire agreement, ending or seeking external support and finally, unilateral political measures. Political negotiations do not figure in this cluster. Myanmar has largely followed the strategies listed in this cluster to demonstrate that both the military junta and military-controlled regime have not developed a preference for negotiated peace. This raises a question, linking the nature of the state and the pattern of conflict management. The different experiences of peace-making in the conflict situations underline the fact that the nature of the state system is a crucial factor in the conflict management process. Both the chosen strategies and their eventual outcomes are determined largely by the nature of state that participates in conflict. Myanmar has laid more emphasis on ending conflicts militarily rather than resolving them through political negotiations, since the autocratic or semi-democratic regimes in the country are least bothered about national and international opinion. On the other hand, evasiveness of Sri Lanka in its commitment to peace even after securing a decisive military victory lies in the illiberal nature of the state and the majoritarian framework within which its ethnic policies are decided.

Expecting an illiberal democracy to produce liberal or positive peace is a difficult proposition. Peace-making record in India is better than other countries. The government has shown deep interest in a negotiated peace and less determination to achieve a military end of any conflict. Better peace-making record does not mean that the quality of peace made in India is better than what other liberal democracies elsewhere have produced. Positive peace is hard to establish even in India.

The outcomes of the conflict management strategies are listed as negative peace, peace with disorder, and persistence of violent conflict. Negative peace means 'absence of direct violence', a condition in which there is no active, organized violence. Further, negative peace can be categorized into stable and unstable conditions. Stable negative peace denotes a condition in that there are no immediate prospects for return of violence. Negative peace is stable in the ethnic conflicts in India's Nagaland and Sri Lanka, and the centralist conflict in Myanmar; it is unstable in the ethnic conflicts in Myanmar and India's Assam. Peace is restored in Nepal, but what marks the post-conflict situation is a durable disorder. The stakeholders are unable to agree on the process and mechanism to create new order in the country. There is bitter contest for power and in the process, the agenda of constitution-making has been politicized, denigrated and delayed. The Maoist conflict in India and some of the ethnic insurgencies in Myanmar persist without an end; even those conflicts where there are peace processes and prevailing negative peace conditions (such as the Naga and Assam ethnic conflicts, and the centralist conflict in Myanmar), post-conflict as a much desired condition appears to be a distant dream. In all these, there is a missing category viz. positive peace. It denotes more than mere absence of violence; it is a condition in which diversity, human emancipation, dignity, equality, democracy, empowerment of people, non-exploitative social structures, etc. are established and sources of structural violence are eliminated. It underlines the establishment of peace with justice.

The analyses of strategies of managing conflicts in these four countries have yielded unclear and mixed outcomes. From the comprehensive assessment, of the conflict management strategies and their outcomes, a number of trends are identified: First, use of coercion is intense and widespread; both adversaries wilfully employ this strategy without worrying much about its consequences for the society and polity. It reflects their deep commitment to their mutually incompatible goals and the value they attach to them. Second, like the conflicts, some of the peace processes are also protracted in nature. They continue as normal events even when conflicts are seen to be persisting. Third, political negotiations, wherever or whenever take place, do not entail generally the higher political leadership, but are between the top or middle level rebel leaders and officials or second-rank political leaders from the government's side. Fourth, external influence or role is a factor in most of the internal conflicts, but the direct participation of influential states in peace-making or conflict management is unusual. In other words, most of the parties do not entertain or even discourage any form of third party role in peace-making. There is no one best policy or strategy for managing internal conflicts. Each conflict is specific in nature although some of the characteristics are common to all conflicts. In the absence of any best policy or strategy, it is important to emulate the available best practices in conflict management. Such an approach should combine coercion with a set of non-coercive instruments and processes, including political negotiations. There are different viewpoints on the extent of use of coercion: some argue for an excessive application of military coercion, to such an extent that a rebel group is *forced* to end violence and exterminated or allowed to survive to negotiate or accept a peace deal. Others emphasize on minimal use of coercion, to such an extent that a militant group is *willing* to hold political negotiations and *accept* a reasonable peace deal based on mutual compromise. Coercion should just be used as an instrument of *facilitating* a peace process rather than a *means* to end a conflict or *impose* an unfair settlement. In this regard, credibility, commitment and sincerity of governments are of importance. A government seeking to use coercion should be equally committed to find a negotiated political settlement.

A peace process should be seen as a 'continuum' in engagement of all stakeholders. It does not just end with a political deal, but proceeds further to transform the society and polity. If it is so, there are possibilities for more than one deal in any internal conflict. He argues that prevention of conflict is a better strategy for the state than managing it subsequently.

Geeta Madhavan in her paper analyses the legal regimes adopted to contain internal conflicts and the role of the judiciary in these countries. The paper also highlights how the judiciary, in some cases, has been subjected to the directions of the executive and thereby rendered inept and such actions have led to the complete loss of confidence by the people. The military coup in 1962 escalated ethnic conflicts in Burma. Human rights violations under the military regime increased and in turn intensified the conflicts. The successive military regimes have consistently dealt with the on-going insurgencies with absolute ruthlessness. During the regime of State Law and Order Restoration Council (SLORC) judiciary was merged with the legislative body. The judiciary was also kept under the executive as it fell within the control of the Ministry of Home Affairs. Thus any law passed by the executive could not be tested for arbitrariness and therefore there was no accountability of the government. The restrictive legal system continued under subsequent Constitutions. The 2008 Constitution did not improve the legal systems or empower the judicial machinery. Article 20 (b) states that the Defence Services has the right to "independently administer and adjudicate all affairs of the armed forces". This places the armed forces above the law and leaves them unquestionably powerful. Article 20 (c) gives the power to the executive administration, which is primarily in the hands of the military, to do all such acts that are required in "safeguarding the non-disintegration of the Union, the non-disintegration of the national solidarity and the perpetuation of the sovereignty". Therefore the military junta is given unlimited power, underlining the fact that the judiciary serves as an arm of the military rule. The 2008 Constitution does not consider the diversity and gives the military clear monopoly and supremacy in every aspect of governance. The 2010 elections which were held as the Fifth Step toward democratization resulted in very few positive changes in the structures of the government.

The legal system in Nepal in the early days was pluralistic law with elements of civil, common, customary law and religious dictums. The Muluki Ain (1854) a compendium of ancient Hindu sanctions and customary laws modeled on British and Indian codes was revised in 1963. Over a period of time, more royal edicts and proclamations were added to it and some piecemeal legislation was also incorporated to create a corpus of laws termed as Ain Sangraha. This remained the substantive law till 1991. Thereafter, the political uncertainty and the eruption of Maoist insurgency had a telling impact on legal system of the country. In 2005, King declared Emergency and assumed all the executive powers. The King suspended several provisions of the Constitution including the freedom of speech and expression and the right to privacy. The right to preventive detention was revoked along with the freedom of the press. The suspension of fundamental rights and the severe curtailments of civil liberties did not augur well for the political stability of Nepal.

Following the ceasefire (2006) between the rebels and the State, elections were held in 2008. New government was installed in Kathmandu and a constitution was to be drafted to guide the nation which had abolished monarchy and adopted the facets of republican structure. However, owing to the difference among the various political parties over issues of form of federalism, the drafting of the new constitution was stalled. There is an urge to ensure that the new Constitution will enshrine the independence of the judiciary. In the past the judiciary was influenced by the autocratic regime and manipulated and corrupted by the system. The current problems with the judiciary in Nepal are: the pendency of cases before various courts, the prolonged time frame for trials and the inordinate delays in delivering judgments. During the state of emergency declared by the King in 2005, the judicial system became subordinate to the King and its powers were altered. Therefore, presently the top priority is to provide a judicial system that assures inclusiveness, accountability and accessibility.

In the bid to tackle the Maoist rebels the Royal Nepalese Army was invested with wide ranging powers and the lack of accountability of the military led to abuse of power for personal gains. Protracted insurgency with associated state of abuse of laws between 1996 and 2006 led to the criminal justice system being severely undermined. During the state of emergency in 2005, civil and political rights were suspended. Subsequent to the peoples' uprising and the Comprehensive Peace Agreement, the House of Representatives was restored. Some of the major changes sought to be carried out by the Interim Parliament in 2008 in the administrative and legal systems were: the protection of individual rights, transparency and communication to the people of the intention and working of the government, reviews and accountability to restore the confidence of the people, reform and transformation of institutions and enhancement of powers of the constitutional institutions.

She points out that drafting a new Constitution and adapting to a new legal system under it would be major challenge for the political leadership of Nepal. The jurists and law makers have called for an integrated system of the judiciary. Although the severity of the conflict situation may have abated, the damage it has caused to the judicial system needs purposeful restoration of the institution. The failure of the judiciary to deliver quick and equitable justice has left the people with no recourse to basic rights. Controversies in appointment of judges, charges of widespread corruption, dismissals and promotions of judges in arbitrary manner has underlined the unfairness in the system and questioned the credibility of the legal structures. She recommends a monitoring system be adopted that not only manages the resources and deals with issues and controversies, but also ensures that the judiciary enjoys the support of the executive branch of the government to function independent of the executive and legislative bodies. The political instability that prevails in the state has done untenable damage to the legal system and the judiciary and it is necessary to create to a stable Nepal that the legal and judicial structures are strengthened.

The three decades long conflict in Sri Lanka damaged permanently many of the structures of the government including the judiciary and the legal systems which were severely eroded by the onslaught of the conflict. Two sets of laws - Public Security Ordinance No.25 of 1947 and the Prevention of Terrorism Act of 1979 - were used by the government to tackle the violent activities that took place during the early days of insurgency and the subsequent civil war in Sri Lanka. Both the emergency laws severely limited the jurisdiction of the courts in Sri Lankan. This was seen as a failure of the Supreme Court to protect constitutional and human rights in Sri Lanka. The Supreme Court did not play any role in constraining the powers of the security forces nor in protecting the rights of the minorities. The ability of the Sri Lankan judiciary to adjudicate in a fair and free manner on sensitive matters and secure political and basic civil rights within the rule of law was severely compromised. The judiciary also failed to protect minority rights and social and cultural rights. The 1972 Constitution, gave the President unrestricted control of the judiciary. The Parliament and the Cabinet Ministers were ranked over the judiciary. All judicial review of executive and administrative actions was terminated thereby curtailing judicial independence. Seventeen sets of regulations were passed on divergent topics dealing with terrorist activities, high security zones, special administrative arrangements etc. The 17th Amendment of 2001 detailed the formation of the Constitutional Council to limit the presidential power over the judiciary but successive presidents ignored the constitutional council and by the powers vested by the emergency regulations kept the judiciary under check and deprived of its ability to function independently.

From the period 1983 to 2001 (except for a five month period) an uninterrupted state of emergency had existed in Sri Lanka. During this period there were no guarantees of personal security and no redress against arbitrary state violence. Even after the end of civil war in 2009, the situation has not changed much as the government and the security forces still enjoy far reaching powers under the Prevention of Terrorism (Temporary Provisions) Act of 1979 and other laws and regulations permitting long detention periods. The repeal of the emergency law does not have any effect for those already in detention, as it does not change the detention practices. Despite repealing of emergency, the government and the security forces will continue to operate as before and without legal authorization. Though the conflict has ended, an air of suspicion that the independence and the powers off the judiciary will not be restored and the legal machinery is still not in a position to secure to all the people fair and equitable justice lurks.

The militant activities and separatist movements and insurgencies in several parts of India have led to different legislations over a period of time. The earliest legislation to deal with the Naxal uprising in the nascent stage was The West Bengal (Prevention of Violent Activities) Act of 1970 passed by the West Bengal government. In Jharkhand, the Prevention of Terrorism Act, now repealed, was used for the arbitrary detention of hundreds of persons. The Special Public Protection Act, which came into force in March 2006, is a vague and overly broad law that allows detention of up to three years for "unlawful activities." The term is so loosely defined in the law that it threatens fundamental freedoms set out by the Indian constitution and international human rights law, and could severely restrict the peaceful activities of individuals and civil society organizations. The law also criminalizes any support given to Naxalites, with no defence given for acting under duress. Thus, persons whom the Naxalites force to provide assistance are subject to detention under the ordinance.

With regard to the Northeast India, she examines the significance and applicability of the Armed Forces (Special Powers) Act (AFSPA) passed by the Parliament of India in 1958. Under this Act, security forces are given wide ranging powers to conduct operations after an area is declared disturbed. While AFSPA gives the armed forces wide powers to shoot, arrest and search for "aiding civil powers", it requires that individuals apprehended in operations along with equipment should be handed over by security forces to the nearest civilian authorities. First applied to the North Eastern states of Assam and Manipur, the Act was amended in 1972 to extend to all the seven states in the north- eastern region of India viz., Assam, Manipur, Tripura, Meghalaya, Arunachal Pradesh, Mizoram and Nagaland. It was withdrawn by the Manipur government in some of the constituencies in August 2004, although the Government of India was not in favour of its withdrawal. The Act has been applied to Jammu and Kashmir since 1990. In the 1958 version of the AFSPA, the authority and power to apply and extend the Act vested in the states. Continued violence in these states led to the extension of this power to the Central Government. Although the enforcement of the AFSPA has resulted in allegations of incidents of arbitrary detention, torture, rape, and looting by security personnel, the legislation is justified by the Indian government on the plea that it is required to stop the Northeast states from seceding from the Indian Union. The antagonism of the populace against misuse of the power conferred under AFSPA has turned into a call for the repeal of AFSPA. The Jeevan Reddy Committee constituted by the government produced a Report that called for the repeal of the act, describing it as "too sketchy, too bald and quite inadequate." It went on to say "The Act, for whatever reason, has become a symbol of oppression, an object of hate and an instrument of discrimination and highhandedness. It is highly desirable and advisable to repeal this Act altogether, without, of course, losing sight of the overwhelming desire of the majority of the region that the Army should remain although the application of the Act should be removed." The committee report also felt that the removal of the application of the AFSPA could create political space for negotiations, dialogue, and peace in the Northeast. In December 2006, responding to the 'legitimate' grievances of the people of Manipur, Prime Minister Manmohan Singh declared that the Act would be amended to ensure it was 'humane' on the basis of the Jeevan Reddy Commission's report.

Along with the AFSPA, the Nagaland Security Regulations Act was enacted to put more sweeping powers in the hands of police and civilian authorities.

There has been no all-encompassing legislation to deal with internal conflict situations throughout the territory of India which could be applied uniformly and interpreted by courts consistently. She posits "the counter terrorist laws which are now used to deal with insurgencies and militant organizations due to their connections with terrorist groups are an absolute necessity for society and it should not be treated as political issues even if the implementation is questioned by human rights forums. Counter terrorist law should be viewed as an efficient response within the rule of law. It has been seen that the policy of military response to terrorism is short lived and does not have long term legal effect. Counter terrorist laws should be viewed as safeguards for collective safety and these should have no partisan or parochial considerations. It should be understood that measured infringement of individual freedom is not violation of fundamental right. It is the duty of the state to prevent the existence of destructive forces within its territorial jurisdiction which endanger the life and liberty of its citizens and the safety and security of other states. A State must defend its territorial integrity in order to protect its citizens and improve their living prospects. Towards this end the state can use military force to fight those who aim to secede or cause other harm to national interests. The paradox of using force against anti-state entities rests in the need for the state to abide by national and international laws of military force while the armed secessionist, terrorist or militant is under no obligation to do so.

India as a democracy introduced and used the maximum legal restraints while Myanmar had none. AFSPA whose enabling clauses were enacted to limit excesses by the military is criticized more for its long application than for its 'draconian' content. Nepal whose army was loyal to Monarch did not have specific laws enacted to meet the Maoist challenge. Sri Lanka today continues to be critiqued for human rights excesses by its army. Internal conflicts will continue to have to be dealt with military force. Application of military force cannot be with the objective of the destruction or elimination of anti-state elements. The use of military force needs essentially to be aimed for obtaining conditions in which a negotiated resolution of the conflict can take place. Towards this end legal safeguards for those conducting military operations and for citizens of the country from excesses should be ensured.

In the age of globalization and the post-globalization phases of economic development and growth, the "maritime-littoral" have emerged to be hubs of development and transportation linking the seas with the hinterland. Lawrence Prabhakar in his paper examines the internal conflicts from maritime perspective - coastal regions shape and influence the discourse of conflicts. The paper analyses internal security challenges and the maritime-littoral nexus 'securitizing' the persistent challenges and perils in the Maritime-littorals and the Exclusive Economic Zone in South Asia, the impact of globalization and maritime security and assess their impact on coastal communities.

The Maritime Regional Security Complex of South Asia envisages the geographical and the political interdependence of the region with West Asia, East Africa and Southeast Asia. The concept of regional security covers how security is clustered in geographically shaped regions. The analysis of the maritime regional security enables to assess the sources and roots of the various non-traditional challenges and threats and how internal conflicts are catalysed by the challenges that come from the adjoining regions through the maritime domain. Lawrence Prabhakar lists out four types of non-traditional challenges in the maritime domain that critically impacts South Asia: piracy and maritime terrorism, human trafficking on the high seas, trafficking of small arms and light weapons and trafficking of narcotics. While the traditional lanes of sea provide for the shipping and communication, there exit parallel networks of sea lanes that are used by pirates and smugglers. They use coastal cities to perpetuate violence and terror on the land as well as sea. Karachi, Mumbai, Jaffna, Chittagong, Maldives have all been sources and recipients of the above mentioned maritime based non-traditional challenges and threats. He briefly gives a profile of these coastal cities and how the maritime medium has been exploited in perpetuating various crimes and terror activities that emanate from the land and are sustained in the sea.

Globalization has spawned the growth of ports, the growth of on-shore and offshore "critical maritime infrastructure" that are critical to the economic growth of the state. These infrastructures are increasingly being targeted by a variety of non-state actors from within the state and external to the state. Low Intensity Maritime Operations (LIMO) suggests application of force, in the maritime domain, against actors that engaged in maritime terrorism, piracy, gun-running, drug smuggling, illegal fishing, poaching, marine pollution and criminal activities at sea that have the potential to disrupt order at sea. The application of LIMOs involves use of force to an extent that it is short of conventional war against targets at sea. The resultant outcome of the hostile operations in the littorals has resulted in the gradual corrosion of the coastal areas with conflicts and collapse of order in the coastal areas. Securing the sea and its expanses is a formidable task as the capabilities are disproportionate to the tasks at hand. Littorals are usually porous owing to the easy access to shore by various users of the sea and the freedom of using the coastal waters. The task of securing this territory usually lies with the local communities who have a better territorial and domain awareness. However with the onset of the variety of asymmetric challenges and threats, this characteristic is being exploited by various non–state actors.

While exploring the existing framework to combat and contain violence at sea, Lawrence points out that various conceptual and operational frameworks have been proposed to combat and contain violence at sea, there has been no rationale of using these to address the littoral interface in this critical challenge and peril. He says that critical to the issue of combating and containing "violence at sea" is the imperative for a viable and robust "Maritime Domain Awareness" and the "Awareness of the Craft / Container" –both material and human contents of ships calling on ports and those in continuous transit or those who employ Crafts of Opportunity (CooP) to infiltrate and beach in the coasts. Maintaining sustained domain awareness is complex, given the opacity of the seas, the vastness of the terrain and the immense difficulties of the authorities to spot the intruders. An iron-clad regime of maritime counter-asymmetric operations is a hugely complex task. Such operations would hamper the freedom of the seas as well as the freedom of trade.

The economic opportunity of trade in the globalization and post-globalization phases in the developing world has produced the polarised sections of littoral populations of the affluent and the desperately poor. Social and economic human development profiles in the littorals are either the novae-rich or the poorest with severe deprivations. This disparity has been exploited by the non-state actors. He suggests that the solution to this problem lies in investing in the littoral populations who are the primary stakeholders of the littoral-maritime commons. Littoral regions lack in human security and human development, the development of these capacities could lead to better governance. He notes that the praxis of building security in the maritime-littorals could emerge from three responses: governance and security; enhanced domain awareness and responses and joint operations. Good governance and social economic development nurtures a vital stake of the citizenry; they constitute the vital synergies as primary stakeholders in combating crime and terrorism. He lists out three requisites for effective conflict resolution in maritime domain– the need for better regional cooperation framework to combat the non-traditional and transnational challenges, the need for interregional protocols to combat piracy, arms and drugs smuggling and the importance to enhance security measures that combat these threats that is combined with human security and human development. In the case of regional cooperation framework, the challenges lie with how SAARC and other regional organizations can be invigorated to specific responses to these challenges and threats.

Ethno-Political Conflicts in Southasia: Changing Dynamics, Common Concerns

Sudha Ramachandran

Ethno-political conflicts are endemic in South Asia. The region is among the most ethnically diverse in the world. It comprises of mostly multi-ethnic states, each of which consist of many groups of people differing along linguistic, regional, communal and sectarian lines. Some of these ethnic groups occupy a distinct geographical region as do the Sri Lankan Tamils; others such as the Karen in Myanmar are scattered. There are ethnic groups too that are not circumscribed by international borders but straddle them as do the Nagas, who live on both sides of the India-Myanmar border or the Baluch, who live astride borders between Pakistan, Afghanistan and Iran.

However, ethnic diversity by itself does not make conflict inevitable. It is when the state identifies with one or a few ethnic groups and excludes others, and the elite of the latter mobilize to access state power that conflict emerges between groups demanding change and a state and entrenched elites reluctant to alter the status quo. Identity politics serve as a means by which excluded political elites seek to access state power. Scores of groups in South Asia have mobilized along ethnic lines to articulate grievances over political, cultural and socio-economic exclusion. Their demands range from affirmative discrimination, recognition of their distinct identity and according of official status to their language to being granted greater autonomy, statehood and even independence. They press their case through non-violent protest, political agitation, parliamentary processes and armed struggle. Far from being issues concerning the peripheries of these countries, ethno-political conflicts are central as they strike at the very heart of the state, challenging the way it was formed.

This chapter examines ethno-political conflicts in Sri Lanka, India's Northeast, Myanmar and Nepal. It draws from five books mainly: *Conflict in Sri Lanka: Internal and External Consequences* ed. by V R Raghavan, *Internal Conflict in Myanmar: Transnational Consequences* ed. by V R Raghavan, *Internal Conflict in Nepal: Transnational Consequences* ed. by V R Raghavan, *Conflicts in the Northeast: Internal and External Effects* ed. by V R Raghavan and Sanjoy Hazarika, and *Internal Conflicts: A Four States Analysis* ed. by V R Raghavan. These books were the outcome of earlier phases of the Centre for Security Analysis' project on Internal Conflicts and Transnational Consequences. This chapter seeks to pull together the findings of various experts who contributed to these books and to build on their insights. It begins with an overview of ethno-political conflicts in the four countries, providing a summary of various aspects of these conflicts, such as the role of the state in triggering conflicts, the evolution of the conflicts and their dynamics, the state's approach to dealing with conflict, etc. It then goes on to draw attention to similarities in these conflicts and finally, makes some recommendations for the future.

The Ethno-political Conflict in Sri Lanka

Analysts have often sought to understand the Sri Lankan ethno-political conflict through the lens of identity politics, minority grievances and rights, majority-minority relations, etc. Scholar Jayadeva Uyangoda argues that while these are important dimensions that exist at various levels of the conflict, the Sri Lankan conflict is primarily a "contestation for state power." Although minority grievances were the original causes of the conflict, the civil war "became a process autonomous of the original political causes of the conflict," he writes. It was "propelled forward by the competing and adversarial imperatives of state formation in the Sinhalese and Tamil ethnic projects" [1]

---

[1] Jayadeva Uyangoda, "Sri Lanka's Ethnic Conflict: Role of the State", in V R Raghavan, ed. *Internal Conflicts: A Four State Analysis.* (New Delhi: Vij Books Pvt Ltd., 2012), pp 221-222

Sri Lanka is a multi-ethnic, multi-religious and multi-lingual country. The two main ethnic groups are the Sinhalese (78 percent) who speak Sinhala and are predominantly Buddhist, and Tamils (18 percent) who speak Tamil and are mainly Hindu. While a Sinhalese Hindu or a Tamil Buddhist is a rarity, there are Sinhalese and Tamil-speaking Christians. Language determines the identity of Sinhalese and Tamils; however, it is religion that determines the identity of Muslims - Sri Lanka's third largest ethnic group[2] . Muslims have added a complicating dimension to the ethno-political conflict.

The roots of Sri Lanka's ethno-political conflict can be traced to colonial rule. Changes introduced by colonial rulers altered the island's ethnic demography, sharpened ethnic identities and introduced a competitive, even conflictual edge to ethnic relations. For instance, English education, which was introduced during British rule, drew more Tamils than it did Sinhalese. Thus Tamils entered the colonial bureaucracy in larger numbers and came to be "slightly over-represented" in the civil services, contributing to a perception among the Sinhalese that Tamils enjoyed an "undue advantage" during colonial rule, researcher S I Keethaponcalan writes.[3] It provided justification for a slew of pro-Sinhalese measures introduced by post-colonial governments to correct the imbalance. The colonial rulers also encouraged Christian missionary activity. This sharpened religious identities and mobilized the island's Buddhists, triggering a powerful revivalist movement that deepened Sinhala-Buddhist consciousness.[4] It generated an "ideological climate" that resulted in the sharpening of Tamil-Hindu and Muslim identities and communal violence.[5]

Sinhala-Tamil elite relations were largely cordial during colonial rule. The formation of the multi-ethnic Ceylon National Congress (CNC) in 1919 marked the highpoint of this ethnic cohesion. However, inter-elite competition

---

[2] Neil De Votta, *Sinhalese Buddhist Nationalist Ideology: Implications for Politics and Conflict Resolution in Sri Lanka*. (Washington DC: East West Center, 2007), p.5

[3] S I Keethaponcalan, "Ethno-Political Conflict and the Civil War: Domestic and International Impact", in V R Raghavan, ed. *Conflict in Sri Lanka: Internal and External Consequences*. (New Delhi: Vij Books, 2011).p 25.

[4] See De Votta, pp. 13-16

[5] Kumari Jayawardena, *Ethnic and Class Conflicts in Sri Lanka*, (Dehiwela: Centre for Social Analysis, 1985)

emerged and culminated in the CNC splitting along ethnic lines in 1921 over the question of reservation of a seat for Tamils in the Western Province. It led to Tamils forming the Tamil Mahajana Sabha. The setting up of an ethnic-based party "marked the beginning of ethnic politics and contestation between the two communities." Thus electoral politics that was introduced during colonial rule set in motion politics along ethnic lines.[6] It paved the way for the emergence of "ethnic identity politics as the organizing framework of political competition and state power" in post-colonial Sri Lanka. [7]

Sinhalization of the State

Within months of independence from colonial rule, the Sinhalization of the Sri Lankan state was set in motion. Two pieces of legislation gave the process momentum. One was the Citizenship Act of 1948, which stripped lakhs of Tamils living in the island's tea plantations of their citizenship and the other was the Official Languages Act of 1956, which made Sinhala the only official language. While the first discriminated against plantation Tamils, the second advantaged the Sinhalese. Together they made the state "more identified with one community - the Sinhalese".[8] The privileging of Sinhala-Buddhism received a further boost in 1972 when the new Constitution affirmed Sinhala as the only official language and accorded Buddhism foremost place. The 1978 Constitution gave Tamil along with Sinhala national language status but Sinhala remained Sri Lanka's only official language and it assigned the state as protector of the Buddhist Sasana.

The Sinhalization of the state was driven by "ethnic outbidding," a phenomenon that defines the politics of parties and politicians on both sides of the Sinhala-Tamil divide.[9] It was the 1956 general election that made apparent the immense electoral gains that were to be made by engaging in ethnic outbidding. In the wake of the Sinhala-Buddhist resurgence of the early 1950s, the Sri Lanka Freedom Party (SLFP) leader SWRD Bandaranaike promised to make Sinhala the only official language if his

---

[6] See Keethaponcalan, pp 24-25

[7] See Uayangoda, p223

[8] Swarna Rajagopalan, *State and Nation in South Asia*. (Boulder, Colorado: Lynne Rienner, 2001), p 36

[9] See De Votta,

party was voted to power. His promise struck a chord with the Sinhalese and the SLFP won a landslide victory. It convinced politicians that pandering to Sinhalese-Buddhist interests guaranteed electoral success. In subsequent decades, parties outdid each other to project themselves as the better custodian of Sinhalese-Buddhist interests.[10] It set off "a parallel process of ethnic politics" among the Tamil and Muslim communities too.[11] Ethnic outbidding among parties of one community thus set off competitive chauvinism in parties claiming to represent another. This in turn fed into another cycle of ethnic outbidding. The result was an ever escalating spiral of ethnic politics and violence.

Parallel to the Sinhalization of the state was the Sinhalization of what Tamils regard as their 'homeland' – the Northern and Eastern Provinces. State-sponsored settlement of Sinhalese in the East changed its demography. It broke the contiguity between Tamil dominated areas in the North and East, diluting the geographical basis of the Tamil demand for independence or autonomy to the Northeast. Over the years, areas with Sinhalese settlers returned Sinhalese politicians to Parliament, contributing to a fall in the number of Tamil parliamentarians.[12] Academic Kalinga Tudor Silva draws attention to the continuing Sinhalization of Tamil areas in post-war Sri Lanka. Sinhalese are being settled in the North and statues of Buddha and Buddhist shrines are being installed here, although the population of the North is largely Hindu or Christian.[13]

The identification of the state with Sinhala-Buddhism entrenched the interests of the majority community, while Tamils were excluded from economic and other opportunities. For instance, 'Sinhala Only' reduced employment of Tamils in the bureaucracy. Their representation in the civil services fell from 30 percent in 1956 to 5 percent in 1975. With the Sinhalese controlling the parliament and the bureaucracy, Tamils were excluded from

---

[10] SudhaRamachandran, 'Towards the imagined haven of Eelam,' *Asia Times Online*, 12 April 2002 available online at http://www.atimes.com/ind-pak/DD12Df01.html

[11] See Keethaponcalan, p 35

[12] Sudha Ramachandran, 'Hopes fade for a Tiger homeland,' *Asia Times Online*. 22 May 2008 available online at http://www.atimes.com/atimes/South_Asia/JE22Df03.html

[13] Kalinga TudorSilva, 'Ethnicity in Post-war Sri Lanka,' in V R Raghavan, ed. *Internal Conflicts: A Four State Analysis*. New Delhi: Vij Books, 2012),

shaping legislation, and the framing and implementing of policies. [14]

The impact of Sinhala hegemony on Tamils would have been less if Sri Lanka was a federal state. It is not. Uyangoda draws attention to the different visions that Sinhalese and Tamils had of the state. While the Sinhalese nationalist discourse "envisaged further entrenchment of the unitary and centralized state, inherited from the British colonial rule, as the ultimate embodiment of the political will of the majority Sinhalese-Buddhist community," that of the Tamils sought "regional autonomy to the Tamil minority within an altered, federalist framework of the state".[15] This clash constitutes the essence of the conflict. Confronted by a centralized Sinhalese-Buddhist state that refused to reform, Tamils opted for armed struggle for an independent state.

Narrow Nationalism

At independence, Tamils saw themselves as one of Sri Lanka's two major ethnic groups. The Sinhalization of the state led to Tamils perceiving themselves as a nation distinct from that of the Sinhalese and the anti-Tamil pogrom of 1983 in Colombo underscored the significance of the 'Tamil homeland' as their refuge. This soon crystallized into demands for self-determination, autonomy and eventually for a separate Tamil Eelam. Emerging as a response to state oppression, Tamil nationalism was an ideology of resistance and thus progressive. However, early in its evolution it displayed reactionary tendencies and over time came to imitate the state in several ways. Like the Sinhalized state, which excluded minorities and equated Sri Lankan identity with Sinhalese identity, Tamil nationalism was exclusivist. The Federal Party claimed to speak on behalf of the 'Tamil speaking people' but in choosing symbols and rhetoric from the Dravidian past it excluded Tamil speaking Muslims. The Liberation Tigers of Tamil Eelam (LTTE) took this exclusion further by expelling Muslims from the Jaffna peninsula and massacring them.[16]

---

[14] SudhaRamachandran, 'Towards the imagined haven of Eelam,' *Asia Times Online*, 12 April 2002 available online at http://www.atimes.com/ind-pak/DD12Df01.html

[15] See Uayangoda, p 226

[16] Sudha Ramachandran, 'Selective Roots to Tamil Nationalism,' *Asia Times Online*, 18 April 2002 available online at http://www.atimes.com/ind-pak/DD18Df01.html

Tamil nationalists, whether moderate or militant, were intolerant of dissent. Those who disagreed with the concept of Tamil Eelam were labelled 'traitors' and killed. For the LTTE, the enemy was not just the Sri Lankan state but anyone, Tamils included, who challenged its methods. If early in the armed struggle it eliminated rival militant groups, over time all dissent was silenced. The LTTE was critical of the 'repressive Sri Lankan state' but emerged as its mirror image.

Reproduction of Conflict

The Sri Lankan ethno-political conflict surged through three phases and de-escalated in the fourth. During the first phase of conflict formation (pre-independence-1960s), Tamil parties tried co-operation with their Sinhalese counterparts and pressed their demand for a federal set-up through political and constitutional means in Parliament and non-violent street protests. Their efforts came to nothing, paving the way for the conflict's escalation in the 1970s. The 1972 Constitution, which ignored the Tamil plea for a federal constitution, and policies such as the 'standarization of education,' which adversely affected Tamil youth and triggered mass protests, contributed to the rise of militant politics among the Tamils. The state responded with an iron hand. It enacted emergency regulations and anti-terrorism legislation, and deployed the armed forces to quell the incipient militancy in the North. While special legislation and military operations are often described as a response to 'Tamil terrorism', these became triggers for further escalation of the conflict.[17] By the end of the 1970s, parliamentary methods and non-violent agitation for a federal constitution gave way to an armed struggle for a separate state. The 1983 violence boosted support for militancy and Tamil Eelam.

The next phase of conflict intensification (1984-2009) saw the island convulsed in civil war with both, the government and the insurgents taking violence to new levels. The enormous civilian casualties and mass displacement generated a flood of grievances and created a new dynamic sustaining the war. The civil war was punctuated by brief pauses in fighting when the government and the LTTE announced ceasefires and engaged in negotiations. However, each of these episodes of 'peace' was followed by

---

[17] See Keethaponcalan, pp 37-38

a surge in violence. For instance, the India-Lanka Accord of 1987 halted fighting for a few months and pushed the Sri Lankan government to agree to devolution of power to provinces and enact the 13th amendment to the Constitution. However, it also "re-defined and re-intensified the conflict." It brought India into the Sri Lankan conflict as a "direct party to the war," "sharpened the country's already intensified political contradictions" and "opened up political space for another anti-state rebellion" – an insurgency spearheaded by the Janata Vimukti Peramuna. Instead of reducing the intensity of the war, India's conflict resolution efforts gave it a "new fillip" (Uyangoda 2012: 235-6).[18]

The fourth phase of the conflict began in May 2009. With the LTTE's military defeat the civil war ended. However, the conflict remains alive although it has mutated considerably over the decades, moving beyond the original minority grievances that sparked it. If in the 1960-70s, education, employment and 'colonization' were the key Tamil grievances, these have receded and issues like security, land and a political solution have surged to the forefront.

Role of External Actors

While the roots of Sri Lanka's ethno-political conflict are domestic, external actors fuelled its militarization, even as they have contributed to the quest for a political solution. This complex role of external actors in internal conflicts is exemplified by India's involvement in the Sri Lankan conflict. India's provision of arms and training to Tamil insurgents between 1984 and 1987 escalated the conflict. However, it also acted as facilitator, mediator and peace enforcer during this period.[19] It provided ideas and input towards political solutions. India understood the "centrality of state reform" in any solution that would meaningfully address Tamil grievances. It pushed the Sri Lankan government and the Tamil nationalists to compromise by seeking a "middle ground," which required the government to move away from its "rigid adherence to the unitary state model" and the Tamil nationalists to

---

[18] See Uayangoda, pp 235 - 236

[19] Sudha Ramachandran, 'India and the LTTE: For Better, For Worse,' in Sumanasiri Liyanage, P Sahadevan and Anisha Kinra, eds. Intra-State Conflicts and Inter-State Relations: Perspectives on India-Sri Lanka Relations. (Colombo: SAPI, 2009), pp 203-08

abandon their goal for a sovereign Tamil Eelam. The 1987 Accord provided for a "significant re-structuring of the post-colonial Sri Lankan state within a framework of quasi-federalism" and eventually led to the 13th Amendment, which has emerged a foundation on which subsequent quests for a political solution have built (Uyangoda 2012: 230-31).[20]

Tamil Nadu's geographic proximity to the war zone made it the destination of Tamils fleeing the fighting. It was an important logistical base for the insurgents. In the course of time, the insurgents' activities undermined the law and order situation in the state (Ramachandran 2009: 201-03).[21] Commentators have often drawn attention to the strong bonds between Tamils on both sides of the Palk Straits. However, journalist N Sathiyamoorthy argues that these were "not as vast and varied" as widely believed (2011: 238).[22] Although the people of Tamil Nadu were moved by the plight of the refugees and supported them, the Sri Lankan conflict "was never really an issue for the Tamil Nadu voter".[23] Over time, conflicts between the locals and the refugees grew. The involvement of refugees and militants in criminal activities and the assassination of former Prime Minister Rajiv Gandhi by an LTTE suicide bomber generated public revulsion with the LTTE's cause and methods and triggered anger against the refugees too. Following the ban on the LTTE in 1992 and the police crackdown on its network in Tamil Nadu, neither the LTTE nor the refugees were welcome any longer.

With Tamil Nadu's support to the LTTE and the Tamil refugees drying up, the significance of the Tamil Diaspora to the LTTE's armed struggle grew exponentially. The Diaspora funded the LTTE's war and facilitated its international logistics and propaganda network. It emerged as the LTTE's "main lifeline," observes Laksiri Fernando (2011: 191)[24]. Describing the transformation of the Diaspora's role following the defeat of the LTTE,

[20] See Uayangoda, pp 230-31

[21] See Sudha Ramachandran, 2009, pp 201-3

[22] N Sathiya Moorthy, 'Sri Lanka: Trans-border Consequences of an Internal Conflict,' in V R Raghavan, ed. Conflict in Sri Lanka: Internal and External Consequences. (New Delhi: Vij Books, 2011).p 238

[23] Ibid p 222

[24] Laksiri Fernando, 'Long Distance Relations to the Conflict and their Ramifications,' in V R Raghavan, ed. *Conflict in Sri Lanka: Internal and External Consequences,* (New Delhi: Vij Books, 2011). p 191

academic Gamini Keerawalla points out that the centre of Tamil nationalist activism shifted from the Wanni, where the LTTE leadership was based, to the Diaspora in North America and Europe. He points to the Diaspora's emergence as a close-knitted "transnational community" and its role post-war in keeping alive the dream of a Tamil Eelam by setting up a 'Transnational Government of Tamil Eelam' (TGTE).[25] Keethaponcalan, however, argues that the TGTE will "hardly have any impact in the absence of an effective local movement." It will only provide an excuse for the state to continue monitoring the Tamils in the name of national security, he warns.[26]

Foreign governments have played an influential role in the conflict although their positions changed over the decades. If in the 1980s the Tamil insurgents enjoyed considerable support abroad, that changed in the 1990s especially after suicide bombers became important weapons in the LTTE's arsenal. Several governments declared the LTTE a terrorist organization thereafter. In the context of the post-9/11 'war on terror,' international tolerance for the LTTE's violence dipped further, forcing it to participate in the Norwegian-brokered peace process. The resumption of fighting in 2006 was internationally condemned but censure of the government was rather muted with many countries not opposed to the government's all-out war against the LTTE. It was only in the final stages of the war that some western countries called for a ceasefire. Countries like India, China, Pakistan and Iran helped the government defeat the LTTE by providing weaponry, intelligence input and other support.

The significance of the external factor in the Sri Lankan conflict has grown post-LTTE. International NGOs, think-tanks and human rights groups have sharply criticized the government's conduct of the war during its final stages. They have accused the government of war crimes and crimes against humanity. Western governments too are putting pressure on the government through the United Nations Human Rights Council (UNHRC). A US-sponsored resolution in the UNHRC called on Sri Lanka to take steps towards reconciliation and to "address alleged violations of international law." While

---

[25] Gamini Keerawella, 'Pursuit of Sustainable Peace after the Military Defeat of LTTE: Insights into Post-War Scenarios,' in V R Raghavan, ed. *Conflict in Sri Lanka: Internal and External Consequences.* (New Delhi: Vij Books, 2011). Pp 78-82

[26] See Keethaponcalan, p52

aimed at getting the government to take steps towards finding a political solution to the conflict, the Sinhala-Buddhist nationalist upsurge it triggered could end up having the opposite effect on the government.[27]

Government's Approach to the Conflict

What has been the Sri Lankan state's approach to the ethno-political conflict? The state used force from the late 1950s to deal with Tamil protests, even when these were articulated peacefully. This was stepped up in 1979 when the government sent the army to the North "to wipe out terrorism." By the mid-1980s, the North was being aerially bombed. Post-war too, the government's approach to the conflict is militaristic. Around 75 percent of the Sri Lankan Army is deployed in the Northern Province. Instead of dismantling military bases in the former conflict zone, these are being strengthened and expanded. Former military personnel are being appointed as governors to the North and reconstruction and rehabilitation work is dominated by the military.[28]

Since the end of the war, the Sri Lankan government has sought to "contain some of the negative consequences" of the war, points out Sri Lanka's Foreign Minister G L Peiris.[29] Displaced Tamils are being rehabilitated and infrastructure is being reconstructed and the private sector is leading economic revival in the war-ravaged North. However, post-war development has focused on construction of roads and infrastructure which ease movement of the military rather than help Tamil civilians. It is Sinhalese entrepreneurs and Tamils who are close to the regime that have benefited rather than the Tamil masses.[30]

---

[27] Sudha Ramachandran, 'Sri Lanka rights vote stirs nationalist passion,' *Asia Times Online*. 27 March 2012 avaiable oneline at http://www.atimes.com/atimes/South_Asia/NC27Df01.html

[28] Sudha Ramachandran, 'War is Over but Tensions run High,' *The Diplomat*, 13 December2012, available online at http://thediplomat.com/2012/12/13/sri-lanka-war-is-over-but-tensions-run-high/

[29] G L Peiris, 'Internal Conflict in Sri Lanka: Managing the Consequences,' in V R Raghavan, ed. *Conflict in Sri Lanka: Internal and External Consequences*. (New Delhi: Vij Books, 2011)

[30] Sudha Ramachandran, 'War is Over but Tensions run High,' *The Diplomat*, 13 December2012, available online at http://thediplomat.com/2012/12/13/sri-lanka-war-is-over-but-tensions-run-high/

While there were attempts at finding a political solution, these have been half-hearted. Some agreements, such as those signed in 1957 and 1966, "had the potential to broaden the ethnic foundations of the Sri Lankan state" but were discarded under opposition protests and pressure from Sinhala-Buddhist hardliners (Uyangoda 2012: 225).[31] Although the present government has the support in Parliament to effect the necessary constitutional amendments to usher in meaningful devolution, it has not acted to find a political solution.

How has India responded to its own ethno-political conflicts? Like Sri Lanka, India is a democracy but one with far greater ethnic diversity. It is to an examination of ethno-political conflicts in India's Northeast that we now turn.

Conflicts in Northeast India

While linguistic and religious differences in Sri Lanka converge along a single fault line, India's demographic profile points to "one source of stability - the absence of a nationwide cleavage along ethnic lines." Consequently, ethno-political conflicts in India tend to be "localized" and therefore "more easily contained" by the state. Besides, India is a federal union. It has 28 states, many of which were demarcated along linguistic lines. While the "promise of federalism" has served to quell ethnic unrest, its flawed implementation – in practice, India is at best quasi-federal with the state having strong centralizing tendencies - has deepened alienation especially in Kashmir, Punjab and the Northeastern states, where some of the strongest and most sustained challenges to India's sovereignty have been mounted.[32]

India's Northeast consists of seven states often referred to as the Seven Sisters - Arunachal Pradesh, Assam, Manipur, Meghalaya, Mizoram, Nagaland and Tripura – and Sikkim, which officially was added to the region in 2003. Characterized by extraordinary diversity, the Northeast has 475 ethnic groups which speak 400 languages and dialects. Demographic composition and majority-minority equations in each of the Northeastern

---

[31] See Uayangoda, p 225

[32] Kanti Bajpai, 'Diversity, Democracy and Devolution in India,' in Sanjib Baruah, ed. *Ethnonationalism in India: A Reader*. (New Delhi: OUP, 2010), pp 24-25.

states have changed over time. For instance, the linguistic and religious composition of Assam's population has changed dramatically on account of migration. Its tribal-non-tribal balance was affected too by the carving out of other states; between 1961 and 1972, Nagaland, Meghalaya, Mizoram and Arunachal Pradesh were carved out of it. With the exception of Sikkim, all the other Northeastern states have experienced some form of violent conflict.

The Nagas were the first to raise the banner of revolt against the Indian state, demanding a sovereign Naga state on the eve of independence in August 1947. Support for independence gathered momentum, erupting in an armed insurgency in March 1956. Although Nagaland was granted statehood in 1963 and a peace accord was signed in 1975, the insurgency continued. Ceasefires with two main groups, the National Socialist Council of Nagalim-Isak Muivah (NSCN-IM) and the rival NSCN-Khaplang, have calmed the insurgency but violence continues due to fratricidal bloodletting. Several rounds of negotiations between the government and rebels have failed to produce a settlement, the NSCN-IM's demand for a 'Greater Nagalim' being an important stumbling block.

The next to pick up arms against the Indian state were the Mizos. The roots of their insurgency can be traced to the failure of the Assam government – the Mizo Hills were at that time part of Assam - to respond sensitively to a famine that ravaged the Mizo Hills in 1958-59. The Mizo National Famine Front, which was formed to provide famine relief, changed its name in 1961 to Mizo National Front (MNF) and demanded an independent Mizoram. In 1966, a powerful insurgency erupted in the Mizo Hills. While a peace accord signed in 1986 ended the insurgency, conflicts between the Mizos and the Hmars, and the Mizos and the Bru/Reang erupted soon after.

Manipur's merger with India in 1949 triggered the emergence of armed groups that demanded restoration of lost Manipuri sovereignty. Their struggle for independence from India is, however, just one axis of the conflict in Manipur. Tensions have flared often between Meitei and Naga, Meitei and Muslim, and Naga and Kuki.

Immigration and the resultant loss of Assamese identity lie at the heart of the multiple conflicts in Assam. In 1979, a powerful mass movement erupted demanding deportation of "illegal migrants" to Bangladesh. A peace accord signed in 1985 provided for detection and expulsion of foreigners who illegally entered Assam after March 25, 1971, and the sealing of the India-Bangladesh border to prevent further infiltration. While the accord ended the agitation and paved the way for elections and a government led by the Asom Gona Parishad, a party that emerged from the Assam movement, migration from Bangladesh has continued. It provided justification for the United Liberation Front of Assam (ULFA), whose goal was an independent and sovereign Assam, to wage an armed insurgency against the Indian state. Parallel to the ULFA insurgency, Assam has witnessed the Bodo insurgency, which saw Bodo groups targeting the armed forces as well as Assamese, tribal Santhals and Muslim migrants. Assam has suffered inter-ethnic violence as well (Baruah 1999).[33]

Migration of Bengali speakers to Tripura has reduced its tribals to a minority. In 1967, tribals set up a political front called Tripura Upajati Juba Samiti, which called for creation of an autonomous district under the Sixth Schedule of the Constitution, restoration of tribal lands allotted to non-tribals, etc. The failure of the central government to address tribal land alienation and arrest influx of Bangladeshis resulted in violence and counter-violence between tribal and Bengali armed outfits as well as the armed forces deployed there.

As complex as the Northeast's demographic composition is the range of issues that drive its conflicts. It is to a closer understanding of these that we now turn.

Forced Integration, Economic Neglect, Alienation, Immigration and the State

While the Northeast is divided along ethnic, tribal and linguistic lines, it is more or less united in its feeling of intense alienation from the Indian 'mainland.' Northeasterners feel they are discriminated against by 'mainland' Indians. Sociologist Vijaylakshmi Brara argues that although Manipuris have tried to build close links with the rest of India – their adoption

---

[33] Sanjib Baruah, *India against Itself: Assam and the Politics of Nationality*. (New Delhi: Oxford University Press, 1999).

of Hinduism is one example of this, she points out – the latter has not reciprocated. 'Mainland' Indians do not look upon Northeasterners as Indians and use words like "*chinki*," "Nepali" or "*chapta*" to refer to Northeasterners, as their features are Mongoloid rather than 'Indian'. Negative stereotypes define the 'mainlanders' perception of the Northeasterner and her way of life. Thus, the Northeast is not just geographically remote from Delhi but also, its people feel distant and isolated from India. The narrow strip of land called 'Chickens' Neck' that connects India to its northeastern states "aptly symbolizes the precarious relation of this region with the mainland India," she observes .[34]

The people of the Northeast argue that their history is distinct from that of the 'mainland.' Nagas, Tripuris and Manipuris, for instance, point out that they were never a part of India. The Nagas were under a special dispensation during colonial rule and resent their land being passed on to Indian hands (Baruah 2010: 239). Tripura and Manipur were princely states during colonial rule. Tripuris and Manipuris resent their "forced merger" with the Indian Union in 1949. Many Northeasterners are angered by Delhi's treatment of them. They describe Delhi's relationship with the Northeast as a 'master-subject' relationship and point to the economic neglect of the region as evidence of its colonial attitude towards the region and its people. India's federalism is "cosmetic," they point out (Hassan 2010: 292-3).

Few issues evoke the kind of despair that migration does in the Northeast. Drawing attention to the impact of migration on Tripura, journalist Jayanta Bhattacharya writes that Partition "permanently changed the demography of the state" by altering the tribal-Bengali balance. The tribal component of Tripura's population fell from 53.16 percent in 1941 to 37.23 percent ten years later. Between 1947 and 1971, 609,998 people – almost the size of Tripura's population in 1951 – migrated from East Pakistan to Tripura. The population pressure on this tiny state was "tectonic." Its impact went beyond changes in the state's demographic profile. It eroded tribal ownership of land. Between 1951 and 1981, the proportion of Tripura's tribal population who were cultivators fell from 62.94 percent to 43.67 percent, while that of

---

[34] N Vijayalakshmi Brara, 'Nongpok Thong Hangba – Towards Cultural Collectives: Manipur and South East Asia,' in V R Raghavan and Sanjoy Hazarika, eds. Conflicts in the Northeast: Internal and External Effects. (New Delhi: Vij Books, 2011).

labourers grew from 9.93 percent to 23.91 percent.[35] Researcher Nani Gopal Mahanta writes that loss of land to Bengali migrants impacted social relations. Tribals saw settlers as "usurpers of their land" and relations between the two deteriorated, even erupting in violence.[36]

Bhattacharya draws attention to the enthnicization of politics in Tripura. 'Vote-bank politics emerged. The Congress party encouraged migration into the state and government schemes provided financial assistance to settlers to buy land in a bid to attract settler votes. In the 1967 general elections, the Congress won both seats from Tripura to Parliament. That year Tripura's first exclusively tribal party and a tribal insurgent group emerged.[37]

Migration changed Assam's demography too. While figures of immigration of Bangladeshis to the state are disputed, that the influx continues whether from other parts of India or Bangladesh is evident from the transformation of the state from one where Assamese speakers were the overwhelming majority to one where they are merely the largest group.[38] Scholar Samir Kumar Das cites a report in *Hindustan Times* to describe migration's impact on voting patterns. As a result of Bangladeshi influx into Assam, minorities have become a "deciding factor" in around 40 of Assam's 126 assembly constituencies.[39]

Analysts have often pointed out that migration lies at the heart of the Northeast's multiple conflicts. However, that the region's ethno-political conflicts quickly turned into insurgencies indicates that the conflicts are

[35] Jayanta Bhattacharya, 'Ramifications of Conflicts in Tripura and Mizoram,' in V R Raghavan and Sanjoy Hazarika, eds. *Conflicts in the Northeast: Internal and External Effects*. (New Delhi: Vij Books, 2011). Pp 77-79

[36] Nani Gopal Mahanta, 'Changing Contours of Armed Violence in Northeast India,' in V R Raghavan, ed. *Internal Conflicts: A Four State Analysis*. (New Delhi: Vij Books, 2012). P 75

[37] Jayanta Bhattacharya pp 80-81,

[38] Sushanta Talukdar, 'Less than 50 per cent Assamese speakers in Assam,' The Hindu, 9 January 2008, avaiable online at http://www.hindu.com/2008/01/09/stories/2008010959461900.htm

[39] Samir Kumar Das, 'ULFA, Indo-Bangladesh Relations and Beyond,' in V R Raghavan and Sanjoy Hazarika, eds. Conflicts in the Northeast: Internal and External Effects. (New Delhi: Vij Books, 2011)., p 106

[40] Ibid, p 8

mainly about state reform.[40] Mahanta points out that while the main issue raised by the Assam movement was that of "illegal immigration" its larger objective was to redefine Assam's relationship with the Indian state.[41]

Conflict Dynamics

Conflicts in the Northeast have changed over the years, whether with regard to their goals, the means adopted to wage the conflict or the issues that agitate the people. Causes that prompted people to take up arms against the state in the first place were put on the backburner as newer causes surged to the forefront. In the case of the Mizos, for instance, anger over the state's poor distribution of famine relief quickly morphed into a full-blown insurgency for independence.[42] Issues have disappeared or changed in priority as circumstances change. The main target of ULFA ire in the 1980s was Bangladeshi immigration into Assam but it changed its stance on the issue in the 1990s. Das draws attention to a 1992 ULFA pamphlet that reflected this change. It praised contributions of immigrants to social life in Assam and their role in making embankments and chars (shifting river islands) cultivable. Rather than blaming immigrants for Assam's woes, the pamphlet depicted them as helpless victims of the machinations of "wicked politicians." ULFA also redefined what it meant by 'the Assamese'. The Assamese were not merely the "Assamese speaking people" but they were the "veritable mixture of all ethnic groups living in Assam," it said. The immigrants of East Bengali origin so far held as potential candidates for expulsion were renamed *Asombasi Purbabangeeya Jangoshthi* (East Bengali ethnic community living in Assam) [43] ULFA's shift in position on illegal immigration from Bangladesh is often attributed to the sanctuary it was getting in that country. However, Das argues that there was more to it than mere "gratitude". ULFA realized that in a globalized world, movement of population across borders was a reality that it had to come to terms with and that migration of cheap and unskilled labour from Bangladesh to India was "unstoppable in the age of globalization." ULFA's

---

[41] See Nani Gopal Mahanta,, p 56

[42] See Samir Kumar Das, p 118

[43] Ibid p 68- 70

[44] Ibid p 28-29

shift, therefore, was an adaptation to changes in the wake of globalization.[44]

As in Sri Lanka, accords in the Northeast have set off new conflicts. Excluded from the Assam Accord of 1985, the Bodos took up arms soon after as did the Hmar and the Bru/Reang following the Mizo Accord of 1986. The way conflicts are waged has changed over the decades in the Northeast. Pointing to Manipur's experience, economist N Mahendro Singh writes that with the insurgency more or less quelled, civil society activists, human rights campaigners and insurgent groups have resorted to *bandhs* (closures), economic blockades and strikes to pressure the government and rival ethnic groups. These have had a crippling effect on the economy besides undermining trust between various ethnic groups.[45] Indeed, the road blockades have deepened anti-Naga sentiment among Manipuris.

Illiberal Nature of Ethnic Movements

A worrying feature about ethnic movements in the Northeast is their illiberalism. Researcher Udayon Mishra draws attention to how the Naga movement sought to overcome the divisions of tribe and clan to forge a Naga identity. It did so not through debate and discussion, which would have resulted in a shared position on issues, but through crushing of dissent and elimination of alternative views and visions. Contrary to Naga National Council (NNC) chief Angami Phizo's claims, support for armed struggle against India was never unanimous either among the Naga people or even within the NNC leadership. Thieyieu Sakhrie, a moderate in the NNC, who advocated peaceful means was reportedly abducted and killed on Phizo's orders. When Imkongliba Ao of the Naga People's Convention reached agreement with the Indian government on formation of Nagaland state, Phizo denounced him.[46] Six months later Ao was assassinated. Das points to similar intolerance in the Mizo movement. MNF leader Pu Laldenga was authoritarian in his style of functioning and often made decisions without consulting his colleagues. The MNF's illiberal culture has produced an

---

[45] N Mahendro Singh, 'Impact of Conflicts in the Northeast with Special Reference to Manipur,' in V R Raghavan and Sanjoy Hazarika, eds. Conflicts in the Northeast: Internal and External Effects. (New Delhi: Vij Books, 2011),

[46] Udayon Misra, 'Internal Strife and External Impacts: The Issues of Nagaland and the Nagas,' in V R Raghavan and Sanjoy Hazarika, eds. Conflicts in the Northeast: Internal and External Effects. (New Delhi: Vij Books, 2011)

intolerant society. Faith-based and community-based organizations in Mizoram indulge in vigilantism and engage in moral policing of society. The Young Mizo Association, for instance, banned the use of drugs and alcohol to deal with addiction and alcoholism and humiliated, beaten, tortured and even killed those who violated the ban.[47]

External Dynamics

The Northeast's ethno-political conflicts have been significantly shaped by external factors. This is not surprising given the fact that 98 percent of the Northeast's borders are international. It was the flood of migrants from East Pakistan/ Bangladesh that prompted the anti-foreigners agitation in Assam and was the main trigger behind the formation of the ULFA and the Tripura National Volunteers (TNV). The escalation of the Naga and Mizo insurgencies in the 1960s owed much to the support they got from Pakistan, China and Myanmar in the form of arms, training and sanctuary. The centrality of such support to the survival of insurgencies in the Northeast was underscored by the MNF's weakening following the liberation of Bangladesh and the loss of its safe havens there.

Such support to ULFA from the Bangladesh state, especially when anti-India coalitions were in power, helped it offset the loss of local support in the 1990s, Mahanta points out. Not only did ULFA take sanctuary and train cadres in Bangladesh but also, it ran businesses there, even intervened in its internal politics. An attack on Awami League chief Sheikh Hasina at a public rally in 2004 was reportedly carried out by ULFA at the behest of anti-Hasina/anti-India forces.[48] Thus groups like ULFA are not only shaped by external factors but also they shape events in the neighbourhood.

Besides neighbouring governments, insurgent groups from the Northeast are drawing support from transnational entities like jihadi groups, writes Das, warning that succour from such outfits is likely to outlive that from governments. ULFA's reported ties with al-Qaeda can be expected to survive the Bangladesh government's severance of support to the organization.[49]

---

[47] See Samir Kumar Das, p 104
[48] See Nani Gopal Mahanta , pp 81-84
[49] See Samir Kumar Das, p 28

The Northeast's neighbours have fuelled insurgencies but they have acted to weaken them as well. In 2003, Bhutan launched military operations to drive ULFA out of its bases on Bhutanese soil. While Indian pressure pushed Bhutan to act against ULFA, there were domestic compulsions too. ULFA extortion was undermining law and order. Officials feared too that ties between Lhotshampas and ULFA would fuel unrest in southern Bhutan. Importantly, ULFA's presence was undermining Bhutan's economy. The Dungsum Cement project had to be shut down, trade routes with India were unsafe and a 900-megawatt Mangdechy Hydropower project was stalled. These compelled Thimphu to crackdown on the ULFA.[50]

Action by neighbouring governments against anti-India insurgent groups has facilitated Delhi's efforts to negotiate with the latter. The Sheikh Hasina government has played a major role in pushing ULFA leaders based in Bangladesh to work out a peaceful settlement with Indian authorities. India sees her government as "an ally" in its "roadmap to peace" in Assam, writes Das.[51]

Three-Pronged Approach

The Indian state's approach to the ethno-political conflicts in the Northeast has consisted of three components – military, political and economic. The military component consists of counter-insurgency operations by the Indian Army, which began in Nagaland in 1956 and expanded thereafter to the other insurgency-hit states. Air power was deployed to crush the Mizo insurgency in 1966 when the Mizo Hills were aerially bombed, the only instance of India ordering its air force to bomb its citizens. An important part of the counter-insurgency operations is the 'grouping of villages,' which began in the Naga Hills in 1956 and was adopted subsequently in other parts of the Northeast. Aimed at isolating the insurgents and cutting their access to villagers, village grouping involved shifting thousands of villages from the remote areas to near main roads and grouping them together to facilitate army surveillance of the people.[52] An important component of India's counter-insurgency strategy in the Northeast has been the enactment

---

[50] See Nani Gopal Mahanta , pp 63-66
[51] See Samir Kumar Das, p 29
[52] Ibid p 98

of special legislations such as the Armed Forces (Special Powers) Act (AFSPA), which come into play in areas declared 'disturbed.' Enacted in 1958 in the context of the Naga insurgency, AFSPA puts extraordinary powers in the hands of the military.[53] In the decades since, it has been imposed in 'disturbed areas' in other parts of the Northeast, particularly in Assam, Nagaland, Tripura and Manipur.

With a view to addressing the Northeast's economic exclusion and eliminate its 'sense of alienation,' the central government initiated the Border Area Development Programme in 1987. Underlining the importance it gives to economic development of the Northeast, it set up a separate ministry called Ministry of Development of North Eastern Region (MDONER) in 2001 to act as the nodal department for the region's socio-economic development. Budget allocations for the Northeast have grown over the years; the budget was raised by 19 percent from the previous fiscal to Rs.1,760 crore in 2010-11.[54] Das observes that the government's extension of financial packages, doles and subsidies to the Northeastern states seem aimed at creating a relationship of dependency between the Northeast and the Centre, rather than address its economic problems. Examining a MDONER document, Das points to "the underlying economism" of its vision, its stress on private sector-led economic development – to attract private investment to the Northeast, the document calls for a shift from the current protective policies of assistance and subsidies to more market-friendly policies including easy credit facilities, tax holidays, export promotion parks and investment subsidies – and enhanced government role in support of private enterprise. An important component of the development approach is aimed at freeing the landlocked region by connecting it to the dynamic Southeast Asian economies.[55]

Analysts say that although the Indian state has used military force often to deal with ethno-political conflicts, its use was "circumscribed by

---

[53] Sudha Ramachandran, 'Hungry for justice in India,' Asia Times Online, 18 March 2010 available online at http://www.atimes.com/atimes/South_Asia/LC18Df02.html

[54] K Yhome, 'Trans-border Effects on Northeast India,' in V R Raghavan, ed. Internal Conflict in Myanmar: Transnational Consequences. (New Delhi: Vij Books, 2011). p 173

[55] See Samir Kumar Das, p 123-126

the clear understanding that the ultimate solution would have to be a political rather than a military one". The intensity of military force was limited in order to leave space open for reaching compromise with the aggrieved ethnic groups. Short of secession, it has been willing to consider and concede political demands. It has carved out new states and created autonomous regions and districts to allow communities a measure of self-rule and taken steps to facilitate the entry of ethnic leaders into the democratic mainstream.[56]

The Indian state has also taken steps to address grievances regarding illegal immigration. But these efforts are "sporadic and ineffectual," writes Kakoty. Listing a series of legislations that were introduced since 1950, he describes them as "toothless," discriminatory, ineffective and unimplemented.[57] As for steps towards a political solution, India has engaged in talks with insurgents and signed accords, granted autonomy ranging from statehood within the Indian Union to autonomous district councils and conferment of recognition to traditional institutions.[58] Critics point to several flaws in the way the Indian government has gone about making 'peace.' Das points out that the government responds to conflict as though it is a game involving just two actors, the state and the main insurgent group, when in fact there are multiple stake holders (2011: 29).[59] In the "rush for settlement with the larger group" the government overlooks what are regarded as 'smaller problems' i.e. issues raised by smaller groups. Over time, these grievances of smaller groups "fester and break out into little rebellions and insurgencies of their own"[60].

Similar ignoring of 'smaller problems' in the hurry for a larger agreement is evident in Nepal too. Whether in 1990-91, when a democratic constitution was being drawn up, or in 2006, when a Comprehensive Peace Agreement

---

[56] Rajesh Rajagopalan, 'Insurgency and Counterinsurgency,' Seminar, no. 599, July 2009 available online at http://www.india-seminar.com/2009/599/599_rajesh_rajagopalan.html

[57] Sanjeeb Kakoty, 'Migration Mantra and the Bangladesh-Northeast Conundrum,' in V R Raghavan and Sanjoy Hazarika, eds. Conflicts in the Northeast: Internal and External Effects. (New Delhi: Vij Books, 2011), pp 49-51

[58] See Kanti Bajpai, p 59-60

[59] See Samir Kumar Das, p 29

[60] Jayanta Bhattacharya, p 86

(CPA) was reached that ended the Maoist insurgency and restored democracy, grievances of ethnic and regional groups were ignored. It set off a wave of violent agitations by an array of ethnic and regional groups across Nepal.

Ethno-political Conflicts in Nepal

Nepal's recent history has been fraught with tension. A powerful Maoist insurgency that lasted ten years was followed up by a wave of ethnic unrest. While the eruption of identity politics to the fore in 2007 took many by surprise, ethnic activism is not new to Nepal. Between 1770 and 1979 Nepal witnessed at least 25 ethnic and region-based mobilizations against the state; most of them occurring among the Limbus and Rais inhabiting the eastern hills.

Nepal is extremely diverse. The 2001 census compiled data for around 102 caste and ethnic groups and tabulated 92 languages and seven religions (Hangen 2007: 3).[61] Nepali Hindus comprise the overwhelming majority accounting for almost 81 percent of the population, followed by Buddhists, Muslims and others. Nepali is the most widely spoken language (89 percent) but Maithili, Bhojpuri, Tharu and Tamang have a sizeable number of speakers too. The Caste Hill Hindu elite (30.89 percent) consist of the Chhetris, Brahmins, Thakuris and others. Dalits account for 7 percent of the hill population. The Newar ethnicity (5.48 percent), also found in the hills, blurs ethnic and caste lines as 84 percent of the group is Hindu. Ethnic groups, also known as *adibasi janajatis* (indigenous nationalities), are found across Nepal and include Magars, Tamangs, Limbus and Rais. People in the Terai (the plains bordering India) or Madhes account for 31.7 percent of Nepal's total population and include Hindu caste groups (19.49 percent), Dalits and Muslims. The Tharu are an important indigenous group here. [62]

Till recently, Nepal was a Hindu kingdom. Following a mass movement in 1990 - often referred to as Jana Andolan-I – Nepal became a constitutional monarchy and a multiparty democracy. However in 2002, King Gyanendra dismissed parliament and took full control three years later. Another mass

---

[61] Susan Hangen, Creating a "New Nepal": The Ethnic Dimension. (Washington: East-West Center, 2007), p 3.

[62] Ibid , p 4-5

movement in 2006 – Jana Andolan-II, this time led by the Maoists and the political parties - resulted in a Seven Party Agreement that culminated in the restoration of democracy and a peace agreement. Monarchy was abolished and Nepal was declared a secular and federal democracy. Elections to the Constituent Assembly in 2007 saw Maoists emerge as the largest group in parliament. Political instability continues as parties have not been able to reach agreement on Constitution and are at odds over proposals to divide Nepal into states along ethnic lines. With another general election unlikely to throw up a clear verdict, it does seem that transforming the state into a federal one – a key demand of the ethno-political groups - will not be accomplished soon.

Why are Nepal's ethnic and regional groups in ferment? The state's identification with one religion – Hinduism - and one language – Nepali, and the efforts of Nepal's rulers to legitimize themselves through religion and homogenize what is an extremely diverse population resulted in exclusion of ethnic and regional groups that were not Hindu and/or spoke a language that was not Nepali. Since opportunities were often closely linked to caste and ethnicity, excluded groups were impoverished.

Hinduization and Nepalization of the State

Use of religion by Nepal's rulers to legitimize themselves or 'unify' the country is not new. Prithvi Narayan Shah, for instance, declared Nepal to be an 'Asal Hindustan,' a pure land of Hindus, to gain legitimacy in newly-conquered lands. But it was with the Ranas imposing the *Muluki Ain*, a civil code that standardised diverse customs, laws and practices in the context of Hindu precepts and laws, in 1854 on all sections of society - Hindu and non-Hindu - that the process of Hinduization of Nepal gathered pace. Researcher Uddhab Pyakurel points out that the *Muluki Ain* accelerated the process of assimilation of diverse ethnic, religious, and linguistic groups. However, it was during the Panchayat period (1960-90) that Hinduization of the state peaked with the 1962 Constitution declaring Nepal to be a Hindu kingdom. Besides, the state sought to assimilate non-Hindus by declaring Buddhism to be a branch of Hinduism (2012: 138-55).[63]

---

[63] Uddhab Pyakurel, 'Changing Patterns of Nepali Ethnic Movement,' in V R Raghavan, ed. Internal Conflicts: A Four State Analysis. (New Delhi: Vij Books, 2012). Pp 138-55

Parallel to the Hinduization of the state was its Nepalizisation. Gorkha Bhasha was named 'Nepali' by the Ranas and declared the official language. Under King Mahendra, only the Nepali language was promoted and other languages were regarded as "local" languages.[64] Nepali was made the sole medium of instruction. State-published school textbooks excluded the cultures, histories and languages of Nepal's ethnic groups and history textbooks provided a unifying 'national history' that emphasized the lives of high-caste Hindu heroes while excluding narratives about noteworthy individuals from other communities.[65] The Panchayat era slogan, 'one language, one nation, one dress,' embodied the state's determination to creating uniformity in a diverse country.

The Hinduization and Nepalization of the state resulted in entrenchment of caste Hindus in the state apparatus. Interestingly, this increased with Nepal's democratization. Comparing representation of various caste, ethnic and regional groups in the House of Representatives in the 1991-2002 period, Pyakurel points out that Brahmin presence rose from 39 percent in the 1991-94 House to 44.4 percent in 1994-1999 and 43.6 percent in 1999-2002. However, representation of hill ethnic groups was 16 percent in 1991, 11.7 percent in 1994 and 12.2 percent in 1999. Madhesi representation too fell from 20 percent in 1994 to 18 percent in 1996 and 17 percent in 1999.[66] Dalit exclusion from cabinets was total; there was not a single Dalit in cabinets in the 1990-2002 period.[67] Representation of indigenous nationalities and Dalits diminished not just in parliament and cabinet but in the bureaucracy and judiciary, as well. "Those who were in the margins continue to remain there and those holding power continue to do so," observes researcher Padmaja Murthy. The excluded groups are thus "not able to participate in policy formulation and implementation to make any difference to their conditions".[68]

---

[64] Ibid , p 49

[65] See Susan Hangen, p 12

[66] See Uddhab Pyakurel, p 158

[67] Mahendra Lawoti, *Looking Back: Looking Forward: Centralization, Multiple Conflicts, and Democratic State Building in Nepal.*(Washington: East-West Center, 2007). P 13

[68] Padmaja Murthy, 'Internal Conflict in Nepal: Implications for India,' in V R Raghavan, ed. Internal Conflict in Nepal: Transnational Consequences. (New Delhi: Vij Books, 2011), p 144

Centralization of the State

The deepening exclusion of ethnic and regional groups despite democratization post-1990 can be attributed to persisting centralization of the Nepali state. The process of centralization set in motion during the so-called unification or rather conquest of Nepal by the Gorkhas in the late 18th century, which gathered momentum under Rana rule and the Panchayat period, continued into the democratic period as the 1990 Constitution retained the unitary state. The near total monopoly of the central government over raising revenue and expenditure kept local governments dependent on the centre. In areas such as education and culture, "Kathmandu had almost monopolistic power over policy formulation and implementation." Not only did the unitary structure concentrate power at the centre but also it did so in one arm – the executive. Power to introduce legislation with budgets was vested by the 1990 Constitution in the Cabinet only; Parliament was thus rendered a mere rubber stamp. The first-past-the-post electoral system too undermined representation of marginalized groups.[69] Thus, although the 1990 Constitution put in place multi-party democracy and recognised the multi-ethnic nature of society, the electoral system and the unitary state militated against the marginalized groups.

Militarization of State and Society

An important feature of Nepali society is its growing militarization. There has been a marked increase in the willingness of state and non-state actors to use violence. Even before the eruption of the Maoist insurgency, the state used force in the form of Operation Romeo to deal with agitation. This and the deployment of the Royal Nepal Army (RNA) in 2001, the Maoist insurgency and the decade-long civilian war contributed substantially to militarizing society, writes researcher Chiran J Thapa.[70] Academic Anjoo Sharan Upadhyaya observes that the Maoists' "legitimization of violence as a political tool" had a demonstration effect on "disgruntled groups" particularly in the Terai. The intimidation used by the Maoists' youth

---

[69] See Mahendra Lawoti. Pp 5-12

[70] Chiran Jung Thapa, 'Nepal's Counter-Insurgency Campaign: Impact and Aftermath,' in V R Raghavan, ed. Internal Conflict in Nepal: Transnational Consequences. (New Delhi: Vij Books, 2011). Pp 24-25

organizations prompted parties and ethnic groups to set up their own militant wings, resulting in a proliferation of armed outfits. Impunity for past crimes that was extended to Maoist cadres as part of the peace agreement has encouraged others to use violence as well .[71]

Ebb and Flow

Ethnic and regional activism in Nepal since 1950 can be divided broadly into five phases. The first phase spanned the 1950s. Activism in this period was spurred by the anti-Rana movement and the end of autocratic Rana rule in 1953. Several ethnic and regional organizations such as the Gurung Kalyan Sangh, the Kirat League and the Nepal Terai Congress (NTC) emerged .[72] When Nepali was made the medium of instruction in 1956, the Terai erupted in protests. However, despite its leading role in the agitations, the NTC's fortunes declined by the end of the decade. Its rout in the 1959 general election was a reflection of its elite bias. The second phase of ethnic activism began with the introduction of Panchayat rule in 1960. Although the 1962 Constitution's definition of Nepal as a Hindu-Nepali state stirred much anger among the ethnic groups, especially those in the eastern hills, organized ethnic and regional resistance did not occur as King Mahendra's co-option of elites left the ethnic movements leaderless. Ethnic organizations existed but they were focused on cultural issues rather than political activism.

The third phase began with the restoration of democracy in Nepal in 1990. Low-key activism of the previous period was replaced by overt mobilization as democratization provided space for such activity. Ethnic organizations proliferated, although ethnic and regional parties were still not allowed. The writing of the Constitution spurred groups to articulate demands before the Constitution Recommendation Commission (CRC). The Mongol National Organization, for instance, called for declaring Nepal a secular state and parity of status for all languages. However, the CRC did not heed the demands of the ethnic and regional groups. The Constitution retained a unitary state with a Hindu-Nepali identity, triggering protests .[73] Indigenous

---

[71] Anjoo Sharan Upadhyaya, 'Conflict in Nepal and its Transnational Ramifications,' in V R Raghavan, ed. Internal Conflict in Nepal: Transnational Consequences. (New Delhi: Vij Books, 2011), pp 125-126

[72] See Uddhab Pyakurel 2012, : p151

[73] See Padmaja Murthy, pp 151-54

groups overcame their extreme internal diversities to construct an *adibasi janajati* identity and several organizations came together to form the National Federation of Nationalities. Meanwhile, militancy was gathering momentum in the eastern hills where an armed movement led by the Khambuwan Rashtriya Morcha for an autonomous Khambuwan state emerged .

During the fourth phase (1995-2006), ethnic and regional movements were eclipsed by the Maoist insurgency. However, they did not suffer on account of the Maoists' class war as the Maoists kept the ethnic movements' demands alive by incorporating several of them in the 40-point charter they put before the government. By tapping into their grievances the Maoists were able to draw on existing networks of the ethnic organizations, especially in the eastern hills. Although relations between the ethnic and regional organizations and the Maoists were never easy, still, the latter's strong espousal of their demands for ethnic autonomy, federalism and secularism resulted in these being positioned centrally in the agenda of the 2006 CPA.

The Maoist insurgency brought about a profound change in the marginalized groups. During Jana Andolan I, although the latter put forward demands it had little impact as they did not "occupy any significant political space." The Maoist insurgency politicized them. They internalized the Maoists' emphasis on the need for constitutional change and the importance of an election to the Constituent Assembly to bring that change. Post Jana Andolan II, various marginalized groups organized themselves more effectively and put forward their demands assertively. The Maoists' successful use of armed struggle convinced them of the efficacy of violence to draw the government's attention to their grievances and concede their demands (Murthy 2011: 160).[74] Researchers Indra Adhikari and Uddhab Pyakurel point out that the Maoists had promised ethnicity-based autonomous states to even those ethnic groups that comprised less than 30 percent of the population in a region. For instance, they proposed a Limbuwan state for Limbus although the community accounts for 27 percent of the population in that area. Expectations were thus raised and when these were not met by the CPA - although state restructuring was an important part of the

---

[74] Ibid , p 160

peace deal, the latter was not explicit on the issue of federalism – it fuelled angry protests (2011: 63).[75]

The fifth phase began with the CPA and saw a surge in ethnic and regional movements. Violent protests in 2007 in the Terai forced the government to include federalism in the Interim Constitution. The demands of various groups clashed with each other. The Madhes movement (Dec 2007-Feb 2008) led by the United Democratic Madhesi Front demanded an autonomous 'One Madhes, One Prades' but this was opposed by the Chure Bhawar movement, which represented the people from the hills living in the Terai. The Tharu agitation (March 2009) demanded the government withdraw its ordinance declaring all communities residing in the Terai as Madhesi. The agitations prompted the government to reach agreements with different groups (Adhikari and Pyakurel 2011: 55-59).[76] The ethnic and regional agitations have subsided over the last couple of years with the tussle over the nature of Nepal's federation moving from the streets to the Constituent Assembly. However, no consensus was reached there. Nepal is likely to go to the polls in 2013 and issues related to federalism, naming of provinces, etc will dominate the election campaign. Several ethnic and region-based parties can be expected to enter the new Parliament/Constituent Assembly.

External Dynamics

India has played an enormous role in shaping political developments in Nepal be it the restoration of democracy or the peace process. Of the various ethnic and regional conflicts in Nepal, it is in the conflicts in the Terai that India's influence and interest is most likely. Although the Madhesi movement is an internal conflict "that emerged from a deep sense of exclusion felt by Madhesis at all levels in polity and society," it was because of their so-called 'Indianness' and their Indian origins that the Madhesis were discriminated against in Nepal, Murthy writes. India's role in the Madhesi movement is one that evokes diverse opinion in Nepal. Some believe that India supports the Madhesi agitation but such support is limited to Indian towns bordering Nepal where people have relatives in the Terai and "this

---

[75] Indra Adhikari and Uddhab Pyakurel 'Internal Conflict in Nepal after the Comprehensive Peace Agreement,' in V R Raghavan, ed. Internal Conflict in Nepal: Transnational Consequences. (New Delhi: Vij Books, 2011).

[76] Ibid

does not get translated into active support." In fact, Madhesis themselves often argue that the Indian government isn't doing much for them as it is keener to cultivate the hill elite [77]

The Terai is notorious for its frail law and order and crime. Agitation and unrest there is of concern to India as the heightened instability would attract anti-India and transnational terrorist groups, mafia organizations, counterfeiters, etc, all of whose activities undermine India's security. There is concern too that Indian business in Nepal will be affected adversely by unrest in the Terai .[78] There are similar concerns in Nepal too as the Terai is crucial to Nepal's economy as well; every major highway, custom point and industry as well as most of Nepal's cultivable land lies here.[79] Thus, India and Nepal have a shared interest in ensuring that agitation in the Terai does not spiral out of control.

Government's Approach

Right until 1990, the Nepal government refused to acknowledge ethnic diversity. It responded to ethnic and regional agitations by co-opting elites. While this was successful in decapitating the ethnic and region-based organizations and in arresting mass mobilizations, it did not resolve the underlying conflict. It only served to postpone the confrontation and contributed to its more violent manifestation subsequently. Post-1990, while the Constitution recognized Nepal's diversity, political parties were preoccupied with forming and bringing down governments and not in addressing the ethno-political conflicts.

From 1995 onwards, the government relied on use of force. Police operations to quell the Maoist insurgency ended up fuelling it. An ill-trained police force resorted to torture and extra-judicial killings of suspected Maoists, contributing to deepening public alienation with the state and growing support for the insurgency. While the army was better trained and equipped to fight insurgents, its disregard for civilian suffering was higher than that of the police.[80] The centrepiece of the government's counter-insurgency strategy was the Integrated Security and Development Programme (ISDP), an army-

---

[77] Padmaja Murthy, pp 166-67

[78] See Anjoo S Upadhyaya pp 133-37).

[79] Padmaja Murthy, p 67

[80] See Chiran J Thapa, and also see

led and implemented programme to introduce security and development simultaneously. It saw the military engage in a wide range of activities ranging from road and bridge repair to electrification, forestry, health, education, agricultural development, food self-sufficiency, micro-credit, and income generation projects. This had the impact of militarizing development activity. Donors and domestic and international NGOs became reluctant to fund or work on these projects as it made them vulnerable to attacks by Maoists.

Since 2007, the effort to find a political/constitutional solution to the ethno-political conflicts has grown. However, while the main parties expressed support to federalism, the deep reluctance of their hill caste elite-dominated leadership to federalize the state and their preoccupation with accessing political power rather than addressing ethnic grievances has undermined the political/constitutional approach to conflict resolution.

Ethnic groups were denied a voice under the monarchy. While the restoration of democracy in Nepal has enhanced ethnic activism, the conflict remains alive. What has been the experience of Myanmar's ethnic nationalities during decades of military rule? What can they expect from their quasi-democracy? The following section throws light on some of these questions.

Ethno-political Conflicts in Myanmar

Since Independence in 1948, Myanmar has experienced multiple conflicts including an armed communist insurgency, an array of armed ethno-political movements for self-determination and a largely non-violent struggle for democracy led by the National League for Democracy (NLD). While the communist insurgency subsided in 1988, the struggles for democratic rights and ethnic self-determination remain alive to date.

Myanmar's ethno-political conflicts are primarily a contention over whether the state should be unitary or federal. Chin activist and academic, Lian H Sakhong argues that differences over "state formation" lie at the root of these conflicts. The ethnic nationalities, he points out, agreed to become a part of the Union of Burma on the condition that it would be a federal state. However, what emerged was a unitary state that became synonymous with the Burman majority. Exclusion of non-Burmans thus underlies the ethno-political conflicts.

Myanmar is among the most ethnically diverse countries in the world. Two-thirds of its population belongs to the Burman ethnic group and they inhabit the country's central and upper plains. The remaining one-third comprises of seven major indigenous ethnic minorities, also called ethnic nationalities - Shan, Karen, Rakhine, Mon, Kachin, Chin and Kayah - and over a hundred other recognized ethnicities. There is some congruence between ethnicity and religion. Buddhism, which is practiced by 89 percent of the population, is the dominant religion of the Burmans, the Shan, the Rakhine and the Mon. Christianity is practiced by 4 percent of the population, mainly by the Kachin, Chin and Karen and roughly 4 percent of Myanmar's population is Muslim.

As in the other conflicts examined above, colonial policies played a role in shaping relations between the various ethnic groups. Colonial administration in Burma was a two-tier system consisting of 'Ministerial Burma' that was established in the areas where the Burmans lived and the 'Frontier Areas' that included areas inhabited by the Shan, Chin, Kachin and others. The British established close relations with the people of the Frontier Areas. Karen, Chin and Kachin were recruited into the bureaucracy and especially into the British Burma Army in large numbers. The Karen played a major role in facilitating the British annexation of Burma, contributing to the Burmans perceiving them as instruments of colonial oppression. Brutal confrontations between the Burman forces and the Karen during World War II deepened the mutual hostility. Thus by the time discussions on the shape of a future independent country began, tensions between the Burmans and the ethnic nationalities were serious .[81]

Panglong's Unfulfilled Promises

Whether the Frontier Areas would be associated with Ministerial Burma in the new Burma and if so in what way was the major question on the eve of Independence.[82] Agreement was reached on the creation of a federal union at a meeting in Panglong between General Aung San representing Ministerial Burma and leaders of the Chin, Kachin and Shan groups representing the

---

[81] Mathew J Watson, 'Conflict and History in Burma: Myths of Panglong,' *Asian Survey*, vol. 48, no.6. November-December 2008. pp. 889-9.

[82] Ibid

Frontier Areas. The ethnic states were promised an equal share in the country's wealth (Walton 2008: 897). While the Shan and Karenni principalities were amalgamated into one state and granted the right to secede after ten years, the Kachin, although granted a state, were not given secession rights. The Chin were given a special division only. Territorial authority of three other major ethnic groups - the Mon, Karen and Rakhine - was left to be decided after independence (ICG 2011: 2). The Panglong Agreement paved the way for a new Constitution and independence. Independence came but not the federal union that was envisaged at Panglong. With Aung San's assassination on the eve of Independence died the federalism he promised. A new redrafted Constitution provided for a quasi-federal union with a strong connotation of a unitary state that was controlled by a single ethnic group – the Burmans. The ethnic nationalities were reduced to "vassal states" of the ethnic Burmans, says Sakhong (2012: 255).

Burmanization and Buddhistization of the State

Successive governments in Myanmar were Burman dominated. They have sought to erase diversity by imposing on all citizens 'one ethnicity, one language, one religion,' these being the ethnicity of the Burmans (*Myanmar lumyo*), their language (*batha-ska)* and their religion (*Myanmar-thatana of Buddha-bata*). Ethnic minorities were thus forced to dissolve their distinct identities and assimilate into the identity of the Burman majority. In excluding Myanmar's minorities, democratic leaders acted no different from the junta. Their paths and methods differed - Prime Minister U Nu took the path of religion and General Ne Win of language – but they complemented each other in homogenizing Myanmar's plural society. The post-1988 junta sought ethnic assimilation as the route to national unity. It changed the name of the country from Burma to Myanmar in 1989.

The privileging of Buddhism began early. The 1947 Constitution recognized the "special position of Buddhism" as the faith of the "great majority of citizens." A Ministry of Religious Affairs was created in 1948 to administer Buddhist affairs and public money was spent on upkeep of Buddhist shrines. These steps culminated in Buddhism being declared state religion in 1961.

Ne Win's nation-building project involved a national language policy that imposed the Burman language on all citizens. It was declared the official language and made the medium of instruction. While ethnic minorities were allowed to use their languages in communications with the central government, restrictions were imposed on publishing in ethnic languages and the rights of minorities to preserving, protecting, promoting and teaching their own language were severely curtailed. Sakhong describes it as "a life and death matter because the survival of ethnic nationalities in Burma as distinctive peoples who practice different cultures, speak different languages, and worship different religions, depends so much on whether they are able to preserve, protect and promote their ways of life as fundamental rights".

Militarized State and Society

Myanmar's state and society is among the most militarized in the world. This is because it has been under some form of military rule for over 50 years. Researcher Kerstin Duell observes that the "military has practically supplanted the state, leaving state institutions inherently weak." It has co-opted most branches of civil society, creating a militarized society.[83]

Militaries are highly centralized in their structure, mindset and outlook. In Myanmar, the military has been more so. Having battled ideological and ethnic insurgencies for decades, the military sees itself as the guardian and guarantor of Myanmar's unity and territorial integrity. It is in favour of a strong state and opposed a federal Myanmar from the start. When U Nu convened a conference on federalism, the military staged a coup alleging that this was necessary to pre-empt a secessionist plot hatched by the Shan princes. It was to prevent Myanmar's disintegration that a coup became necessary, the generals pointed out. After assuming power, Ne Win put in place a highly centralized, one-party dictatorship with the military at its core. The 1962 coup thus drove the final nails into the coffin of Panglong's federalizing promises.

Researcher Tin Maung Maung Than describes Myanmar as a "national security state" where the generals "have conflated national interest with

---

[83] Kerstin Duell, 'Non-Traditional Security Threats, International Concerns and the Exiled Opposition,' in V R Raghavan, ed. Internal Conflict in Myanmar: Transnational Consequences. (New Delhi: Vij Books, 2011)

the armed forces' corporate interests defined and represented by them. To them nation and state become interchangeable and regime and state are conflated." The military says it upholds national interest by protecting what it describes as the "three Main National Causes: the non-disintegration of the Union, non-disintegration of national i.e. multi-ethnic solidarity, and perpetuation of national sovereignty".[84]

Journalist Larry Jagan provides insights into the junta's mindset and how this feeds into their approach to conflict resolution. "Myanmar's military leaders cannot compromise and do not understand the notion of a win-win situation," he writes. "For them, any concession means some-one else gains and they lose. In their minds, there are only winners and losers, no matter what the case is. Everything is seen in terms of a military battle or campaign." Consequently they do not favour negotiations or compromise solutions.[85]

Nation-building Projects of Ethnic Movements

Myanmar's ethnic nationalities have fiercely opposed the state's nation-building approach and the Burmanization and Buddhistization of the state. Yet, their own approach to nation-building is no different. The KNU's approach is illustrative. The Karen are highly diverse. While they are overwhelmingly Buddhist, around 20 percent are Christian and a small number are animists and Muslims. The Karen speak a dozen related but mutually unintelligible languages. Most Karen do not live in the conflict zone and large numbers, though critical of the state, are not necessarily supportive of the armed rebellion. In a bid to paper over this extreme diversity, the overwhelmingly Sgaw-speaking Christian leadership of the KNU sought to project a Sgawized Christian Karen identity. In the process, they have excluded the Buddhists, paving the way for alienation of Karen Buddhists, their breakaway from the KNU and subsequent emergence of rival Karen-Buddhist armed organizations. Thus the nation-building projects of the ethnic nationalities have in turn triggered new conflicts.

---

[84] Tin Maung Maung Than. 'Tatmadaw in Transition: Dealing with Internal Conflict,' in V R Raghavan, ed. Internal Conflict in Myanmar: Transnational Consequences. (New Delhi: Vij Books, 2011).p 17

[85] Larry Jagan, 'Myanmar's Military Mindset Intensifies Internal Conflicts,' in V R Raghavan, ed. Internal Conflict in Myanmar: Transnational Consequences. (New Delhi: Vij Books, 2011).

Conflict Dynamics

Myanmar's ethno-political conflicts have ebbed and flowed over the past six decades. The first phase coincided with democratic rule in Myanmar and extended for a decade after Independence. The first to pick up arms were the Karen, Mon, Pao and Rakhine. So powerful was their challenge to the state that vast swathes of territory fell to the ethnic armies. The KNU made rapid advances initially taking control of several key towns, including Insein, near the capital .[86] An attempt at peace talks in 1949 brought a brief pause in fighting but the KNU's rather ambitious demands led to a resumption of fighting. [87] During this period, the Chin, Kachin and Shan, explored political means to address their grievances and rallied around the government through the turmoil of those years. The Chin and Kachin Rifles, who were deployed against the Communist Party of Burma (CPB) and the Karen insurgents, in fact played an important role in preventing the country's disintegration .

During the second phase (1958-88) fighting intensified. When the government declared Buddhism as the state religion, Kachin and Shan youth turned to militancy. The enraged Kachin set up the Karen Independence Organization (KIO) in 1961. Meanwhile, the 'Federal Movement' of the Chin, Kachin and Shan, which aimed at amending the constitution, forced U Nu to call a meeting at Taunggyi to discuss the federal question. Even as the meeting was in progress, the military staged a coup and flickering hopes for federalizing Myanmar were snuffed out (Smith 2007: 31).[88] The coup proved the last straw for the Chin, Kachin and Shan, who now joined the ethnic insurgencies. The military's counter-insurgency operations during this period saw the adoption of the 'Four-Cuts campaign,' which took violence to unprecedented levels.

The 1988-2010 period witnessed dramatic changes. Prior to 1988, the issues and main defenders of the struggle for democracy and those for ethnic rights were separate. The struggles were in fact seen to be "detrimental

---

[86] Martin Smith, State of Strife: The Dynamics of Ethnic Conflict in Burma. Singapore: Institute of Southeast Asian Studies; (Washington: East-West Center, 2007). P 27

[87] Ashley South, Burma's Longest War: Anatomy of the Karen Conflict. (Amsterdam: Transnational Institute, 2011), p 8

[88] See Martin Smith, p 31

to each other" [89] Many pro-democracy activists – they were mainly Burman – blamed the ethnic insurgencies for the failure of democracy, arguing that it was because of the threat they posed to Myanmar's territorial integrity that the generals staged a coup. Post-1988, pro-democracy activists fled to areas under the control of ethnic armies. This brought the two struggles closer to each other. "Differing political agendas were aligned into one set of overarching movement objectives. Pro-democracy activists came to regard federalism as essential for nation-building. This change ultimately influenced the wider Burman population. In return, the ethnic armies officially declared in 1990 not to break away from the country under a real federal union, forfeiting their traditional right to secession," observes Duell .[90]

To pre-empt co-operation between the pro-democracy activists and the ethnic armies, the government initiated ceasefires with the latter. Between 1989 and 1993 ceasefires with 17 groups were reached. The ceasefires freed the military to crush the pro-democracy movement as well as focus on groups like the KNU, who rejected the ceasefire. While the ceasefires did see a winding down of several insurgencies, violence in the border areas continued as militias clashed with each other over control of resources and the drug trade. The fragility of the ceasefires was exposed repeatedly. In 2009, for instance, when the government ordered the ceasefire groups to transform their armies into Border Guard Forces under the command of Myanmar's army, most groups rejected the offer. The military then initiated operations against smaller groups like the Myanmar National Democratic Alliance Army (MNDAA).

The present phase of the conflict began with a quasi-civilian government dominated by the military and led by a former junta leader took charge in 2011. While it has reached out to the ethnic minorities, entering into a ceasefire agreement with groups like the KNU, for instance, recent clashes between the Buddhist and the Rohingyas and the reported role of the military in fuelling the violence raises questions over how far President Thein Sein will go to resolve the ethno-political conflicts.

---

[89] See Kristen Duell, p 40
[90] Ibid, p 70

Role of External Actors

Although the military is inward-looking and followed a policy of isolating the country from even the neighbours, external actors have played an important role in shaping the conflicts' dynamics. Thailand hosts the largest number of refugees. It is the most important base from which pro-democracy exile groups and Karen and Mon armies have operated. Its support to the Karen insurgents stems from its buffer zone policy, which is based on a perception of Myanmar's ethnic minorities as "bulwarks" against possible "physical and ideological intrusions." Successive Thai governments believed that supporting conflicts in Myanmar would prevent it from emerging stronger and posing a threat to Thailand's security. Hence, it "went along with the American plan to contain communism in Burma by supplying arms and funds to ethnic rebels," writes researcher Pavin Chachavalpongpun .[91] Thailand's fuelling of ethnic insurgencies in Myanmar has carried heavy costs. As violence escalated, so did the flow of refugees. Thailand has borne the financial burden of providing for them. Conflicts over resources have erupted between the refugees and local communities and problems like prostitution, HIV-AIDS, and easy availability of narcotics and arms have undermined Thai society and security. "It is thus ironic that in an attempt to block any threat from the military regime in Myanmar ... [Thailand] has made itself vulnerable to other kinds of threats brought by the refugees".[92]

China's policy towards Myanmar has changed significantly over the decades. If in the early post-Independence decades it was keen to export communism to Myanmar and to this end provided robust support to the CPB insurgency, its burgeoning economic interests in Myanmar compelled it to withdraw such support from the 1980s. Its policy towards the ethnic insurgencies has been confused, swinging from arming insurgents to nudging them to halt the violence. It facilitated the ceasefires in 1989. Two factors determine China's interest and involvement in Myanmar's ethnic

---

[91] Pavin Chachavalpongpun, 'Exporting Threats, Transmitting Instability: Conflict in Myanmar and its Effects on Thailand,' in V R Raghavan, ed. Internal Conflict in Myanmar: Transnational Consequences. (New Delhi: Vij Books, 2011).

[92] Ibid

insurgencies. One is that most of the Sino-Myanmar border is under the control of groups like the MNDAA and the United Wa State Army (UWSA) making it imperative for China to cultivate good relations with them if only to ease trade through territories they control. The other is the presence of ethnic groups straddling the Sino-Myanmar border. Beijing fears that ethnic unrest in Myanmar could spark turbulence among their kin in China. It is thus opposed to Myanmar granting autonomy to its ethnic groups as that would prompt similar demands from their Chinese kin. This presents Beijing with a dilemma. Too much autonomy for ethnic minorities could spark ethnic uprising in China. However, military operations to crush the ethnic insurgencies, such as the offensive against the MNDAA in 2009, result in refugees fleeing into China. As researcher Li Chenyang argues besides the financial burden of providing for refugees, Chinese-owned businesses and crops in Myanmar are destroyed in the fighting.[93]

International NGOs working in refugee camps along the Thai-Myanmar border have shaped perceptions of the conflicts. Even as they provide voice to the refugees, they project the Sgaw-Christian version of the conflict as that of the Karen community, when in fact this represented only the perception of the KNU's leadership. The flawed perception of the Karen identity as a homogenous one too was driven by foreign accounts of the conflict as seen through the eyes of the Thailand-based refugees (South 2011: 32).[94] An important source of support for ethnic insurgents comes from the exile community, the Diaspora and human rights activists. Think tanks in Europe that are working on ethnic minority issues have provided rich input on the nature of the ethno-political struggles. Besides, western governments, while focused on the pro-democracy movement, supported the ethnic nationalists struggle indirectly through their opposition to the government.

Overwhelmingly Military Approach

Successive governments viewed Myanmar's diversity as divisiveness and sought to impose unity through military coercion. The conflicts were seen

---

[93] Chenyang Li, Effects of the Conflict between the Ceasefire Groups and the Military Government on China,' in V R Raghavan, ed. Internal Conflict in Myanmar: Transnational Consequences. (New Delhi: Vij Books, 2011).

[94] See Ashley South, p 32

as requiring a military approach, evident in the military-led counter-insurgency operations since 1948. In the 1960s, the junta implemented the 'Four-Cuts' strategy to cut off insurgents' access to food, funds, recruits and intelligence by cutting their access to civilian populations. While this strategy weakened the insurgents, it resulted in massive displacement and "completely transformed the human landscapes of the Mon, Karen, Karenni, and Shan areas in particular." Its failure to cut off insurgent supply lines became apparent in the areas bordering China, India, Thailand and Bangladesh where insurgents could access supply lines across borders. The army also created militias in areas under its control. Set up to guard villagers against insurgents and to support the army in its operations, the militias were allowed to "rule their areas relatively undisturbed." Soon, militia leaders were trafficking drugs, often with the support of the military. When Ne Win abandoned the scheme in 1973, the militias went underground and joined hands with their former adversaries from the armed groups to build drug syndicates (Duell 2011: 63-64).[95] Thus, the counter-insurgency strategy directly fuelled the narcotics trade and set off new conflicts.

Rarely has the government engaged in serious talks with ethnic insurgent groups. When it did, these were driven by motivations of divide-and-rule and more in the nature of deal-making and opaque. The post-1988 ceasefires are illustrative of this. The ceasefires were mere verbal deals done with ethnic army leaders, which allowed them to retain their militias and run businesses (Duell 2011: 65).[96] While there was less war in the post-1988 period, there was no peace as the ceasefires were not followed by negotiations towards a political solution.

The ceasefires paved the way for the government to gain access to the remote borderland areas, which were hitherto under the control of the ethnic armies. It enabled the government to exploit the natural resources of these regions (Duell 2011: 65).[97] Large-scale projects in hydro-electric power production and mining were set up with investment from China, India and Thailand. But these did not bring socio-economic improvement in the lives of local people. Projects in areas bordering China saw an influx of Chinese

---

[95] Kristen Duell, pp 64-65
[96] Ibid p 65
[97] Ibid

labour. Displacement of local populations, their exclusion from the benefits of these projects and the impact of these projects on local environment has triggered new conflicts as in the case of the Myitsone Dam project. The government has also sought development in border areas through border trade with the neighbours. While some of these initiatives have expanded civilian activities in the borderlands, criminal mafias dominate much of the trade.[98] Both the military and the ceasefire groups have approached development to mean business deals that enrich them and their cronies rather than the local populations.

The above examination of ethno-political conflicts in Sri Lanka, India's Northeast, Nepal, and Myanmar reveals broad similarities in their origin and evolution as well as in the state's role in and response to these conflicts. It is to a summarizing of these similarities that we now turn.

Commonalities in the Conflicts

There are similarities and differences in the historical experiences of India, Sri Lanka, Nepal and Myanmar. While India, Sri Lanka and Myanmar underwent long periods of direct colonial rule, Nepal did not. There are differences too in the political systems they have had over the last 60 years. But for a short period in the 1970s when a political emergency was declared and fundamental rights suspended, India has been a democracy. Sri Lanka is Asia's oldest democracy but is increasingly turning authoritarian. Nepal is a young democracy, which only recently shook off monarchical rule. As for Myanmar, it has only begun taking small steps towards democratization. Their different political systems notwithstanding, all four countries studied in this chapter have witnessed a surge in identity politics and ethnic insurgencies.

All four countries are ethnically plural. Their political elites have viewed this diversity with apprehension, seeing it as divisiveness that would culminate in disintegration. It prompted them to set out on a process of nation-building that was often contentious as it raised in these plural societies difficult questions regarding the definition of the nation and its constituents, the relationship between state and religion, which language/s would be the official

---

[98] K Yhome, p 175

and/or national language/s, etc. These questions evoked furious debate on whether the state would be centralized or federal. The political elites turned to consolidating the nation-state through some variant of majoritarianism, which privileged the identity and rights of the majority group, and centralization of power. They were also willing to use coercion to enforce their homogenization of society.

Of the four countries, India was the only one to resist crafting a majoritarian state. It did not declare Hinduism to be the state religion and avoided declaring any language to be the 'national language,' although Hindi and English were declared official languages. In contrast, Myanmar, Nepal and Sri Lanka constitutionally privileged one religion, language and ethnicity, usually that of the majority or the largest group. In this, Nepal and Myanmar went the furthest, declaring the state to be Hindu and Buddhist, respectively. The 'national integration' that South Asian countries set out to achieve, was unitary in its connotations. It saw political elites reject federalism and embrace centralization of power to varying degrees. Again, India is the least centralized of the four countries, although its federalism is still work in progress. In Sri Lanka and Myanmar, federalism is seen as the first step towards secession; so intense is the fear of devolving meaningful power to excluded ethnic groups.

While political elites in the four countries turned to homogenization and centralization to hold their diverse societies together, it was this very approach that triggered ethno-political conflict, with ethnic groups that are excluded from the political and economic power structure engaging in struggles against their respective states for recognition of their cultural, social and political rights, rights over land, and so on. The response of the states in South Asia to these demands has in turn spurred groups to escalate demands and methods, sometimes resulting in armed struggles for separate states. The centrality of the state in triggering conflict and escalating it is apparent from the accounts of the conflicts in the four countries under study.

Interestingly, in all four countries, organizations and movements that emerged to protest the exclusion of ethnic groups were exclusionist themselves. If the state responded to ethnic diversity through homogenizing the population, the ethnic organizations sought to forge a unified identity by denying diversity within the group. The KNU projected the Sgaw-Christian identity of its leadership, excluding in the process the Karen Buddhists. Likewise, the Tamil nationalist parties and the LTTE claimed to represent the Tamil-speaking people but in their actions they excluded the Tamil-speaking Muslims, even the Tamils from the Eastern Province. Commanders and fighters of the LTTE felt that while it was Tamils from the North who dominated the leadership and crafted strategy, it was Eastern Tamils who did the fighting and bore the brunt of the war. The failure of Karen and Tamil nationalist organizations to forge an inclusive identity not only undermined their claims to speak on behalf of their communities, but also it had implications for their survival. Buddhist Karen left the KNU to form the Democratic Karen Buddhist Army (DKBA). The DKBA then co-operated with the military against the KNU. The fall of Manerplaw, the headquarters of the KNU, in 1995 and the decline of the KNU thereafter was in large measure the outcome of intra-ethnic conflict. Similarly, in Sri Lanka, the exclusion of Eastern Tamils culminated in the LTTE's split in 2004 and in its former eastern commander Karuna joining hands with the army. It was an important factor in the LTTE's defeat. The South Asian experience reveals that ethnic and nationalist organizations often become mirror images of the state - coercive, hegemonic and centralized – and this has severely weakened their struggle.

The experiences of India, Nepal, Sri Lanka and Myanmar underscore an intriguing relationship between democracy and ethno-political conflicts. On the one hand, electoral politics have encouraged mobilization, competition and conflict along ethnic lines. Democratization has triggered heightened ethnic activism and a proliferation of ethno-political organizations as was evident in Nepal. It has given a new lease of life to ethnic identities. However, authoritarian rule gives a fillip to violent eruption of ethnic activism as democratic and political channels for articulation of demands and grievances are blocked. It leaves aggrieved groups with no option but to pick up arms to press their demands.

A striking feature of South Asia's ethno-political conflicts is their protraction; many of them have festered for decades. Myanmar and India are home to some of the world's longest running ethnic insurgencies. This protraction of ethno-political conflicts can be attributed in part to their being contestations over state power and hence not easily amenable to solution.

But also, South Asian governments have avoided addressing the underlying causes of the conflict and the issues that fuelled them subsequently. They have failed to grapple with conflict in all its complexities, to respond to and understand its changing dynamics as well as to tackle consequences, which often fuel escalation of violence.

In all four countries studied in this chapter, governments have adopted a 'carrot and stick approach' to the ethno-political conflicts, with extension of economic development packages to the restive region constituting the 'carrot' and the use of coercive force comprising the 'stick'. They have been willing to use extreme force, including deployment of the armed forces, to stamp out secessionist aspirations and insurgencies but also, against non-violent articulation of demands. Special legislations criminalizing dissent and giving the police and army extraordinary powers have been enacted in all four countries. Governments have also sought to develop the economies of alienated regions by extending aid packages, building infrastructure and taking steps to jump-start the economy. While enhancing employment opportunities and development plays an important role in blunting grievances, it does breed dependency instead of building local capacity. Moreover, it triggers new conflicts. This is largely because development encouraged by South Asian governments in conflict zones is a private sector-led business model. This has generated new conflicts by accentuating poverty, destroying local environment through aggressive resource extraction and deepening the existing economic divide. Besides, the economic development initiated in conflict zones is rarely owned and led by locals. Take Myanmar, for instance. Infrastructure development and business in the former conflict zones bordering China are Chinese-owned. The beneficiaries are Chinese. This has triggered violent protests among groups like the Kachin against the Myanmar government as well as the Chinese. Economic development that is not locally driven does not result in locals developing a sense of ownership over the process or projects or in building local capacity. This is becoming evident in post-war Sri Lanka, where reconstruction and economic activity in the North is a top-down process that is military-driven and Sinhalese-owned. Tamils feel little ownership over the reconstruction process. It is laying the foundation for renewed conflict.

Of the four countries studied in this chapter, only India seems to have pursued political solutions with some seriousness. However, the way it has carried out negotiations or reached settlements has generated new conflicts and paved the way for a return to violence. The record of Sri Lanka, Nepal and Myanmar vis-à-vis political solutions has been abysmal, with their governments reluctant to concede even minimum political demands. Myanmar's 'talks' with ethnic groups has been more in the nature of striking business deals with leaders rather than sustained dialogue towards resolution.

What is the way forward then for South Asia? The above discussion provides some pointers and it is to a summarization of this that we now turn in the final section of this chapter.

Thoughts for the Future

This study chose to use the word 'ethno-political' to describe what are often termed as 'ethnic conflicts' as it captures better the essence of these conflicts, underscoring their political component even as it acknowledges their ethnic dimension. Recognizing this political component is essential not only for a better understanding of these conflicts but to prevent their violent escalation and their effective resolution. It is this failure or unwillingness of South Asian political elites to recognize the political core of ethno-political conflicts that lies at the heart of the protraction, proliferation and often violent manifestation of these conflicts. Instead, South Asian governments have tended to frame ethno-political conflicts as a terrorist problem that requires a military solution and/or understand the alienation of ethnic groups as the outcome of a lack of economic development. This understanding of ethno-political conflicts through the terrorism-development prism is flawed, even dangerous as it delegitimizes political grievances. It results in a perception of pacification as peace and assumes that ethnic alienation will subside once the problem is 'fixed' by an injection of economic aid to develop the restive region's economy.

It is not our argument that economic development of conflict zones is unwelcome. Creation of jobs for instance is an important step in rebuilding lives and livelihoods shattered by the conflict. However, South Asian governments need to facilitate development that is inclusive and empowers local communities. Development that does not enhance human security will generate new conflicts.

Most South Asian countries are multi-ethnic. As discussed above, political elites have tended to view not only ethnic diversity with apprehension but the assertion of identities with concern. Instead of defining nationalism in terms of a language or religion, South Asian states should move towards civic nationalism. Instead of debating whether an individual is an Indian or Muslim first, Nepali or Limbu first and so on and feeling threatened by people's assertion of their Naga or Kashmiri identity, South Asian states should adopt an approach that allows an individual to define and articulate his/her identity in any way he/she chooses so long as he/she carries out his/her obligations and duties of being a citizen of India or Sri Lanka or Myanmar, he/ she should be able to define and articulate his/her identity as she chooses.

Experience shows that policies which homogenize identities with a view to prevent disintegration of ethnically diverse societies have, in fact, the opposite effect. They set off ethno-political demands that could even culminate in violent secessionist movements. Given the central role that the state plays in the emergence of ethno-political conflicts and in their proliferation, protraction, intensification and often violent manifestation, state reform is imperative. South Asia's diverse societies predicate inclusive and pluralist politics. To this end states must become inclusive and more open to power-sharing arrangements.

Federal or autonomy provisions have been successful in mitigating secessionist demands. However, such provisions have also set off new conflicts that are triggered by anxieties of minorities within the new territorial arrangements. Hence, states must be open to considering a repertoire of responses to ethno-political conflicts, including non-territorial arrangements that could, for instance, meet self-governance demands of scattered ethnic groups.

South Asian governments tend to ignore peaceful movements and take more seriously demands that are violently articulated. This has encouraged non-state actors to resort to violent means. They need to engage in dialogue and take it seriously.

What is more, governments must avoid treating talks as a game between two actors, itself and the main armed group. Talks must be inclusive and allow participation of civil society, women's groups, trade unions, religious leaders, etc. The quest for a solution to ethno-political conflicts is largely an elite process in South Asia, with government officials speaking to leaders of ethno-political groups. Rarely are the people included in the process. A sustainable peace predicates a bottom-up process and the building of peace constituencies among the people. South Asia's experience shows that peace accords that follow inclusive peace processes are more likely to succeed.

Preventing ethno-political conflicts from turning violent is not the responsibility of the state alone. Civil society can play an important role in preventing clashes between various ethnic groups. Studies of Hindu-Muslim violence in India show that cities that have intercommunal or interethnic civic engagement are less likely to experience communal riots.

Across South Asia there is a perception that ethno-political conflicts are divisive and undermine democracy. As we saw earlier, the struggle for ethnic rights in Myanmar was seen to be detrimental to the struggle for democratic rights. The ethnic insurgencies were in fact blamed for creating conditions that supposedly paved the way for the military coup. In Nepal too, there is a perception that raising ethno-political demands distracts attention away from the democratization process. However, struggles for ethno-political rights cannot be separated from those for democratic rights. Restoration of democracy in Myanmar will be meaningless as long as ethnic nationalities are denied equal rights. Far from eroding democracy, Nepal's ethno-political organizations are seeking deepening it by making it more inclusive and egalitarian.

Select Bibliography

Adhikari, Indra and Uddhab Pyakurel. 2011. 'Internal Conflict in Nepal after the Comprehensive Peace Agreement,' in V R Raghavan, ed. *Internal Conflict in Nepal: Transnational Consequences*. New Delhi: Vij Books.

Bajpai, Kanti. 2010, 'Diversity, Democracy and Devolution in India,' in Sanjib Baruah, ed. *Ethnonationalism in India: A Reader*. New Delhi: OUP.

Baruah, Sanjib, ed. 2011. *Beyond Counter-Insurgency: Breaking the Impasse in Northeast India.* New Delhi: Oxford University Press.

Baruah, Sanjib. 2010. 'Confronting Constructionism: Ending the Naga War,' in Sanjib Baruah, ed. *Ethnonationalism in India: A Reader.* New Delhi: OUP.

Baruah, Sanjib. 1999. *India against Itself: Assam and the Politics of Nationality.* New Delhi: Oxford University Press.

Bhattacharya, Jayanta. 2011. 'Ramifications of Conflicts in Tripura and Mizoram,' in V R Raghavan and Sanjoy Hazarika, eds. *Conflicts in the Northeast: Internal and External Effects.* New Delhi: Vij Books.

Brara, N Vijayalakshmi. 2011. 'Nongpok Thong Hangba – Towards Cultural Collectives: Manipur and South East Asia,' in V R Raghavan and Sanjoy Hazarika, eds. *Conflicts in the Northeast: Internal and External Effects.* New Delhi: Vij Books.

Chachavalpongpun, Pavin. 2011. 'Exporting Threats, Transmitting Instability: Conflict in Myanmar and its Effects on Thailand,' in V R Raghavan, ed. *Internal Conflict in Myanmar: Transnational Consequences.* New Delhi: Vij Books.

Choudhury, Iftekhar Ahmed. 2011. Effects of Conflicts in Myanmar and their Consequences on Bangladesh,' in V R Raghavan, ed. *Internal Conflict in Myanmar: Transnational Consequences.* New Delhi: Vij Books.

Das, Samir Kumar. 2012. 'India's Northeast: The Post 'Pacification Era,' in V R Raghavan, ed. *Internal Conflicts: A Four State Analysis.* New Delhi: Vij Books.

Das, Samir Kumar. 2011. 'ULFA, Indo-Bangladesh Relations and Beyond,' in V R Raghavan and Sanjoy Hazarika, eds. *Conflicts in the Northeast: Internal and External Effects.* New Delhi: Vij Books.

Das, Samir Kumar. 2007. *Conflict and Peace in India's Northeast: The Role of Civil Society.* Washington: East-West Center.

De Mel, Deshal. 2011. 'Economic Dimensions of the Conflict,' in V R

Raghavan, ed. *Conflict in Sri Lanka: Internal and External Consequences*. New Delhi: Vij Books.

De Votta, Neil. 2007. *Sinhalese Buddhist Nationalist Ideology: Implications for Politics and Conflict Resolution in Sri Lanka*. Washington DC: East West Center.

Duell, Kerstin. 2011. 'Non-Traditional Security Threats, International Concerns and the Exiled Opposition,' in V R Raghavan, ed. *Internal Conflict in Myanmar: Transnational Consequences*. New Delhi: Vij Books.

Fernando, Laksiri. 2011. 'Long Distance Relations to the Conflict and their Ramifications,' in V R Raghavan, ed. *Conflict in Sri Lanka: Internal and External Consequences*. New Delhi: Vij Books.

Hangen, Susan. 2007. *Creating a "New Nepal": The Ethnic Dimension*. Washington: East-West Center.

Hassan, M Sajjad. 2010. 'Secessionism in Northeast India: Identity Wars or Crises of Legitimacy?' in Sanjib Baruah, ed. *Ethnonationalism in India: A Reader*. New Delhi: OUP.

Jagan, Larry. 2011. 'Myanmar's Military Mindset Intensifies Internal Conflicts,' in V R Raghavan, ed. *Internal Conflict in Myanmar: Transnational Consequences*. New Delhi: Vij Books.

Jayawardena, Kumari. 1985. *Ethnic and Class Conflicts in Sri Lanka*. Dehiwela: Centre for Social Analysis.

Kakoty, Sanjeeb. 2011. 'Migration Mantra and the Bangladesh-Northeast Conundrum,' in V R Raghavan and Sanjoy Hazarika, eds. *Conflicts in the Northeast: Internal and External Effects*. New Delhi: Vij Books.

Keerawella, Gamini. 2011. 'Pursuit of Sustainable Peace after the Military Defeat of LTTE: Insights into Post-War Scenarios,' in V R Raghavan, ed. Conflict in Sri Lanka: Internal and External Consequences. New Delhi: Vij Books.

Keethaponcalan, S I. 2011. 'Ethno-Political Conflict and the Civil War: Domestic and International Impact,' in V R Raghavan, ed. Conflict in Sri

Lanka: Internal and External Consequences. New Delhi: Vij Books.

Kramer. Tom. 2009. Neither War nor Peace: The Future of the Cease-fire agreements in Burma. Amsterdam: Transnational Institute.

International Crisis Group (ICG). 2011. Nepal: Identity Politics and Federalism. Asia Report No199. 13 January.

International Crisis Group (ICG). 2011. Myanmar: A New Peace Initiative. Asia Report No 214, 30 November.

Lawoti, Mahendra. 2007. Looking Back: Looking Forward: Centralization, Multiple Conflicts, and Democratic State Building in Nepal. Washington: East-West Center.

Lawoti,Mahendra. 2003. Towards a Democratic Nepal: Inclusive Political Institutions for a Multicultural Society. New Delhi: Sage.

Li, Chenyang. 2011. 'Effects of the Conflict between the Ceasefire Groups and the Military Government on China,' in V R Raghavan, ed. Internal Conflict in Myanmar: Transnational Consequences. New Delhi: Vij Books.

Mahanta, Nani Gopal. 2012. 'Changing Contours of Armed Violence in Northeast India,' in V R Raghavan, ed. Internal Conflicts: A Four State Analysis. New Delhi: Vij Books.

Manchanda, Rita. 2008. 'Partition as Conflict Resolution,' Himal Southasian, July http://www.himalmag.com/component/content/article/760-.html

Misra, Udayon. 2011. 'Internal Strife and External Impacts: The Issues of Nagaland and the Nagas,' in V R Raghavan and Sanjoy Hazarika, eds. Conflicts in the Northeast: Internal and External Effects. New Delhi: Vij Books.

Moorthy, N Sathiya. 2011. 'Sri Lanka: Trans-border Consequences of an Internal Conflict,' in V R Raghavan, ed. Conflict in Sri Lanka: Internal and External Consequences. New Delhi: Vij Books.

Murthy, Padmaja. 2011. 'Internal Conflict in Nepal: Implications for India,' in V R Raghavan, ed. Internal Conflict in Nepal: Transnational Consequences. New Delhi: Vij Books.

Peiris, G L. 2011. 'Internal Conflict in Sri Lanka: Managing the Consequences,' in V R Raghavan, ed. Conflict in Sri Lanka: Internal and External Consequences. New Delhi: Vij Books.

Phadnis, Urmila and Rajat Ganguly. 2002. Ethnicity and Nation-building in South Asia. New Delhi: Sage.

Pyakurel, Uddhab. 2012. 'Changing Patterns of Nepali Ethnic Movement,' in V R Raghavan, ed. Internal Conflicts: A Four State Analysis. New Delhi: Vij Books.

Raghavan, V R. 2012. Internal Conflicts: A Four States Analysis. New Delhi: Vij Books.

Raghavan, V R. 2011. Conflict in Sri Lanka: Internal and External Consequences. New Delhi: Vij Books.

Raghavan, V R. 2011.Internal Conflict in Myanmar: Transnational Consequences. New Delhi: Vij Books.

Raghavan, V R. 2011. Internal Conflict in Nepal: Transnational Consequences. New Delhi: Vij Books.

Raghavan, V R and Sanjoy Hazarika, 2011. Conflicts in the Northeast: Internal and External Effects. New Delhi: Vij Books.

Rajagopalan, Rajesh. 2009. 'Insurgency and Counterinsurgency,' Seminar, no. 599, July. http://www.india-seminar.com/2009/599/599_rajesh_rajagopalan.htm

Rajagopalan, Swarna. 2001. State and Nation in South Asia. Boulder, Colorado: Lynne Rienner.

Ramachandran, Sudha. 2009. 'India and the LTTE: For Better, For Worse,' in Sumanasiri Liyanage, P Sahadevan and Anisha Kinra, eds. Intra-State Conflicts and Inter-State Relations: Perspectives on India-Sri Lanka Relations. Colombo: SAPI.

Ramachandran, Sudha. 2012a. 'War is Over but Tensions run High,' The Diplomat, 13 December http://thediplomat.com/2012/12/13/sri-lanka-war-is-over-but-tensions-run-high/

Ramachandran, Sudha. 2012b. 'Sri Lanka rights vote stirs nationalist passion,' Asia Times Online. 27 March http://www.atimes.com/atimes/South_Asia/NC27Df01.html

Ramachandran, Sudha. 2010. 'Hungry for justice in India,' Asia Times Online, 18 March http://www.atimes.com/atimes/South_Asia/LC18Df02.html

Ramachandran, Sudha. 2008. 'Hopes fade for a Tiger homeland,' Asia Times Online. 22 May http://www.atimes.com/atimes/South_Asia/JE22Df03.html

Ramachandran, Sudha. 2002a. 'Selective Roots to Tamil Nationalism,' Asia Times Online, 18 April http://www.atimes.com/ind-pak/DD18Df01.html

Ramachandran, Sudha. 2002b. 'Towards the imagined haven of Eelam,' *Asia Times Online*, 12 April http://www.atimes.com/ind-pak/DD12Df01.html

Silva, Kalinga Tudor. 2012. 'Ethnicity in Post-war Sri Lanka,' in V R Raghavan, ed. Internal Conflicts: A Four State Analysis. New Delhi: Vij Books.

Singh, N Mahendro. 2011. 'Impact of Conflicts in the Northeast with Special Reference to Manipur,' in V R Raghavan and Sanjoy Hazarika, eds. Conflicts in the Northeast: Internal and External Effects. New Delhi: Vij Books.

South, Ashley. 2011. Burma's Longest War: Anatomy of the Karen Conflict. Amsterdam: Transnational Institute.

Smith, Martin. 2007. State of Strife: The Dynamics of Ethnic Conflict in Burma. Singapore: Institute of Southeast Asian Studies; Washington: East-West Center.

Steinberg, David. I. 2011. Myanmar's Perpetual Dilemma: Ethnicity in a "Discipline Flourishing Democracy." Honolulu: East West Center.

Talukdar, Sushanta. 2008. 'Less than 50 per cent Assamese speakers in Assam,' The Hindu, 9 January http://www.hindu.com/2008/01/09/stories/2008010959461900.htm

Thapa, Chiran Jung. 2012. 'Nepal's Armed Conflict – A Narrative of Political

Mismanagement,' in V R Raghavan, ed. Internal Conflicts: A Four State Analysis. New Delhi: Vij Books.

Thapa, Chiran Jung. 2011. 'Nepal's Counter-Insurgency Campaign: Impact and Aftermath,' in V R Raghavan, ed. Internal Conflict in Nepal: Transnational Consequences. New Delhi: Vij Books.

Tin Maung Maung Than. 2011. 'Tatmadaw in Transition: Dealing with Internal Conflict,' in V R Raghavan, ed. Internal Conflict in Myanmar: Transnational Consequences. New Delhi: Vij Books.

Upadhyaya, Anjoo Sharan. 2011. 'Conflict in Nepal and its Transnational Ramifications,' in V R Raghavan, ed. Internal Conflict in Nepal: Transnational Consequences. New Delhi: Vij Books.

Uyangoda, Jayadeva. 2012. 'Sri Lanka's Ethnic Conflict: Role of the State,' in V R Raghavan, ed. Internal Conflicts: A Four State Analysis. New Delhi: Vij Books.

Watson, Mathew J. 2008. 'Conflict and History in Burma: Myths of Panglong,' Asian Survey, vol. 48, no.6. November-December. pp. 889-9.

Yhome, K. 2011. 'Trans-border Effects on Northeast India,' in V R Raghavan, ed. *Internal Conflict in Myanmar: Transnational Consequences*. New Delhi: Vij Books.

Managing Internal Conflicts in India, Nepal, Sri Lanka and Myanmar: Strategies and Outcomes

P. Sahadevan

Peacemaking in internal conflict is inherently an arduous task. It essentially entails a complex process of negotiations in that both state and groups adopt multiple strategies in pursuit of their conflict goals. Yet, the outcome tends to be uncertain or ambiguous in many cases. An internal conflict may have a clear beginning gradually, makes a steady progress evident in its incremental escalation and shows predictable trends, but its end or eventual termination is often unclear. It is possible that a conflict, which is apparently settled through negotiations, either continues or resumes under a different leadership excluded from the peace process. This underlines the need for an inclusive approach to peacemaking. However, this approach in reality constraints and limits the task of accomplishing peace since leaders representing different groups and interests in a conflict may not easily agree on a common framework of solution. Thus, in either way, conflict tends to continue as a protracted event until a genuine solution, based on mutual compromise by both parties and supported by their constituencies, is arrived at and implemented fully. Differently, use of coercion by the state dominates the conflict process and thus peacemaking receives a low priority in the strategy of one or both parties. This leads either to intractability of conflict or its end in a military victory of the state until or unless it is revived by new leader(s) who adopt violent or nonviolent means to accomplish a set of redefined goals. The trends and experience in many of the conflicts analyzed in this chapter corroborate the above arguments.

This chapter analyzes the strategies of managing ethnic conflicts in four countries—India, Nepal, Sri Lanka and Myanmar—and assesses their outcomes in a comparative perspective. Important questions in this context are: what have been the principal or preferred strategies of states and how have the rebel groups responded to them? Has conflict management as a process and strategy yielded the desired outcome viz. peace to the satisfaction of all stakeholders—states, groups and members of their respective constituency who have willy-nilly become participants in conflicts and thus victims of violence by both adversaries. What were the conditions under which they made their preference for a negotiated peace? And, why have some states and groups refused to engage in political negotiations? What is the structure of political settlement? And, what is the state of internal conflicts now? In answering these questions by making a comparative assessment of conflict and peace processes, the chapter relies on the case studies conducted by the Centre for Security Analysis (CSA)[1]. These interesting studies provide a comprehensive account of the causes and consequences of each conflict dealt with in this chapter from a management or peace perspective. The task here is to develop a comparative analysis on how these conflicts have been managed or mismanaged. It must be noted that comparative studies on internal conflict management in South Asia is scanty, whereas case studies are plenty. From a methodological standpoint, studies based on comparative analysis yield variety of insights on behavior of state and group in any conflict situation. They are not only useful for theory-building but also peace policy-making in divided societies. Therefore, using the arguments developed in the chapter, a set of broad policy recommendations on internal conflict management will be made in the last section to achieve peace in South Asia.

---

[1] V R Raghavan, ed. (2011), *The Naxal Threat: Causes, State Responses and Consequences*, (New Delhi: Vij Books India Pvt. Ltd, 2011), V.R. Raghavan, ed., *Internal Conflict in Nepal: Transnational Consequences*, (New Delhi: Vij Books India Pvt. Ltd, 2011), V.R.Raghavan, ed., *Internal Conflicts in Myanmar: Transnational Consequences,* (New Delhi: Vij Books India Pvt. Ltd, 2011), V R Raghavan, ed, *Internal Conflicts: A Four State Analysis India, Nepal, Sri Lanka and Myanmar*, (New Delhi: Vij Books India Pvt. Ltd, 2013), Sanjoy Hazarika and V.R. Raghavan, eds., *Conflicts in the Northeast: Internal and External Effects,* (New Delhi: Vij Books India Pvt. Ltd, 2011).

Internal Conflict Management: A Conceptual Explanation

The burgeoning literature on internal conflict and peacemaking offers rich conceptual insights and explanations. This section provides a conceptual analysis by defining two principal concepts—'internal conflict' and 'conflict management'—and identifying the strategies and process of peacemaking.

Categorizing Internal Conflicts

Internal conflict is a generic term and broad category; it refers to a variety of political (non-violent) and armed (violent) struggles and movements within a state. An internal conflict can be classified according to its goals and nature of parties involved. Goals of each conflict vary and parties are many. An internal conflict based on ethnicity involves issues such as autonomy and secession *versus* centralization or consolidation of state and also maintenance of its (lopsided) structure and (exclusionary) policy. In the contemporary period, this is a dominant category of conflict involving state and its disgruntled ethnic community. Beginning as political campaigns, an ethnic conflict attains violent dimensions (such as insurgency, terrorism and ethnic war) in response to state repression and its refusal to redress ethnic combatants' legitimate grievances. Differently, an ideology driven revolution or insurrection entailing a state and radical group(s) can have the objective of capturing state power or dismantling the existing state structure and reforming state. Confrontation between the two determined parties can gradually grow to become a civil war, costing them enormously both in terms of men and materials. Disorder and instability unleashed in the process tends to weaken the fundamental fabric of polity. Communal or sectarian conflict is less widespread but more prevalent in many polarized multi-ethnic societies. Involving groups divided along linguistic or religious lines, this set of conflict is mainly driven by their strong desire to preserve and promote their sectarian interests. While seeking socioeconomic and political privileges and concessions, each group seeks to deny the same things to other. Rioting is another mode of group behavior; it can be both organized and spontaneous. Group leaders engineer riots, but rumors contribute to its intensity and spread. Lastly, coup d'etat involving a legitimate government and a section of military is a contest for state power. In seeking to depose an elected government and usurp power illegally, power-hungry military elites take measures including imprisonment and even killing of top political leaders with the aim of neutralizing their current and future challenges.

Table 1: Categories of Internal Conflicts

Nature	Parties	Goals	Dimensions
Ethnic conflict	State versus ethnic group	Autonomy & secession	Insurgency & ethnic war
Centralist conflict (Insurrection, revolution, reform movement)	State versus radical/moderate group	Capturing state power & socio-political reform	Civil war
Communal/sectarian Conflict	Group versus group	Promoting sectarian interests	Riots
Coup d'etat	Government versus military	Capturing or controlling state power	Captivity & killing

Inherent difference in nature and dimension of each internal conflict indicates that its varied causes are distinguishable from other. Causes are both principal and proximate: the former denotes those underlying sources of conflict and the latter refers to those facilitating factors/conditions that interplay with the former to onset conflict or make it manifest. Issues in contention between ethnic groups are multifarious and their mutually competing interests are strong. Deeply rooted in institutional, political, economic and cultural factors[2], outbreak of an ethnic conflict is a symptomatic of prevalence of 'mass hate'[3] or mass hostility[4] between two ethnically divided communities which perceive each other as a competitor first and adversary then in course of their bitter experience at each other's hand. Mass hostility is indeed a domino-effect of unresolved ethnic grievances and a fear of ethnic extinction that one or both groups face or perceive. In this, the state plays a dominant role. Being an arbiter of material fortunes and socio-political interests of communities, states contribute towards sharpening ethnic chasm by pursing discriminatory policies aimed at favoring

---

[2] Michael E Brown,ed., *The International Dimensions of Internal Conflict*, (Cambridge, Mass: The MIT Press.1996).pp, 12-32

[3] John Mueller, "The Banality of 'Ethnic Wars'", *International Security*, 25(1): 42-70, 2000

[4] Stuart J Kaufman, "Spiraling to Ethnic War: Elites, Masses and Moscow in Moldova's Civil War", In Michael E. Brown, ed., *Nationalism and Ethnic Conflict: An International Reader*, (Cambridge, Mass: The MIT Press, 1997), pp 169-99

one at the cost of the other. This develops into a majoritarian state polity to undermine the multi-ethnic character of society, create an acute feeling of relative deprivation among weaker/minority ethnic group members, alienate them from the national mainstream and also set an exclusive national ideology based on the majority community's ethnicity.[5] Ethnic conflict has a greater spatial dimension.[6] Groups invariably identify themselves with part of territory where they are concentrated and demand for its exclusive political recognition as their traditional homeland. If a country's territorial compartmentalization along ethnic lines develops conditions for a state to create socioeconomic and political discrepancies among its ethnic communities, it also increases the prospects of ethnic conflict easily taking a secessionist or autonomist dimension.

Underlying sources of conflict become accentuated and attain a violent dimension due to the interplay of several factors. Since the state is the principal arena of competition for access to power and control of scarce resources,[7] its structural characteristics assume greater salience. Locating ethnic conflicts in structures of weak states, many argue that ethnic assertion in violent terms become greater when the state's legitimacy declines and its control over ethnic regions dwindles[8] Perhaps, states that use total force to repress groups may "appear strong, but their reliance on manifest coercion rather than legitimate authority more accurately implies weakness"[9]. It is not merely weakness of state that fuels conflict but also its blatant partisan

---

[5] Ted Robert Gurr, *Why Men Rebel*, Princeton, (N.J.: Princeton University Press, 1970), Donald L.Horowitz, *Ethnic Groups in Conflict*, (Berkeley: University of California Press. 1985),Joseph Rothschild, *Ethnopolitics: A Conceptual Framework* ,(New York: Columbia University Press, 1981).Russel Hardin, *One for All: The Logic of Group Conflict*, (Princeton: Princeton University Press, 1995), Ted Robert Gurr, "Why Minorities Rebel: A Global Analysis of Communal Mobilization and Conflict Since 1945", *International Political Science Review*, 14(2): 161-201. 1993

[6] John Agnew, "Beyond Reason: Spatial and Temporal Sources of Ethnic Conflict", In Kriesberg, Louis, et.al. eds., *Intractable conflicts and their Transformation*, (Syracuse: Syracuse University Press, 1989)

[7] Milton Esman, "Political and Psychological Factors in Ethnic Conflict ", in Joseph V. Montville, ed., *Conflict and Peacemaking in Multiethnic Societies*, (Lexington, Mass: Lexington Books, 1991), p 57.

[8] See Michael E.Brown, 1996,

[9] David A. Lake and Donald Rothchild,"Containing Fear: The Origins and Management of Ethnic Conflict," In Michael Brown, ed., *Nationalism and Ethnic Conflict: An International Reader*. (Cambridge, Mass: The MIT Press, 1997), P 100.

policy.[10] In deeply divided multi-ethnic societies, the state behaves more as an agent of the dominant/majority ethnic community than as an arbitrator among conflicting groups. In many cases, it is virtually taken captive by the majority group to serve its ethnic interests while minority/weaker groups face a threat from those institutions on which they rely for protection, equity and justice. In fact there are hardly any neutral institutions that can mediate between various conflicting groups and between a disgruntled minority and the majority ethnic group-dominated centre. The relevant intermediary institutions are primarily those bodies of popular representation (such as parliament) and adjudication (judiciary) which, instead of providing mediating structures and playing a arbitration role, function like a mere rubber-stamp of the dominant/majority community.

This exemplifies the "breakdown of normal politics".[11] Ethnicity is politicized and polity is ethnicized so that the majority ethnic group leaders' strategy of "ethnic outbidding"[12] to win and maintain in power is considered as a part of democratic process. Resultantly, competing ethnic communities tend to face a "commitment problem".[13] Since each group perceives the other as a threat to its interests and survival, promises of the dominant group and commitment of the weaker group are mutually suspected. The fear of betrayal haunts the latter more than the former; it is based on a premise that one group will renege on its obligations under an agreement and exploit the other at an opportune moment. In such adverse situations, both parties redefine the pattern of their interactions by involving themselves in mobilization and counter-mobilization—defined as a process by which a

[10] Paul Brass, *Ethnicity and Nationalism: Theory and Comparison*, (New Delhi: Sage Publications, 1991), Rodolfo Stavenhagen, *The Ethnic Question: Conflicts, Development, and Human Rights,* (Tokyo: UN University Press, 1990) and Judith D Toland, *Ethnicity and the State*, (New Brunswick: Transaction Publishers, 1993).

[11] William I Zartman, *Elusive Peace: Negotiating an End to Civil Wars*, (Washington, DC: Brookings Institution, 1995), p 5.

[12] Giovanni Sartori, "European Political Parties: The Case of Polarized Pluralism", In Joseph LaPalombara and Myron Weiner, eds., *Political Parties and Political Development*, (Princeton: Princeton University Press, 1966),

[13] See Lake and Rothchild, 1997. pp 104-8; also see [3] James D.Fearon, "Commitment Problem and the Spread of Ethnic Conflict", In David A. Lake and Donald Rothchild, eds., *The International Spread of Ethnic Conflict: Fear, Diffusion, and Escalation.* (Princeton: Princeton University Press, 1998), pp 107-26

mere member becomes an active participant in any collective venture.[14] Collectively, all these contribute to a serious security dilemma, a situation in which each group's defensive steps are construed as a threat to the other which in turn reacts to make the former less secure and thus the spiral of measures continues to cause hostility.[15] What ensues is violence as an inevitable cumulative outcome of all these factors.

Though insurrection, revolution and reform movements are different from ethnic conflict, the difficulty in isolating underlying sources makes the distinction sometimes elusive.[16] While each category is distinct in its characteristics, issues in both categories are often common. Some ethnic secessionist conflicts attain a revolutionary character and many revolutions have a strong ethnic base or are caused by intermixing of ethnicity with class (ethno-class struggle) or accentuation of the class grievances (ideological movement). Thus, there are many types of revolutions[17] and all of them are collectively known as "centralist conflicts"[18] because they seek a change in the structure of authority or a new system of government or even introduction of socio-economic changes in the society. Explanations of outbreak of insurrection and revolution are essentially social and structural. A social explanation underlines the socioeconomic processes marked by societal dysfunction, inequitable social and economic structure, mass socio-psychological disturbance and competition for comprehensive power (economic and political) among different social/class groups in a society.[19] The structural explanation locates revolution in the state system itself (a feudal-imperial variety with relatively inaccessible and elite-monopolized institutional structure whose goal is incompatible with that of society), intrusion of international political and economic forces into the structures of state, nature of peasant communities' relations to their landlords and state, conditions

---

[14] See Esman, 1989 pp 53-63 and Gurr 1993

[15] Barry R.Posen, "The Security Dilemma and Ethnic Conflict", *Survival*, vol. 35, no. 1, pp. 27-47.1993

[16] Roy Licklider, ed., *Stopping the Killing: How Civil Wars End*. (New York: New York University Press, 1993), p 304.

[17] Raymond Tanter and Manus Midlarsky,"A Theory of revolution*", Journal of Conflict Resolution*, 11(3): 264-280.1967

[18] see Zartman, 1995, p 121

[19] Jack A Goldstone, "Theories of Revolution", *World Politics*, 32(3): 425-53, 1980.

of military coherence and structural constraints on state's use of military, and the nature of elite (isolated, marginal or intransigent) and also range of their behaviors and interactions.[20] As each explanation is exclusive in nature, it makes our understanding of the phenomenon of insurrection and revolution limited and partial at best. An inclusive and broad-based explanation should combine both social and political factors whose close linkages are demonstrated in revolutions or insurrections. For instance, socio-economic discontentment of a community or class is rooted in discriminatory state structures and policies. Outbreak of violence, which tends to be intense and often takes a civil war dimension, depends on the monopoly of power that the state enjoys vis-à-vis the aggrieved and agitated group.

Coup d'etat is different from revolution and insurrection both in terms of processes and causation.[21] As a process it entails a swift action by military to seize power from a civilian regime, in that while participation of masses is either totally absent or extremely limited, they support or oppose depending on their interest and benefits. In terms of causes, coups occur in varied situations and circumstances; it is the cause that determines the goal of a coup. One perspective relates coups to the chronic breakdown of political authority. They are revolutionary or reform coups.[22] By seeking to play a political role and act as a major agent of political development, the military's goal is to cleanse the polity and restructure the decayed political institutions.[23] In contrast, the modernization perspective emphasizes the role of process of modernization of society in kindling the interest of military in political processes.[24] It is maintained that in transitional societies, tensions and cleavages (along ethnic, class and ideological lines) inevitably develop to undermine and challenge institutions. The military is susceptible to any such developments in society. Given its "great sense of citizenship" characterized by its "unique position" as members of "highly organized social and political unit", military often feels that it has a solution for achieving what its country

---

[20] Ibid

[21] Manus I Midlarsky, *On War: Political Violence in the International System*, (New York: Free Press, 1975). P 184

[22] See Tanter and Midlarsky, 1967, p 265

[23] Lucian W.Pye, "The Roots of Insurgency and the Commencement of Rebellions", in Harry Eckstein, ed., *Internal War: Problems and Approaches*, (New York: The Free Press,1964).

[24] Samuel P.Huntington, *Political Order in Changing Societies,* (New Haven: Yale University Press, 1968).

has failed to accomplish.[25] If these constitute the military's general interests, self-interests of some of its officers are also a motivating factor. To these the corporate interests of the armed forces can also be added. Being a "trade union" itself,[26] the military nurtures certain ambitions and moves to protect its core interests by seizing power when they are virtually affected or undermined. The varied causes of coup identified here underscore the point that it is a context specific incident and each one can be characteristically distinguished from the other by linking the socio-political conditions and the motives of military.

The final category of internal conflict is related to sectarianism and communalism—the latter term lacks clarity. Some scholars use both terms 'communal' and 'ethnic' conflicts interchangeably. Varshney[27] gives a communal label to ethnic conflict which, in Midlarsky's[28] view, is communal. However, in popular understanding and discourse in South Asia, the two terms carry different connotations. Whereas an ethnic conflict entails two or more linguistically or racially different groups, basically a communal conflict is between two or more different religious communities, who may even speak the same language. There are many competing perspectives on the causes of communal/sectarian conflicts. The instrumentalists blame the political elite for exploitation of illiteracy and gullibility of people who, in responding readily to their mobilization strategies, become candidates for "obscurantist agitation". Here, the emphasis is not on illiteracy and backwardness but on the politicization of religious differences. On this, Varshney and Wilkinson have proved that there is no systematic and clear linkage between literacy and communal/ sectarian violence. For anti-secularists, modernization is considered as a major cause of communal conflict. Besides flattening traditional cultures, it seeks to homogenize the society and makes the political class totally immoral. Alternatively, perceived or real economic competition between traders of different religious groups can also contribute to communal conflict. Lastly, the civil society-centered argument of Varshney[29] locates the principal causes of communal violence

---

[25] See Midlarsky, 1975, pp 180-81

[26] Donald L. Horowitz, *Ethnic Groups in Conflict*, (Berkeley: University of California Press, 1980), p 5.

[27] Ashutosh Varshney, Ethnic *Conflict and Civic Life: Hindus and Muslims in India*, (New Delhi: Oxford University Press, 2002).

[28] Manus I. Midlarsky, ed., *The Internationalization of Communal Strife*, (London: Routledge, 1992).

[29] See Varshney, 2002

mainly in the absence of inter-communal civic network and engagement in multi-religious societies. Whatever may be the underlying and proximate causes, communal/sectarian conflict becomes intense and widespread if the religious passions are evoked and consequently, a sense of fear and threat perception is created among the competing communities. Nevertheless, as compared to other type of internal conflicts, communal/sectarian conflict does not become protracted.

The characteristics and dimensions of internal conflicts highlight the following points: First, state is a principal actor or participant in a variety of internal conflicts occurring largely within its domain. Its role, direct or indirect, has an objective of maintaining institutional structures and preserving its ideology. Promoting the interests of a particular community with which the state identifies itself or a section of elite that nurtures and controls the state can be also its major goal. At the same time, dissidents aim at seizing state power or sharing it with others. Secondly, internal conflicts involve groups with strong ethnic, political and communal interests as parties, which support or oppose the state. In the process they play a combatant role which cost them at the end heavily in terms of men and materials. Thirdly, despite the denial of justice being an underlying cause, some conflicts taking a civil war dimension are motivated by economic interest of the leaders. Greed and grievance thus form together a major factor in determining the process of conflict.[30] Fourthly, since internal conflicts tend to be intensely violent and consequently create humanitarian crisis (generally marked by widespread human rights violations, hunger and internal displacement of civilians and influx of refugees to many foreign countries), they tend to draw into their vortex a variety of external actors with different goals. Thus, internationalization is a dynamic feature of an internal conflict process.[31]

---

[30] P Collier and A Hoeffle, "On Economic Causes of Civil War", Oxford Economic Papers, 50: 563-73, 1998 and Charles King, "The Benefits of Ethnic War: Understanding Eurasia's Unrecognized States", *World Politics*, 53: 524-52, 2001

[31] David Carment, "The International Dimensions of Ethnic Conflict: Concepts, Indicators, and Theory", *Journal of Peace Research*, 30(2): 137-50, 1993; Alexis Heraclides, "Secessionist Minorities and External Involvement", International Organization, 44(3): 341-378, 1990; C R Mitchell, "Civil Strife and the Involvement of External Parties", *International Studies Quarterly*, 14(2): 166-194, 1970; Stephen M.Saideman,"Explaining the International Relations of Secessionist Conflicts: Vulnerability Versus Ethnic Ties", International Organization, 51(4): 721-53, 1997; Patrick M.Regan, "Choosing to Intervene: Outside Interventions in Internal Conflicts", *The Journal of Politics*, 60(3): 754-79, 1998.

Defining Conflict Management

Management is one of the widely used terms in conflict studies to mean peacemaking. A generic term that denotes achieving a number of end-results and activities, 'conflict management' entails efforts to prevent, limit, contain, or resolve conflicts, especially violent ones, even while "building up the capacities" of all parties to undertake peace- building. It is assumed that "conflicts are a normal part of human interaction and are rarely completely resolved or eliminated, but they can be managed by such measures as negotiation, mediation, conciliation, and arbitration". Besides ending violence and creating peace, conflict management "supports the long-term development of societal systems and institutions" that are meant for enhancing "good governance, rule of law, security, economic sustainability, and social well-being, which helps prevent future conflicts".[32] Thus, the list of expected or desired outcomes of any conflict management process is long but, in practice, it is not easy to achieve all of them under a single phase or process. Further, no one set of strategy or measures will help realize the desired outcomes outlined above. Rather, any conflict management process entails multiple strategies and instruments, adopted in accordance with the nature of conflict and the level and pattern of power relations between the adversaries. States make their choice first and groups invariably respond or chose not to respond. This underscores the point that state is the initiator of conflict management process either in response to (*internal*) pressure in military terms from its adversary or (*external*) pressure brought to bear upon one or both adversaries by actors (states and organizations) outside to the original conflict structure. Importantly, while state enjoys a pivotal position directly in managing ethnic and centralist conflicts, it seeks to mediate communal conflicts even while deploying its administrative machinery to maintain law and order. Incidentally, the question of political management of coup d'etat does not arise since the event has led to overthrowing of one set of forces (democrats) by another (authoritarians). What is, therefore, desired is an end forthwith of the latter's rule on which there cannot be any compromise from the democratic standpoint. A successful political management of coup d'etat denotes restoration of the concerned state system to its original position (from dictatorship to democracy).

---

[32] Dan Snodderly, ed., *Peace Terms: Glossary of Terms for Conflict Management and Peacebuilding*, (Washington, D.C.: USIP, 2011).

The conventional conflict management strategy merely involves political negotiations between government and dissident or rebel leadership. While negotiations as a mode of conflict management is still important to work out peace deals, the strategy is broad enough to include a number of unilateral political measures that a government prefers to undertake either to strengthen a negotiation process or strengthen its position at the negotiating table vis-à-vis dissidents or avoid any serious negotiations. Thus, political measures work to compliment or supplement or prevent the process of negotiations in internal conflicts. Two important measures that governments invariably undertake are aimed at ending any external patron role and eroding dissidents' support base so that they are weakened by their own constituency members.

In many internal conflicts, the support of external patrons forms a critical component of dissidents' power structure. In such cases, they are not only important for initiation and sustenance of conflict but also for its ending. If involving patrons is a crucial part of every weaker party's conflict strategy, ending or denial of any external military or political intervention is an important condition for achieving a military victory (by a stronger party) or a negotiated settlement. In numerous cases, governments consider it important to wean away its opponent's patrons from conflict, not so much to their side but against the latter's conflict strategy and goal, through constant use of bilateral or multilateral diplomatic persuasion or pressure. The underlying assumption is that, though ending the partisan role of an external patron does not directly contribute to power and capability of the government in conflict, it indirectly enhances its strength vis-à-vis the dissidents. A government is more inclined to win its opponent's patron when the protracted conflict threatens to alter the military balance, with the militants registering a series of successes in battles, or when they reject an offer of negotiations and remain committed to their goal even after the conflict is stalemated or when there is less likelihood of creating a hurting stalemate in the prolonged conflict process.

The success of this strategy depends upon the extent of pressure exerted, the nature of client-patron relationship, and the cost and benefit of ending the patron's support or continuing it. It is easier to end an external patron support extended for instrumental considerations than an intervention by a kin-state for affective reasons. The kin-states cease or moderate their patron role when the cost of it is seemingly much higher than their non-intervention. A successful weaning of a kin-state patron may also include modifying its original role to become an interested intermediary or facilitator of peace process. Outcomes of this strategy vary. It is possible that dissidents suffer a jolt when their patron(s) are pressurized to withdraw their support so crucial for sustaining their conflict efforts. It means that the asymmetry is further deepened to create a situation for deescalating the conflict that ultimately leads to a military end. If the dissidents enjoy the popular support of their local constituency and display a strong commitment to their goal, the conflict continues without hurting the government until it reaches a simple stalemate that forces them to negotiate a peace deal. Or, the patron enters into an informal deal with the government under which it withdraws support to the rebels and in return, extracts a promise from the government that it would negotiate with them. It is possible that even after the withdrawal of patron support, status quo ante in the conflict process continues because the rebel leadership, besides its local resources, finds alternative sources of external support, possibly from their diaspora. Ending of patron support does not mean an end of the conflict itself in every case; also this is not the only strategy that governments adopt. If at all this strategy succeeds in changing the power equation between adversaries, it may be due to the fact that the government further resorts to other steps. Eroding the rebels' support base assumes importance because, in the absence of any patron support, the local support becomes crucial both for their conflict efforts and survival.

The other strategy seeks to target at the militant group's structure. The general assumption is that the strength of a group lies in its cohesive structure: it means that the greater the group cohesion, the stronger it is to fight its adversary. When challenged by militants and trapped endlessly in an internal war without any prospect for a political dialogue, governments seek to target the groups' structure with a view to dividing them further and thus weaken them on the battlefield. Generally, the dominant/intransigent group that holds the key for the success of a peace process or challenges the government the most is targeted by its adversary. Since insurgent groups in internal wars are mostly internally divided even without any contribution from their adversary, embarking on the strategy of divide-and-engage would mean creating more focal parties in a given conflict/internal war which pursue different sets of goals. Thus, governments tend not only use the existing structural cleavage of groups to their advantage, but also work towards dividing them further for the success of their war-ending strategy.

It must be noted that dividing militants is one aspect of a government strategy, and driving a wedge between them and the moderates is another. By encouraging or even inducing the moderate leaders to accept political negotiations, governments seek to isolate militants from their own society and constituency. Cumulatively, the purpose of the divide-and-engage strategy is to either end an internal conflict/war without any settlement, or initiate and advance a peace process with the objective of reaching a negotiated settlement. As it is an externally induced division, governments obviously offer certain incentives and rewards. It may be in the form of an offer of general amnesty to the militant cadres and their leaders and a promise of rehabilitation and political position in the governmental structure. The divide-and-engage strategy may not always be beneficial to governments. If group cleavages and creating more focal parties in an internal war can weaken the parent group and also de-concentrate power, it can also increase the contest and challenge to the concerned government from many angles. It means that instead of weakening the targeted group to achieve an end of the war or initiate a peace process with dissidents, the concerned government may end up in intensifying the war as the new groups seek to show their determination to fight for their cause. In many situations, it is easier for a government to deal with a small group either militarily or politically rather than a plethora of groups with different goals and strategies. Of course, this is not a definite proposition applicable to every internal war situation.

Measures to erode rebels' support base assume importance invariably in the strategy of almost all governments. When internal conflicts become intense and widespread, the difference between combatants and non-combatants is hardly recognizable.[33] Civilians, who are otherwise not the direct participants in violence, find themselves bracketed with militants and targeted by the security forces. The aim is to break the insurgents' strategic link with their people and erode their support base. "If and when active support [of the community] dries up", Gurr[34] observes, "the group finds it

---

[33] Charles King, *Ending Civil Wars*, Adelphi Paper 308, (London: Oxford University Press, 1997), pp16-17.

[34] Ted Robert Gurr. "Terrorism in Democracies: Its Social and Political Bases", In Walter Reich, ed., *The Origins of Terrorism: Psychologies, Theologies, States of Mind*, (Cambridge: Cambridge University Press, 1990). P 95.

increasingly difficult to attract new recruits, to get material resources, to find refuge among reliable sympathizers". But violence against civilians cannot be endless, and using all-out military tactics to alienate them from the insurgents will be counterproductive to the government's war efforts. The latter therefore adopts various political measures to win the insurgents' constituency while waging the conflict or after its end in the government's favour. If political steps follow military victory, they are simply part of measures of reconciliation. Otherwise, pursuing them along with the conflict will have the aim of securing civilian support for the government's efforts to achieve a military victory if the patron support dwindled, or to start negotiations if the conflict reaches a stalemate without hurting the parties after the end of the patron support.

Politico-economic measures by governments for eroding rebels' support base include the following: (i) Announcement or undertaking of economic development works in conflict afflicted areas or where the militants' support base is located or concentrated; (ii) Effective relief and rehabilitation measures for the conflict affected people, and reconstruction of the strife-torn areas; (iii) Protection of the human rights of non-combatants by instructing the state security forces to spare civilian targets; publicized punishment to those who violate human rights; (iv) Conduct of good civil-military relations in conflict zones by making the security forces to undertake various civil duties and functions; (v) Unilateral announcement of a peace package with guarantees to the dissident groups' interests; (vi) Initiation of political process by, for instance, holding elections in the war-torn areas and establishing civilian-controlled administrations.

It is assumed that these measures, if implemented, create opinion favourable to the government. But they work more in those situations marked by a capitulation of the insurgents after the decline of their power, coupled with cessation of violence against civilians and de-escalation of the conflict. Thus, these are reconciliation measures at best. Communities concerned do not just get carried away by the government's politico-economic steps and change their loyalties in an internal conflict, especially if they live with memories of their repression by the state security forces, feel that their government is untrustworthy as its prime interest lies in ending the conflict without redressing their legitimate grievances, and take an intransigent position that their demands are not negotiable. This, therefore, leaves out only a few situations under which these measures work. Of course, civilians tend to get deviated from the cause for which the insurgents started the conflict if they are not so successfully mobilized or the level of their mobilization is low. It occurs mostly in an elite-led mobilization process where the role of the masses is absent.

At this point, it is pertinent to interrogate the role of coercion in conflict management. In a definitional sense, coercion does not constitute a conflict management strategy. It is at best a strategy that parties in a conflict use to create propitious condition or 'ripe moments'[35] for peacemaking when their original desire for zeros-sum outcome (win-lose) becomes difficult. Thus, coercion is a strategy meant for conflict-waging, whose outcomes and efficacies determine the conflict management process. Coercion is therefore seen as a tool to soften one party's demands, or to make another give up its tough position on accommodating the rival party's interests. In either way, peace is considered as the most valued goal of the parties, which they seek to achieve according to their own terms and conditions and through negative means of violence. It means that in their frame of mind and strategy, violent coercion alone is considered to be the most appropriate means of managing or ending conflict. This is a strategic choice that the top leaders make on the basis of certain capability-related assumptions and interest-oriented compulsions. For those government and insurgent leaders who are worried about their position and power, negotiated peace is "less desirable than an outright victory", even if the "immediate cost" of attaining it "outweighs the cost of a negotiated settlement". "When victory is uncertain, leaders may reason that pushing for an uncertain victory on the battlefield is preferable to the certainty of *de facto* defeat at the bargaining table".[36] If one adversary openly declares its intention of securing a military victory for peace by foreclosing the option for negotiations, it is inevitable for the other to follow the suit even if the probability of success in the conflict is low.

But politics of personal interest cannot always guide the conflict process. Since the parties in internal conflicts are rational actors despite their irrational

---

[35] William I Zartman, *Ripe for Resolution: Conflict and Intervention in Africa,* 2nd edition, (New York: Oxford university Press, 1989).

[36] See King, 1997, pp 30-32

tendency of using violence, they tend to become more realistic when the use of force fails to bring about their desired result. This means that for government, the level of its power asymmetry remains the same and its desire to elevate its position to acquire a complete monopoly over the use of force is not fulfilled. In such a situation, it is normal for the same government to adopt the above discussed strategies to supplement its coercive tactics if it is committed to the goal and confident of securing a military end of the conflict—the original objective of the coercion -for-peace strategy. Such an end may eventually come without any negotiated settlement or by following the imposition of a settlement by government. Insurgents seek to achieve the same, if the results of coercion favour them in power terms. Both parties scale down their objectives if they are faced with a simple stalemate or "hurting stalemate": the former situation may open up ways for a peace process involving the government and the moderate leaders (of the insurgents' community) whereas the latter creates opportunities for direct negotiations between the combatants. Coercion may become a means of one adversary to exert pressure on another to accept negotiations when it (the weaker side mostly) achieves some sort of strategic advantages without, at the same time, drastically tilting the power balance. In all, therefore, what determines the changing objective of a conflict is the conflict process itself, in which losses and gains of the adversaries are the critical factors. But whatever may be the objective of the adversaries, coercion alone cannot be the tactics to achieve their desired end.

Process of Negotiating Peace

Stalemate that hurts parties offers both opportunities (for negotiations) and challenges (for peace). Negotiating peace is more difficult than waging a conflict; the former process is hard and cumbersome due to some structural and functional attributes of a conflict. Stedman[37] identifies some of them. First, the leaders, who seek to keep power, often place their personal interests over general interests; their fear of losing power arises from power sharing with the opponent and also internal struggle. Changing the parties from this position to benefit negotiations is an important task. Second, security dilemma

---

[37] Stephen John Stedman, *Peacemaking in Civil War: International Mediation in Zimbabwe, 1974-1980,* (Boulder: Lynne Rienner Publishers, 1991), pp 11-20.

that fueled the conflict needs to be removed; thus the task is to evolve a settlement that guarantees security both to the leaders and supporters. Still, many may be fearful of settlement more than continuing the conflict Third, given the loose structure of militants, the diverse factions in them with competing goals can render negotiations impossible; a unified settlement with them involves harmonizing all differences, a task that is beset with many difficulties. Fourth, each adversary may suspect the other of using negotiations solely for tactical advantage; that is, to wriggle out of a hurting stalemate. Enlisting their good faith in negotiations as a precondition for a solution is a daunting task. Fifth, the conflict parties may be pessimistic about a solution because of each one's bad experience with other in the past or their feeling of "entrapment", which implies that negotiated outcome is not in commensurate with the investment made for the cause. This negates the possibility of a compromise.

Also, there are other constraints in negotiating a peace settlement. Since stalemate in a conflict is "perceived rather than objective reality" and it hurts one party more than the other because of asymmetry of power,[38] the pattern of negotiations itself can become asymmetrical. Asymmetrical negotiations are not the ideal type for a compromise solution, and the hindrances to acceptable alternatives are hard to remove. Furthermore, insurgents tend to create a situation where commitment far exceeds the level of grievances,[39] leading to their hardened position. Finally, agreeing to negotiate means, willing to compromise on the original goals of the parties. But dissidents may stand against their leaders' decision and work towards de-legitimizing any settlement. Hence, people from both the sides are to be mobilized for a successful negotiation process.

These constraints tend to develop difficulties for initiation, sustenance and conclusion of negotiations even if the parties have interest in a negotiated peace. In a situation of stalemate, there is no victor and vanquished; both parties enjoy the same position and, therefore, none can be forced into a political process. Militants may see themselves important for peace, whereas government finds itself in a dilemma of recognizing its adversary. Both have

---

[38] William I Zartman , *Elusive Peace: Negotiating an End to Civil Wars,* (Washington, DC: Brookings Institution, 1991) pp 8 and 18

[39] Ibid , p 9

their own egos to be mollified; they like to stand strong in their bargaining position. Direct communication between them, broken during the conflict, is not automatically restored even when the conflict reaches a hurting stalemate. This brings in a mediation role for third parties that can convert a hurting stalemate into a meaningful negotiation process for a positive-sum solution at the end.

The framework of solution to internal conflicts varies according to their nature and dimensions. Whereas there is no standard formula for managing sectarian or centralist conflicts, peacemaking in ethnic conflicts follows a particular pattern and framework. If an ethnic conflict is a struggle for political power, then it is only logical to expect that a reasonable and viable political solution will address the fundamental issue of powerlessness of the aggrieved minority group which, in a situation marked by the "breakdown of normal politics"[40], has been forced to take up arms against their own government to redress the inherent structural imbalance of power in the political system. Thus, political negotiations tend to focus on creating new balanced institutional structures, autonomy within a federal system and power-sharing arrangement. Peace accords in ethnic conflicts are, therefore, about power-sharing and autonomy, though their ambit is much wider than what is being generally understood. How much power an aggrieved ethnic minority is able to secure under a power-sharing framework at the centre, how greater the regional autonomy structure it has managed to put in place and what is the extent to which the majority group has accommodated the minority's aspirations by decentralizing the state power depend upon how effectively both have bargained in an atmosphere of hurting stalemate in the conflict process.

There are many notable theoretical perspectives on the framework of managing ethnic conflicts, including the theory of consociational democracy[41] and the integrative approach (Horowitz, 1985: 563-680).[42] In varying terms, both have fundamentally laid emphasis on redefining the majority-minority power relations within the ambit of the state. They complement each other

---

[40] See Zartman, 1998, P 319

[41] Arend Lijphart, "Consociational Democracy", *World Politics*, vol.21, January, 207-25, 1969 , *Democracy in Plural Societies,* (New Haven: Yale University Press, 1977).

[42] See Horowitz, 1985, pp 563-80

in certain respects while being totally different on some others. It is outside the scope of this chapter to make a systematic comparison of the two perspectives. Suffice to state, in additional to the subsidiary provisions to cover some of the issues such as reconstruction of the strife-ravaged territory, amnesty and rehabilitation of militants, etc., a solution to an ethnic conflict will have two main components essentially dealing with aggrieved minority's direct participation in governance and decision-making at the national and regional levels. One component covers territorial solution at the regional level if the rebel ethnic group is congregated in a contiguous area and non-territorial solution, known as corporate federalism,[43] if they are geographically scattered. They specify political and cultural autonomy under which two centres of powers are established both at the national and regional levels with the former enjoying some overriding powers vis-à-vis the latter. The other component focuses on creating a new national political system by reforming the state and restructuring the existing lopsided institutions which have kept the minority excluded from the national power structure. The state reform is to change its ethnic exclusive character and make it more inclusive and broad. The principal idea is to develop a joint ownership of the state and end the monopolistic control of it hitherto exercised by one ethnic group. A durable ethnic solution will also spell out a new social and political contract among all the ethnic stakeholders. It provides them more space to maintain their socio-cultural, political and financial autonomy whilst, at the same time, developing interdependent inter-ethnic relations for their existence as autonomous ethnic communities with a shared destiny. Institutional restructuring aimed at new power-sharing arrangement tends to accommodate the minority in the configuration of national power. It is, in the words of Rothchild and Lake[44], a significant "effort by the state to build representative coalitions. In conceding to ethnic minority members a proportionate share of cabinet, civil service, military, and high party positions, the state voluntarily reaches out to include minority representatives in public affairs, thereby offering the group as a whole an important incentive for cooperation".

---

[43] Arend Lijphart, *Democracies: Patterns of Majoritarian and Consensus Government in Twenty-One Countries,* (New Haven: Yale University Press, 1984), pp 183-85

[44] David A. Lake and Donald Rothchild, eds., *The International Spread of Ethnic Conflict: Fear, Diffusion, and Escalation.* (Princeton: Princeton University Press. 1998), p 207

What are the conditions under which negotiations succeed? Negotiated peace is better achieved when the function of the given conflict structure changes with the changing fortunes of the conflict and a third party controlled effective negotiation process leads to radical change in the objectives of the conflict. Here, the relevance of the conflict structure, efficacy of conflict-strategies and influence of the mediator should not be missed. If the first turning point in the conflict process comes with the decision of the parties to negotiate (agreeing to compromise on their original goals), the ultimate one is achieved when the actual compromise occurs under a negotiated settlement. For this certain preconditions at the structural level should exist: the purpose of the patron support should change from conflict to peace, the local constituency must redefine its role in support of peace and the commitment of the parties is diluted so much that it does not exceed the level of their grievances. Alongside, importantly, the situation of hurting stalemate should continue with no escape route available for the parties except the path of negotiated peace. It is assumed that the longer the duration of the hurting stalemate, the greater are the chances for a negotiated peace. Perhaps, the government may feel more hurt from a prolonged stalemate than its opponent does when its international image is tarnished on account, for instance, of bad human rights record, effect on its development programmes, its continuing domestic disorder, etc. These conditions do facilitate a negotiated outcome.

Case Selection and Conflict Mapping

South Asia is popularly characterized as a conflict-ridden region. In the post-colonial period, India has experienced over a dozen internal conflicts and Pakistan ranks next with half-a-dozen conflicts. Many of the internal conflicts in South Asia are not only protracted but also intensely violent. Most of them are ethnic conflicts, articulating a set of autonomist or secessionist goals. Centralist conflicts have centered on the goal of capturing state power. Whereas many conflicts have attained a civil war dimension or become insurrections, some of them have remained low-key insurgent movements. Communal riots have occurred more frequently in India than in any other South Asian states; Pakistan has developed a deep divide along sectarian lines, leading to frequent violence between Shia and Sunni groups. In their post-independence political history, both Pakistan and Bangladesh have experienced military coup d'etat.

Table 2: Nature and Dimensions of Internal Conflicts

Country	Name of conflict	Nature of conflict	Principal Sources of conflict	Conflict goal	Major Parties (Non-state)	Dimension
India	Naga	Ethnic	Feeling of betrayal; fear of loss of identity	Secession	NSCN (I-M) NSCN (K)	Internal war
	Assam	Ethnic	Sense of relative deprivation; feeling of powerlessness	Secession	ULFA	Internal war
Sri Lanka	Sri Lankan Tamil	Ethnic	Fear of ethnic extinction; sense of relative deprivation; sense of powerlessness	Secession	TULF & Militants	Internal war
Nepal	Maoist	Centralist	Exclusion from the power structure	State power	CPN (Maoist)	Internal war
Myanmar	Kachin, Shan, Karen, etc.	Ethnic	Feeling of betrayal; sense of powerlessness	Secession/ autonomy	KIO, SSA, CPB, etc.	Internal war
	Pro-democra-cy movement	Centralist	Structural deformity; exclusion from the power structure	Democrati-zation	NLD	Political agitation

This chapter deals with some of the major ethnic and centralist conflicts in four states stated earlier. Both communal conflicts/sectarian and coup d'etat are not included in the analytical purview since they are invariably short-lived and non-structured events in that only a small section of society or a tiny group of interested people participates. Three centralist conflicts chosen for the analysis here are: the Maoist insurgencies in Nepal and India, and the movement for democracy in Myanmar. The cases of ethnic conflict are: Naga and Assam conflicts (India); Sinhalese-Sri Lankan Tamil conflict (Sri Lanka), and ethnic insurgencies (including the Shan and Kachin ethnic groups) in Myanmar. Thus, we have chosen some of the prominent conflicts that are continuing as violent or nonviolent events and some of those which have just ended in political settlement or military victory, yet have failed to create a stable peace in a post-conflict situation.

Ethnic conflicts have originated from a myriad of sources related to the post-colonial state structure, ideologies and policies. On a broader level, the fundamental source is found in the hegemony of one group (majority/dominant) and, resultantly, the fear of extinction of another (minority/weaker). Here, the majority/dominant ethnic groups—Sinhalese (Sri Lanka) and Burmans (Myanmar)—and caste groups (such as Brahmin and Chhetri in Nepal) have exhibited their ethnic/caste pride out of an acute sense of insecurity or extreme fervor along nationalistic and caste lines, and demonstrated their utter intolerance or indifference towards the minority/weaker groups in the process of consolidating their power or hegemonic rule and institutionalizing the majoritarian ideology. When the threatened minority/weaker groups—Sri Lankan Tamils, Shan, Kayin and other ethnic groups (Myanmar), and *Janajatis* (Nepal)—responded with the same level of desire and fervor to assert their identity and sought to change the existing pattern of the unequal relations, the majority/dominant groups have showed greater determination to strengthen their position further and uphold their ethnic/caste pride. In the process, ethnic intolerance has bred more intolerance and ethnic fear has grown out of proportion. This is evident in Sri Lanka where both the Sinhalese and Sri Lankan Tamils share the same psychological structures of fear of annihilation, resulting in a strident ethnic competition marked by offensive-defensive tactics in order to ensure their survival. The argument is that both groups have been driven to violence by their minority fear complex. One is fearful because of its actual minority status in a society dominated by an ethnic/caste hegemon, and another is numerically a majority with a streak of minority psychology and also a strong sense of ethnic pride and superiority that stems from their culture and civilizations. Thus, the Sri Lankan Tamils fear that they, as a distinct ethnic group with a long history in the island and a rich cultural heritage, are under threat of marginalization and eventual extinction by the Sinhalese. At the same time, the Sinhalese majority seeks to justify their blatantly discriminatory policies as defensive measures to ensure their survival perceivably from a combined threat of a larger Tamil population living both in Sri Lanka and India's Tamil Nadu. Thus, one group's defensive measures have become offensive to another group whose counter response has in turn further threatened the former group.

The reinforcement of the majoritarian Sinhalese ideology in Sri Lanka as a part of the group's survival strategy was made in several ways. The first step was to promote a Sinhalese-Buddhist way of life by providing constitutional primacy and protection to the language and religion. This was accomplished through the Sinhala only official language legislation in 1956[45] and the 1972 Constitution, which had touched a raw nerve among Sri Lankan Tamils who felt alienated and relegated to a secondary position in the society. Subsequently their feeling got aggravated by the government's discriminatory educational and employment policies,[46] which had a crippling effect on their economic interests. They saw in the lopsided developmental policies[47] the Sinhalese ruling elite's uncanny agenda of denying economic self-sufficiency to the Tamil provinces, thereby enhancing their dependence on the majority group. Worse, the Sri Lankan Tamils' forcible attempt to relate their identity to the island's north-eastern province evoked strong countermeasures of

---

[45] Robert. Kearney, *Communalism and Language in the Politics of Ceylon*. (Durham: Duke University Press, 1967).

[46] K.M de Silva, "University Admissions and Ethnic Tension in Sri Lanka, 1977-82" In Robert B. Goldman and A.J. Wilson, eds., *From Independence to Statehood: Managing Ethnic Conflicts in Five African and Asian States*, (London: Frances Pinter, 1984), pp 97-110 and S.W.R.D. Samarasinghe, "Ethnic Representation in Central Government Employment and Sinhala-Tamil Relations in Sri Lanka: 1948-1981", In Robert B. Goldman and A.J. Wilson, eds., *From Independence to Statehood: Managing Ethnic Conflicts in Five African and Asian States*, (London: Frances Pinter, 1984), pp 173–84.

[47] Neelan Tiruchelvam," Ethnicity and Resource Allocation" In Robert B. Goldman and A.J. Wilson, eds., *From Independence to Statehood: Managing Ethnic Conflicts in Five African and Asian States*, (London: Frances Pinter 1984).

successive governments to invalidate their claim for ethnic territoriality. This is meant, in a way, to validate the Sinhalese identity, constructed on the narratives of Mahavamsa, which compulsorily seeks to associate itself with the whole of Sri Lanka. In a measure perceived as a grave threat to the survival and stabilization of the minority identity the centre has misused the land settlement policies to vitiate the basic ethnic character of the eastern province by resorting to state-sponsored resettlement of landless Sinhalese under various colonization schemes (Manogaran 1994: 84–125).[48] The hard-core Tamil nationalists realized that the root cause of their problems lay in the powerlessness of the community and, therefore, demanded a power sharing arrangement under a federal constitution as a safeguard structure against contingent Sinhalese majoritarianism (Oberst 1988: 175–94).[49] Given the majoritarian thrust and centralizing tendencies of the state and the Sinhalese ruling elite's desire to contain the fissiparous tendencies among the Tamils, the rejection of the federal autonomy scheme was not unexpected. Cumulatively, these measures worked to raise the level of ethnic antagonism in which the Tamils found a strong motivating force for collective political movement first and a military campaign later to arrest the group's decline and demise.

The minority psychology that operates in Sri Lanka cannot be found clearly in other ethnic conflicts. Rather, grievances of some ethnic groups are rooted in their feeling of betrayal or legacy of British colonial rule. The secessionist goal of the Nagas has its origin from their historical antecedents. It is a case of an ethnic group which seeks to regain what is termed as its 'lost ethnic territory', thereby re-establishing its ethnic sovereignty and adding a territorial component to strengthen its identity. The group's grievance is that it controlled the Naga Hill tracts before its subjugation by the British colonial rule, and as a corollary, its territory should have been set free with the ending of colonialism. The Naga nationalists under Z. A. Phizo alleged that the post-colonial 'national territorial formation' in India has been unjust and arbitrary: it ignored their pre-colonial history. This, in their interpretation,

---

[48] C Manogaran, "Colonization as Politics: Political Use of Space in Sri Lanka's Ethnic Conflict", In Chelvadurai Manogaran and Bryan Pffaffenberger, eds., *The Sri Lankan Tamils: Ethnicity and identity*, (Boulder: Westview Press, 1984).

[49] Robert C Oberst, "Federalism and Ethnic Conflict in Sri Lanka", *Publius,* 18(3): 175-94, 1998.

amounted to continuing the British colonial policy of subjugating the minority ethnic territories. Independence to India, therefore, did not mean freedom to the border ethnic minority group, which related its freedom to restoration of independence to its own ethnic territory. But achieving this through a normal political process appeared difficult for the Naga nationalists who had to confront a powerful Indian state controlled by ardent advocates of national integration by all means. Prime Minister Nehru's popular national image of being a liberal democrat carried little appeal in the Naga Hills where people, guided by the experience of the Naga National Council's (NNC), found a tinge of authoritarianism in his approach towards the Naga problem. What lent credence to this feeling was his statement that "You can never hope to be independent. No state, big or small, in India will be allowed to remain independent. We will use all our influence and power to suppress such tendencies".[50] The tone of his argument did not leave any scope for the NNC to expect a positive political deal to promote its ideal. Facing an insurmountable challenge from the Indian state and its hegemonic leadership, it had made tactical retreat when it agreed for the integration of the Naga Hills into the Indian Union on the condition that the agreement would be renewed after ten years. The militant segment of the NNC had nurtured a hope to secede at the end of the mandatory period, but the Indian government insisted that Nagaland could discuss its relations with the Indian Union only within the framework of the Indian Constitution. To legitimize its claim to a separate statehood, the aggrieved NNC held an unofficial plebiscite in 1951, whose result was deliberately ignored by the central leadership. This culminated in the use of violence by the NNC, to which the Indian government responded with military deployment and operations.

A somewhat similar situation is the one under which the conflict in Assam originated, even though the context that gave rise to the conflict was the anti-foreigners agitation (popularly known as 'Assam movement') and its consequences seen in terms of state repression.[51] Since there is a strong territorial element in the armed contest, the United Liberation Front of Assam

---

[50] Maxwell, Neville (1973), *India and the Nagas,* Minority Group Report no.330, (London: MRG, 1973), P 8

[51] Samir Kumar Das, "India's Northeast: The Post 'Pacification' Era, In V.R. Raghavan, ed. *Conflicts: A Four State Analysis (India, Nepal, Sri Lanka and Myanmar)*, (New Delhi: Vij Books India Pvt. Ltd, 2013). P. 107

(ULFA), which came to the fore only in 1983 even though it was formed in 1979, has harped on the 'glorious past' of the Assamese people (who formed an independent political entity until 1826) to develop its ideological premises. The historicity that the ULFA believes, nurtures and glorifies questions the very fact of integration of Assam into the Indian Union and, in the process, the Indian state is implicated for what is called as its 'internal colonialism'. Assam is, in its view, an Indian 'colony' because the structure of capitalism that is imposed on the country has led to a colonial-type extraction of resources (such as oil, tea, timber, etc.) from the state. It is the economic exploitation of Assam that is seen as the fundamental cause for its underdevelopment.[52] A sense of 'powerlessness' has been cultivated in the minds of the Assamese who attribute the non-implementation of the Assam Accord (1985) on the migration issue to their weak position vis-à-vis the much powerful centre. The liberation of Assam and restoration of its "lost independence"[53] has, therefore, become an ideological slogan of the ULFA, to which the hard-core Assamese nationalists have responded with militant nationalistic fervour. In so doing, they seek to stop the Indian state's exploitative and manipulative control of their state, recover their wealth for their own benefits and also empower themselves to arrest their decline as an ethnic community. In this context, it is debatable whether the ULFA insists on full sovereignty for Assam or it is only using its sovereignty demand as a bargaining chip to end the Indian state's domination and exploitation. According to Das,[54] the ULFA does not view sovereignty as an 'end in itself', but a "means" to the "end of establishing a state free from repression and exploitation".

Like the ethnic groups in India's northeast, a strong feeling of betrayal coupled with a sense of powerlessness have gripped the minority ethnic communities in Myanmar. In their determination to win freedom, every ethnic minority has resorted to a sustained armed movement, separately and also

---

[52] Jyotirindra Dasgupta, "Ethnicity, Democracy and Development", In Atul Kohli, ed., *India's Democracy: An Analysis of Changing State-Society Relations*, 2nd Edition., (Princeton: Princeton University Press, 1990). Pp 165-67

[53] Baruah, Sanjib, "The State and Separatist Militancy in Assam", *Asian Survey*, 34(10): 863-877, 1994

[54] Samir Kumar Das, "India's Northeast: The Post 'Pacification' Era, In V.R. Raghavan, ed. *Conflicts: A Four State Analysis (India, Nepal, Sri Lanka and Myanmar)*, (New Delhi: Vij Books India Pvt. Ltd, 2013).p 108

in a coordinated manner, against the Burman-dominated hegemonic Myanmar state. However, the armed challenges of the ethnic minorities, though highly protracted and created multiple fronts against the state, have not altered its ethnic policy. Rather, the state has emerged very strong to consolidate the brand of majoritarian nationalism it has sought to promote even in the midst of a durable national disorder lasting for over half-a-century. Yet, some ethnic minorities, particularly the Karen and the Shans, have refused to surrender abjectly to the state. For these ethnic communities, their history as 'independent people in the pre-colonial period' is unalterable or indestructible at least from their collective consciousness and memories; it remains a source of not just their ethnic ideology but also their identity and power vis-à-vis the state.

Thus, the fundamental issue relates to how the Burman-controlled post-colonial state, through skillful political machinations and deceitfulness, has changed the status of the 'pre-colonial independent peoples' viz. the Chins, Kachins and Shans, who co-founded the Union of Burma (now Myanmar), into second-class citizens without equal rights, powers and privileges.[55] Historically, these minorities had virtually remained independent political entities with well-demarcated territories and also well-established institutions of power and authority until they were forcibly integrated into the British Burmese state. Therefore, at the time of transition to independence, their hope and desire was to secure independence simultaneously with the Burmans, but changed their mind when the Anti-Fascist People's Freedom League (AFPFL) leader, Aung San, offered a liberal ethnic policy that would have "embraced all the people living in the country, indigenous and alien, on a basis of equality and that it intended to create a political structure that would be erected jointly by Burmans and minorities.[56] The apparent mutual goodwill and understanding between the majority and the hill minorities resulted in an accord—the Panglong Agreement of 12 February 1947—under which the Shans, Kachins and Chins agreed to join the Union and, in

---

[55] Lian H. Sakhong, "Ethnic Conflict in Burma", In V.R. Raghavan, ed. *Conflicts: A Four State Analysis (India, Nepal, Sri Lanka and Myanmar)*, (New Delhi: Vij Books India Pvt. Ltd, 2013).

[56] Josef Silverstein,, "Fifty Years of Failure in Burma", In Michael E. Brown and Sumit Ganguly, eds., *Government Policies and Ethnic Relations in Asia and the Pacific*, Cambridge, (Mass: The MIT Press.. 1997). P 176

return, extracted an assurance that their political equality, right to internal self-determination and autonomy under a federal system would be guaranteed. The right to secede from the Union after ten years of independence was also provided to all ethnic nationalities that formed the Union (Sakhong 2013).[57] However, the post-colonial state, which has come under the military control for the most part of its political history, has deviated hugely from the promised path to become a centralized institution that has developed a strong commitment to promote the Burmans' interest while, at the same time, subjugating the ethnic minorities. The hegemonic majoritarian policy has deeply fractured the society, militarized the state and deepened the crisis of governance. The prominent minorities have chosen to rebel against the state, to which the latter has responded with its brute force to quell the ethnic insurgencies. It has been a protracted internal war that the state is unable to end through political means.

In ethnically diffused Nepal, categorization of group identities based on racial origin, language, religion, region and culture is difficult.[58] Along the regional lines, ethnic groups are divided into two principal groups—the Tarai and non-Tarai people. In terms of the historical antecedents, a large section (over 35 per cent) of the country's population is known by a generic name, *Janajati* ('indigenous nationalities'). It encompasses several of groups whose identity invariably cross-cuts with each other. About one- quarter of the *Janajati* live in the Tarai region of Nepal; the Madhesis are considered as the largest *Janajati* group in Nepal.[59] Since the early 1990s, particularly in the wake of the Maoist insurgency, which highlighted the ethnic grievances of minorities, the Madhesis have been assertive of their distinct identity by demanding autonomy and federalism. When the Maoist movement resulted in virtual capitulation of the Nepali state, the Madhesi ethnic assertion became visibly strong to a new level that some of their representative organizations resorted to violence against the same battered state. Thus, the Maoist insurgency and the resultant peace process, which has changed drastically

---

[57] See n 55

[58] Phadnis, Urmila, *Ethnicity and Nation-building in South Asia*, (New Delhi: Sage Publications, 1989).

[59] Uddhab Pyakurel, "Changing Patterns of Nepal's Ethnic Movement", In V.R. Raghavan, ed. *Conflicts: A Four State Analysis (India, Nepal, Sri Lanka and Myanmar)*, (New Delhi: Vij Books India Pvt. Ltd, 2013).

the fundamental nature and character of the state (from a 'monarchy' to a 'federal democratic republic') and enabled the Communist Party of Nepal (Maoist) to come to the national political mainstream to enjoy power and shape the national political development, have "inadvertently encouraged more violence" as the number of known and unknown armed groups has "surged exponentially".[60] Many of them operate in the Tarai region and some of the prominent ones represent the Madhesis, who consider the state as unequal and discriminatory. In their view, the state has neglected their welfare for too long and deprived them of power and development that a large section of the hill people could enjoy. Thus, what lies in the heart of their demand for a federal autonomy is their deep sense of powerlessness and relative deprivation. They seek to change their relations with the state by finding a space in its fold and make the latter to recognize them as one of the stakeholders on par with other communities.

Unlike the ethnic conflicts, the centralist conflicts have different set of sources rooted or connected to the political system or structure. Such conflicts can also be termed as 'systemic conflicts'. All three centralist or systemic conflicts dealt with in this chapter have originated essentially from one or more of such structural factors as deformity, lopsidedness, malfunctioning, inefficiency, exclusion, etc. From the standpoint of the ideological leaning and disposition, the forces that have challenged the states in India, Nepal and Myanmar can be categorized into extreme leftists (the Maoists) and liberal democrats. Whereas the Maoists have threatened violently both the Indian and Nepali states, the state in Myanmar has experienced the political wrath of liberal democrats led by Aung San Suu Kyi of the National League for Democracy (NLD). The causes of these conflicts are different, but their goals are similar; every movement has sought to bring about a radical structural change or comprehensive transformation of the state system in terms of ideology and governance principles. The rebels or dissidents think that their goal is justifiable and the path they choose to follow is hard but winnable.

---

[60] Thapa, Chiran Jung (2013), "Nepal's Armed Conflict: A Narrative of Political Mismanagement", In V.R. Raghavan, ed. *Conflicts: A Four State Analysis (India, Nepal, Sri Lanka and Myanmar)*, (New Delhi: Vij Books India Pvt. Ltd, 2013). 193.

The Maoists in India, as the CSA study explains,[61] are engaged in a 'protracted people's war' against the state. Though the origin of their insurgency can be traced back to the 1940s, the current spate of their armed campaign began in the late 1990s. Deeply rooted in the irreconcilable ideological (ultra leftism versus liberal democracy) antipathy between the Indian State and the Maoists, the movement has successfully capitalized on the growing sense of alienation among the dispossessed sections of Indian (tribal) society and also the general discontent of people over the undesirable effects of the contemporary socio-political and economic reality. Both developments form a proximate cause/source of their armed struggle. Of course, the unalterable ideology determines the Maoist actions and goals; it is their guiding force. In their perception and understanding, the Indian State is thoroughly capitalist, whose neoliberal economic policies have led to deprivation and exploitation of the tribal population, endemic corruption at all levels, and protection of the economic interests of the political class, entrepreneurs and multinational corporations at the cost of the dispossessed tribal people's interests. In challenging the Indian State, therefore, the Maoists have set two sets of goals: one denotes their level (minimalist and maximalist) and the other indicates the period (short- and long-term) within which they are to be achieved. Ending under-development and exploitation of the tribal population is their immediate, short-term and minimalist goal; capturing the state power through 'armed agrarian revolution' is their ultimate, long-term and maximalist goal.[62] In achieving these goals, they depend on the tribal population; it is their sole reliable constituency. Both of them have forged an interdependent relationship that the Indian State has sought to break through its varied political and military strategies.

In Nepal the ultra left ideology-driven Maoist insurgency was quite powerful to shake the foundations of the modern state and achieve its radical transformation along their desired and determined lines in a matter of about ten years.[63] Like their counterpart in India, the Nepali Maoists had used the

[61] Raghavan, V.R., ed., *The Naxal Threat: Causes, State Responses and Consequences,* (New Delhi: Vij Books India Pvt. Ltd, 2011).

[62] Ramachandran, Sudha (2011), "The Maoist Conflict in Dandakaranya", In Sanjoy Hazarika and V.R. Raghavan, eds. *Conflicts in the Northeast: Internal and External Effects,* (New Delhi: Vij Books India Pvt. Ltd., 2011)

[63] V R Raghavan,ed., *The Naxal Threat: Causes, State Responses and Consequences,* (New Delhi: Vij Books India Pvt. Ltd, 2011)

deep-seated socioeconomic and political grievances of some of the ethnic/ caste communities (excluded from the power structure controlled by the Kathmandu-based elite largely from the hill region) for mobilization of local support and articulating their high-end goals, which include the capture of state power to establish a 'new republican democracy'; restructuring the centralized political system by abolishing the entrenched monarchy; introduction of socio-economic reforms for a just and equitable society; development of a new form of assertive nationalism to strengthen Nepal's autonomy and independence in national and international affairs (Muni 2003).[64] Though the Maoists' main target was the state, whose reform remained at the core of their agenda, the monarchy, whose abolition was considered necessary for achieving the former goal, came under their direct attack. In the process, the monarch himself came to spearhead the counter-insurgency campaign after sidelining the democratic political forces which, on their part, were inclined to turn the insurgent movement into a conflict between the King and the Maoists for political power and supremacy. Ultimately, it worked to the advantages of the Maoists, whom the political parties had engaged in a peace process, which resulted in the unexpected demise of the monarchical system. One of the unintended consequences of the Maoist movement is that it has opened a new space, and also kindled the dormant ethnic/caste forces, to assert their identity and interest in sharing the state power.[65]

Unlike the violent centralist conflicts in India and Nepal, the NLD-led pro-democracy movement in Myanmar is basically a political conflict between the military oligarchy and liberal democrats. Yet, various forms of violence and coercion mainly by the state forces have marked the conflict. The other difference is that whereas the Maoists have sought to capture the state to bring it under their control to enjoy power themselves, the liberal democrats in Myanmar have waged political campaigns to liberate the state from the clutches of the military junta, bring it to the people's control and vest powers in them to enjoy. In terms of duration, the Myanmar conflict can be considered as one of the protracted political events—the current phase can

---

[64] S D Muni, *Maoist Insurgency in Nepal: The Challenge and the Response*, (New Delhi: Rupa & Co, 2003).

[65] See.note 63

be traced to the 1988 student movement for democracy; but the evolution of strong democratic sentiments is as old as the usurping of power by the military junta in the early 1960s. Together with many ethnic movements, the centralist conflict has contributed to protracted disorder in the country. The combined transnational implications of both sets of conflicts have been serious: For political, economic and security reasons, the neighboring countries such as India and China have shown deep interest in Myanmar; their passive or active role has helped the military junta to survive and repress the pro-democracy forces who, as a result, developed a sense of alienation. However, the larger international community has exerted pressure on the regime to relent. Thus, the centralist conflict has remained an internationalized event although it has marked a low level of external involvement especially of the West and the United Nations. But the international human rights community has played an active role in support of the repressed people —ethnic groups and the pro-democracy forces. [66]

From a brief mapping exercise undertaken in the preceding pages, a number of salient points regarding the distinct characteristics and dynamics of conflict can be deduced. First, power asymmetry, a given trait of an internal conflict, is markedly evident in all the conflicts discussed above. The states have enjoyed far superior firepower than that of the insurgents, who have possessed the minimum deterrence capabilities defined in terms of their power to withstand the military pressure of (and sometimes harass) the security forces. The insurgents have not accepted power asymmetry as an unalterable situation; they have constantly sought to increase their power and capabilities through a variety of means (political and strategic) and from a number of sources (internal and external), not with the intention of developing a symmetrical power relationship but to narrow their existing power asymmetry with their adversary—the state. In this context, the topography of the theatre of conflict has helped some of the rebel organizations to increase their power to deter the state forces. For long, the Sri Lankan Tamil militants derived invaluable strategic advantage from the peculiar geographical area (with thick jungles, vast coastline and huge lagoons) where they were concentrated and carried out their insurgent

---

[66] Ibid

activities. Likewise, India's northeast insurgents and Maoist rebels have found hilly terrain and jungles in the tribal areas most suitable for their guerrilla attacks. The Nepali Maoists felt constrained by the absence of direct access to the sea or base facilities in a neighboring country, but took advantage of the country's eastern and western hilly regions where they were concentrated to mount attack on the army (Muni 2003: 27).[67] Many ethnic insurgent groups in Myanmar have also operated in the same kind of geographical region bordering with China, thereby limiting the military's operational capabilities.

Besides the geographical advantages obtained naturally, some of the insurgent groups have also found external support a vital source of their power to bridge the asymmetry gap. External sanctuaries in the neighboring countries are the type of external support the insurgent groups have generally enjoyed. Almost every militant group in India's northeast enjoyed the patron support of either China or Bangladesh at different levels. Many insurgents have made use of India's porous borders with Bhutan and Myanmar, where they set up sanctuaries. As early as in 1986, the ULFA received training from the Kachin Independence Army (KIA). Coupled with the external state support has been the inter-group solidarity and operational network involving some insurgent groups in the northeast region, which brought tremendous strategic advantages to the militants by reducing their power disparity on the battlefield with the government forces. In the mid-1980s, the Sri Lankan Tamil militants had an uncontrolled access to Tamil Nadu, where they established sanctuaries for training and arms procurement.

Second, most of the ethnic conflicts have involved multiple warring factions from the minority/weaker ethnic group's side even though they share a common goal. The deep cleavage has occurred generally because of power or personality rivalry or ideological or tactical differences either before the outbreak or during the course of conflict. Thus the Naga conflict has involved two major factions of the National Socialist Council of Nagaland (NSCN); the Sinhalese-Sri Lankan Tamil conflict has incorporated several moderate and militant groups, and a plethora of groups are competing with each other to represent the interests of the Madhesi community. Unlike these ethnic conflicts, the centralist conflicts are known for relatively cohesive or unified structure. Factionalism is not absent in organizations fighting against the state, but it is contained to present a united challenge to their adversary.

---

[67] See Muni, n 64.

Finally, except the political movement for democracy in Myanmar, all other conflicts have attained an internal war dimension. Therefore, they can be described as 'internal wars', not just internal conflicts. We use the term in a restricted sense to mean a 'large-scale violent incident entailing a constant and prolonged military engagement and confrontation between insurgents/militants and security forces of a state' (Sahadevan 2000:6).[68] There is a certain degree of organization and organized fighting on the part of both adversaries and continuity in armed clashes and operations extended over a considerable part of a country's territory. While the criteria set by this definition has differentiated internal wars from other types of incidents occurring in internal settings, there is only a thin dividing line between civil wars and internal wars.

Many analysts use both 'internal' and 'civil' war interchangeably,[69] and some actually mean 'internal war' when they employ the term 'civil war'.[70] This, in a way, does not appear to be erroneous because every civil war is fought within a national territory and, therefore, it qualifies to be an 'internal war'. However, this chapter seeks to make a conceptual delineation by emphasizing the delicate functional, if not structural, distinctions between the two phenomena and argues that while every civil war can technically be an internal war, not all internal wars are civil wars. The main assumption is that governments cannot possess, at the outbreak of a civil war, either a "monopoly of violence or political control". There may occur an almost "equal division" within government forces that play a combatant role against each other by even adopting 'conventional military techniques'.[71] In some cases, it is said, "warlords declare their independence, military headquarters lose control of the warring groups as the government loses political control". A regional internal war can transform itself into a civil war when violence

---

[68] P Sahadevan,. *Coping With Disorder: Strategies to End Internal Wars in South Asia*, RCSS Policy Studies 17, (Colombo: Regional Centre for Strategic Studies, 2000), p 6.

[69] James N. Rosenau, ed., *International Aspects of Civil Strife*, Princeton, (NJ: Princeton University Press, 1964).

[70] Roy Licklider, S*topping the Killing: How Civil Wars End*.(New York: New York University Press, 1993) and Charles King, *Ending Civil Wars*, Adelphi Paper 308, (London: Oxford University Press, 1997)

[71] Martin Edmonds,"Civil War, Internal War, and Intrasocietal Conflict: A Taxonomy and Typology", In Robin Higham, ed., Civil Wars in the Twentieth Century, (Lexington: The University Press of Kentucky), pp 18-21 and Melvin Small and David J Singer, *Resort to Arms: International and Civil Wars, 1816-1980*, (Beverley Hils: Sage Publications, 1982), p 214.

spreads and the rule of law in the 'society as a whole' breaks down or loses its foundation, leading to a state of anarchy.

Strategies of Conflict Management

The dynamics of conflicts analyzed in the earlier section reveals their complexity and the inherent challenges to their management. As stated in the conceptual section, there is no one single/unified strategy that can bring an end to violence or restore peace. In fact, every state including the ones analyzed in this chapter invariably adopts multiple strategies in a sequential manner. In other words, as demonstrated in this section, each strategy is linked to the other; one is tested before another is adopted, and one failed strategy (from the standpoint of state and its adversary) gives way for another failed or successful one at the end until the dominant party's desired goal in a given conflict is achieved. Strategy can be unilateral or bilateral or multilateral: a unilateral strategy entails unitary decision-making by the state to manage conflict, in that an assessment of its strength and weakness and also that of it adversary is factored. Bilateral conflict management strategy involves a joint decision-making (by both adversaries) process, while a multilateral strategy enlists an external (direct or indirect) role that can take one or more of the following forms: pressure for peace (push) or facilitation of peace process or mediating conflict or peace-building (during the conflict and/or in the post-conflict period). How have the governments in India, Nepal, Sri Lanka and Myanmar dealt with their internal conflicts?

Coercion

As stated in the conceptual section, coercion is not considered as a strategy of conflict management. Yet, its link and importance to the conflict management process cannot be ignored altogether. The argument is that initiation, progress, sustenance, success or failure of such a process is invariably determined or influenced by use of coercion by both adversaries. It essentially has two aspects: military coercion is exercised through violence and counter-violence; political coercion entails non-military pressure tactics used against each other. As mentioned earlier, both coercive tactics serve the different purpose of parties: states use coercion either to achieve an outright military victory or force their rebellious adversaries to accept political negotiations; insurgents' coercive or counter-coercive tactics have similar objectives—denial of a military victory to their adversary or subject itself to a military defeat or force it to accept a negotiated peace. Against this backdrop, this section explores why have the states (whose conflicts are analyzed in this chapter) employed coercion against the insurgents? Has it been for a military victory or a negotiated peace? Have they changed their original objectives—from military victory to political negotiations and vice versa? The discussion below to answer these questions focuses on the behavior of each state separately.

Table 3: Conflict Management Strategies

Conflict	Strategies	Outcome
Naga conflict	Coercion Ceasefire Ending or seeking external support Divide and engage Development work Political negotiations	Negative peace; continuing peace process
Assam Conflict	Coercion Ending or seeking external support Divide and engage Development work Political negotiations	Continuing conflict and peace talks
Indian Maoist	Coercion Divide and engage Development work	Violence
Sri Lankan Tamil	Coercion Ceasefire Ending or seeking external support Divide and engage Unilateral political measures	Negative peace
Nepali Maoist	Coercion Ceasefire Ending or seeking external support Political negotiations	Peace without order
Myanmar's ethnic conflict	Coercion Ceasefire	Negative peace; continuing conflict
Myanmar's pro-democracy movement	Coercion Ending or seeking external support Unilateral political measures	Partial democratization

Though a liberal democracy, the Indian State has never been averse to use of coercion (both military and political) as a preferred instrument against the disgruntled sections or groups (violent and non-violent) of society. Experiences from India's conflict zones (located in Nagaland, Assam and the tribal regions) substantiate this argument. Let us take the Naga conflict first. Coercion was India's principal strategy in response to the militant Naga nationalists' entrenched position on their secessionist goal, sought to be achieved through a long-drawn insurgency. Independence was not negotiable. In the 1950s, the spirit of freedom remained strong; it was demonstrated in 1956 when the Naga National Council (NNC) had established a federal government and promulgated a constitution, whose preamble said that "Nagaland is a people's sovereign republic". Through its intense guerrilla warfare, the Naga Army showed its determination to defeat the Indian security forces. The Indian government responded with an equally militant posture, demonstrating its total resolve to fight the militants until they gave up their secessionist goal. Nehru took a firm stand that Naga nationalist Z.A. Phizo's demand for independence was unreasonable and futile and that his government would deal firmly with the "hostile elements". "This is an unpleasant but necessary task", he added.[72]

As a part of its counter-insurgency tactics to bring the militants to heel, the army had grouped villages under their control with the aim of cutting off supplies to the former.

By 1960, the Naga Army began to crack up under mounting military pressure. The NNC realized the futility of military engagement and in order to prevent a total defeat, Phizo offered to discuss a ceasefire with the government, which the latter had turned down. While sustaining its military pressure on the insurgents, the Indian government engaged the moderate leaders in negotiations and accepted some of their demands. But this double-track approach did not yield any result. Contrary to the government's expectation, the militants could neither be isolated from the mainstream Naga society nor be defeated by the security forces.

[72] Ministry of External Affairs, *The Naga Problem*, New Delhi: Government of India. 1963, p 13.

At this point, Nehru realized the constraints of his government's strategy and hence changed its objective. Defeating the militants was not the operational task of the army any more, but their weakening, so required for a negotiated settlement. Though he did not survive to implement the new approach, his successors Lal Bahadur Shastri and Indira Gandhi continued the peace process initiated by him for a ceasefire agreement, leading to negotiations with the Federal Naga leaders since August 1964. The fact that the ceasefire continued for about eight years even after the breakdown of peace talks indicated the limitations of the conflict strategy, which the adversaries acknowledged. The resumption of hostilities in 1972 was inevitable, since the long lull in the Hills became symptomatic of a deadlock, which both parties wanted to break. Despite the army's territorial consolidation in the Hills and its military confidence gained after the Bangladesh war, the government did not seek a military solution. Instead, it sought to use military coercion to bring the insurgents to a negotiating table: that it worked to yield a definite result was evident from the Shillong Accord (1975), which five NNC representatives signed with the Indian government.

For the loyalists of Naga nationalism, who formed the NSCN, the accord was "the most ignominious sell-out in history" by "downright, reactionary traitors".[73] It meant that the opportunity to win freedom through a sustained armed struggle was lost because, in the words of Th. Muivah, the NNC renegades had overestimated the adversary's strength and at the same time, underestimated theirs'.[74] The self-made setback suffered by the movement in the past was therefore attributed to the absence a correct tactics and strategy. Insisting on national remorse, he declared that the Indian government could no longer "crush us" in spite of its "military pride in its mighty might".[75] Thus, what the NSCN proposed in the early 1980s was a fight for a total military victory. The government responded with equal militant fervour and strove to defeat the NSCN. Once again, the war raged in most parts of the Hills, and continued without any success for either of the parties. The no-win situation made the militants sit pretty, for it vindicated their earlier

---

[73] B G Verghese, India's *Northeast Resurgent: Ethnicity, Insurgency, Governance, Development*, (New Delhi: Konark, 1996), p 67.

[74] (http://www.angelfire.com/mo.Nagaland.num)

[75] Ibid

assessment of the state's capability. They felt themselves to be in a position of strength, so that Muivah declined to even respond favourably to peace offered by the government in 1993. He was determined to push his group's strategic advantage. When the war dragged on for about 17 years, the government gave up its earlier preference for a total military victory in favour of substantive weakening of the militants so that they would be pressurized to negotiate. This is what happened in 1997 when the government and the NSCN (I-M) declared a ceasefire and then held talks to end their internal war.

The outcome of state coercion is different in Assam. Both the Indian government and ULFA, given their determination to defeat each other, have used violence for a zero-sum outcome. Despite its admission of weakness vis-à-vis the security forces, ULFA is committed to its secessionist goal— Swadhin Asom (Independent Assam). It has linked the restoration of peace in the state to the grant of independence to Assam. The internal war was therefore waged in pursuit of peace, since negotiations on their demand were unacceptable to the government, whose resolve to fight the secessionist forces stemmed from their very goal-rigidity. In other words, one party's preference for coercion as the only instrument of peace has compelled another to follow suit. If the secessionist goal was non-negotiable for ULFA, India's territorial integrity is non-negotiable as far as the government was concerned. The government's strategy was to defeat or neutralize the insurgents to the extent that they would abjure violence and accept the Indian Constitution, either as a result of political negotiations or of military coercion. Its desire to exercise both the options was demonstrated on many occasions. The failure of coercion to subdue the militants has increased the government's interest in negotiations, but it inevitably reverted to the former strategy when they refused to respond positively.

Thus, the Indian government's strategy has given priority for military victory. This is tried in many ways. Besides targeting the militants to wear them out psychologically and physically, the security forces have destroyed their camps and forced them to be out of their hideouts in the dense forest to surrender. They have also virtually sealed India's international borders with Bhutan and Bangladesh with the aim of disrupting the militants' supply lines, and arrested some of their leaders while crossing over to India.

Sustained military pressure has kept some of the top ULFA leaders in exile, thereby creating a vacuum of leadership on the ground. All these military measures have demoralized the cadres. Yet, the war has not led to a logical end. Making use of the local constituency support and terrain to their strategic advantage, the ULFA have launched surprise attacks at the security forces. Its main goal is not register a military victory, but to deny the same to the government and also to save itself from a defeat. After its recent split, the weakened ULFA seems to be lacking confidence in taking on the government forces. Yet, the hard-line faction led by Paresh Barua has not given up its original secessionist goal. It favours a prolonged militancy till the government is forced to accept its demand. Until the split, the ULFP leadership kept the cadres' fighting spirit alive even when they were cornered and made to be on the run by the security forces. As a morale-boosting exercise, they periodically targeted politicians, bureaucrats and police officials.

Coercion remains the single most dominant strategy of the Indian government against the Maoists. Its singular objective has been to defeat them militarily and thus end their insurgency. The central paramilitary forces, in coordination with the Maoist-affected states, have launched a sustained military campaign. Since 2009, the 'operation green hunt', which has seen massive deployment of paramilitary forces across the Maoists-infected states, has taken the war deep into the jungles to hit at the Maoists. But this has produced mixed results. Both the government forces and Maoists have suffered in their exchange of violence and counter-violence, and they together subjected a large number of civilians to death and debilitation. As far as both adversaries are concerned, it is a fight to finish. There seems to be no room for complacency and compromise. The government has created an internal war structure: a unity of command for the forces operating in the Maoist-hit states of Orissa, Chhatisgarh, Jharkhand and West Bengal is meant to provide the much needed coordination among the forces operating on the ground. In addition, the government has extended assistance for modernization of the police and reimbursed fully the security-related expenditures incurred by the state governments. These measures point to the direction the government's counter-insurgency operations is permitted to take and the outcome it is keen to accomplish at the end.

In Sri Lanka's internal war (1983-2009), successive governments tried to use military coercion as an instrument primarily to defeat the militancy first and then settle the Sri Lankan Tamils' ethnic grievances unilaterally in accordance with their state's ethnic policy. Only when coercion became an unworkable strategy, they had shown interest in using it to force the Sri Lankan Tamil militants to negotiate for a political deal. All four executive Presidents—J.R. Jayewardene, R. Premadasa, Chandrika Kumaratunga and Mahinda Rajapakse—who executed the twenty-six year long war, had the same objectives. The same applies to the militants especially the Liberation Tigers of Tamil Eelam (LTTE), who had all along resisted the Sri Lankan military's pressure to save themselves from a defeat or deny a victory to the government, but accepted political negotiations merely as a tactics. In 1983, when President Jayewardene, who classified the ethnic conflict as a military problem that needed a "military solution",[76] launched military operations, his strategic aim was to defeat the militants. However, following many reverses and losses suffered by the security forces, his government gave up its determination for a military victory. Since 1987, therefore, it sought to use military coercion to weaken the LTTE, so as to pressure its leadership to negotiate peace. As a tactical step, initially LTTE leader V. Prabhakaran seemed to have accepted the 1987 India-Sri Lanka peace accord, but backtracked later by fighting against the Indian peacekeeping force (IPKF), whose military task during its operations (1987-90) was to implement the accord. It was, therefore, not a fight to finish but an attempt to weaken the LTTE (after capturing territory from their control) to the extent that it would be forced to seek peace under the accord.

At the end of the IPKF-LTTE war, the government tried to extend olive branch to the LTTE out of political and military expediency. But political negotiations between the two broke down within one year, leading to resumption of hostilities between them in June 1990. Each adversary was determined to defeat the other. The government's firm resolve to score a military victory was evident in Ranjan Wijeratne's (Deputy Minister of Defence) statement in parliament that there was no "half way house" with him and that he would go "all out for the LTTE" and "annihilate them".[77]

---

[76] *The Times of India*, 27 January 1986

[77] Bradman Weerakoon, *Premadasa of Sri Lanka: A Political Biography*, (New Delhi: Vikas Publishing House, 1992), p 71.

But what the army managed to win was territories from the Tigers, and not their total annihilation. Even the territorial victory was temporary because the army did not have sufficient manpower to hold on to the recaptured areas against a determined Tiger attack. As the battlefield fortunes were shifting constantly to the favour of both combatants, the government had changed its hard-line position on its military objectives. President Premadasa spoke of reconciliation: "In war, no one wins, all are losers. It is in peace that all are victors. It is through consultation that we can find solutions to human problems".[78] The government's candid admission of its weakness prompted LTTE chief V. Prabhakaran to characterize the Tigers as an undefeatable force. Rejecting Colombo's coercive strategy, he said in an interview to the BBC that it should "learn a lesson" that it would "never resolve the Tamil issue by opting for a military solution".[79] Since both adversaries were pinning their hopes on a military victory and thus reluctant to compromise on their position, there could not be any prospect for a purposeful peace process. It means that the stalemate that continued in the war did not have any impact on the attitude and strategies of the parties.

However, the new government of Chandrika Kumaratunga, which was voted to power in 1994 on the plank of ethnic peace in the island, did not endorse the Premadasa government's approach. Realizing that the army could not make a forward momentum in the war process, she needed to give a fresh chance for political negotiations with the LTTE. A break with the previous regime's war strategy was, therefore, made out of a conscious political decision, which seemed to have found support in the military largely because of war-weariness among the soldiers. But the failure of the peace talks in 1994–95 made the resumption of war inevitable. Thus, the third eelam war began with all intensity in April 1995 which, according to the government, was fought for peace: the declared objective had been to force the LTTE to accept the devolution proposals of 1995. Waging war to implement a peace package was a novel method, but its inordinately high cost had raised the question of its endurance. Nevertheless, it seemed to be the best bet for the government. On the method of accomplishing the task—whether to defeat the Tigers militarily or weaken them sufficiently to enlist

[78] *Frontline*, 17–30 August 1991, p 41

[79] *Frontline*, 28 September–11 October 1991, p. 38

their strong commitment to political negotiations–the government's changing position was conditioned by the battlefield outcomes. The Kumaratunga government had nurtured a deep desire for a military victory, but in view of the battlefield limitations, it had set a limited task for the military—weakening the Tigers militarily: The idea was to force them to accept the devolution package that would turn them into democrats. By 2001, both the government and LTTE prepared themselves for a peace process facilitated by Norway under the influence of stalemate in the war process. But its failure within one year (by 2003) of its beginning and the consequent resumption of hostilities (by 2006) led to revision of the government's strategy.

President Rajapaksa's war objective was different from that of his predecessors; he was firm in his determination to exterminate the LTTE militarily and end the ethnic conflict thereafter. In setting this goal, he was deeply influenced and greatly helped by the changed global security situation, in the post-September 2001 period, marked by the international community's strategic cooperation and support to defeat terrorism in any part of the world. Hence, the regime considered its military operations against the LTTE as a war against terrorism and successfully earned the support and endorsement of the international community until it realized that Sri Lanka's 'war-on-terror' did not spare the civilians who were treated along, if not on par, with the Tigers—the original combatants. Massive human rights violations by the military made the West to rethink on its earlier support to the war. Yet, rejecting the widespread international outcry and condemnation, the determined Rajapaksa regime had allowed the military to launch a series of well-coordinated operations in phases since 2006, which yielded unexpected strategic gains. It first captured the entire Eastern province from the LTTE control and then marched into the Northern province (the Wanni region, covering Kilinnochi, Mullaitivu and parts of Jaffna, Mannar and Vavuniya districts) where it conducted a conventional warfare (indiscriminate use of artillery, tanks and air power), which not only crippled the LTTE thoroughly but also killed thousands of civilians. At the end, the government has become victorious by defeating and exterminating the LTTE. The death of the Tigers has signalled not only the end of a protracted armed resistance to the Sinhalese majoritarian state's ethnic policy but also emboldened it sufficiently to deny a negotiated permanent political solution to the ethnic conflict.

Like in other cases, coercion constituted a strategy of the Nepali state. The difference is that it did not privilege the government in terms of gaining strategic advantages vis-à-vis the Maoists. In the initial phase, the government seemed to have underestimated the Maoists' strength and firepower. Therefore, until 2001, it relied on the police force whose defensive strategies increased the state's vulnerabilities and, at the same time, expanded the Maoists control over a large chunk of territories across the country. It was only after an army post was attacked in November 2001 that the government had decided to employ them in counter-insurgency operations. Yet, the army maintained a "defensive posture", seldom undertaking concerted offensive missions to neutralize or defeat the Maoists.[80]

At the end, the government's coercive strategy appeared weak while the Maoists succeed in developing tremendous counter-coercive capabilities. This outcome had exerted the government to negotiate a peace deal with the willing Maoists.

The use of coercion in Myanmar has been severe and widespread. The military junta became a repressive enterprise that defied the international opinion on democracy and human rights in the country. It has used political repression against the pro-democracy leaders and military coercion against the ethnic insurgent groups that challenged the state. The military junta kept Aung San Suu Kyi under house arrest for several years and subjected her to other civil disabilities. It denied the fundamental rights and civil liberties to the people. In countering the ethnic challenges, the regime has consistently used the military against the insurgents, leading to large-scale human rights violations and displacement of people.[81] Clearly, there is greater continuity in the approach and strategy of the current regime headed by President Sein and the earlier military junta in dealing with the ethnic insurgencies. Both have shown resoluteness in using military coercion as the preferred strategy to destroy the ethnic insurgents. No insurgent group has managed to escape from the authoritarian state's fury. This has been the main reason for proliferation of ceasefire agreements in Myanmar.

---

[80] Ashok K. Mehta,*The Royal Nepal Army: Meeting the Maoist Challenge,* (New Delhi: Rupa & Co, 2005), p 59.

[81] See note 63

Ceasefire

Ceasefire denotes a pause in skirmishes or fight between the adversaries in a conflict. It seeks to suspend violence between them to end the conflict through a peace process. As such, ceasefire does not itself create permanent peace or resolve a conflict; rather, it paves the way for a negotiated peace, if the parties themselves are willing to adopt an alternate approach in pursuit of their interest in conflict and commit themselves to end violence. In sum, ceasefire is a condition for peacemaking, and not necessarily an instrument of peace. What stems from this argument is a point that ceasefires are "by their nature reciprocal,"[82] yet, in practice, it is possible that one party makes an unilateral offer of ceasefire either as an incentive to the other to accept a peace process or out of military pressure from the dominant adversary— in the latter case, it is to ward off a potential threat of defeat or escape from an adverse military situation. A distinction can also be made between "armistice agreements that aim to stop the fighting but do not purport to settle the conflict, and peace agreements that address the political dispute underlying the conflict.[83] Here again, one should note that not all ceasefires are written agreements; they can be merely political declarations or unwritten commitments by both parties. The purpose of the section is to analyze the link between coercion and ceasefire; whether the ceasefire agreements have resulted in peace processes, and whether ceasefire-driven peace processes led to permanent settlement of conflicts in India, Nepal, Sri Lanka and Myanmar.

In a number of conflicts analyzed in this chapter, ceasefire has been a chosen strategy for one or both parties. In most cases, the outcome of the use of military coercion has largely determined the adoption of this strategy. As such, there is a close link between the use of military coercion and the parties' preference for a ceasefire agreement. The Naga conflict is an interesting case. As early as in 1963, under tremendous military pressure, the NNC leader Phizo had shown interest in a ceasefire agreement with the Indian government. He proposed a meeting with Nehru to discuss this matter, but the latter declined to meet him. Subsequently, he suggested a joint

---

[82] Virginia Page Fortna, *Peace Time: Ceasefire Agreements and the Durability of Peace*, (Princeton: Princeton University Press, 2004), p 3.

[83] Ibid

declaration of a cease-fire, which Nehru also rejected. Then Phizo pushed the proposal through Michael Scott (an Anglican churchman and human rights activist) who pleaded unsuccessfully with Nehru. Finally, Phizo sent feelers to Chief Minister Shilu Ao, seeking his help to visit Nagaland. Later, consultations between the state and central governments led to acceptance of Phizo's plea on the condition that they would not entertain him for any discussion if he espoused the cause of Nagaland's secession.[84] Phizo did not accept the conditional offer, but other leaders from the Naga Federal Government had utilized the Indian government's changed attitude towards a peace process. Their interest in talks was either a tactical step to ease military pressure on the Naga Army, or to secure political legitimacy for their movement from New Delhi. It was in this situation that the Baptist Church launched a peace offensive by urging the central government to set up a peace mission to find ways and means to end the war. Now, New Delhi's stand on cease-fire had changed and with the peace mission interacting with the government and the underground Naga Federal leaders, a draft ceasefire agreement was prepared by May 1964 and signed in August. It came into effect on 6 September initially for one month and extended thereafter for another eight years, until the government had unilaterally terminated it on 1 September 1972. Importantly, the cease-fire continued much longer than the peace talks (which lasted until October 1967), indicating the weakening position of the Naga Army vis-à-vis the Indian security forces.

The breakdown of ceasefire made the use of coercion the readily available strategy for both combatants. Though the Shillong Accord of 1975 brought a moderate section of the Naga nationalist to the mainstream, the militant nationalists continued the internal war until the NSCN (I-M) declared a three-month ceasefire with effect from 1 August 1997. It has been extended since then, initially for every six months, then every year (since 1998 onwards), and now indefinitely (since July 2007). The NSCN (K) has also accepted ceasefire (since November 1998), which is now extended to a faction led by Kitovi (since August 2011). In 2001, the government and the insurgent leaders agreed on a set of 'ground rules' for their functioning during the

---

[84] Y.D Gundevia, *War and Peace in Nagaland*, (Dehra Dun: Palit & Palit, 1975), p 105.

ceasefire period; a ceasefire supervisory board has also been constituted to monitor and implement them. The long drawn ceasefire has enabled the parties to engage in protracted political negotiations, but their progress remains retarded.

In Nepal, ceasefire appeared intermittently between insurgency and the peace process, which resulted in a comprehensive peace accord in November 2006. For the first time, both the government and Maoist declared ceasefire on 29 January 2003—seven years after the outbreak of insurgency in February 1996. Despite their strong determination to achieve an outright military victory, the parties exhibited their mutual interest in ceasefire, clearly indicating their inability to advance their desired military objectives in an adverse situation marked by a stalemate in the conflict process. For the Maoists, accepting the ceasefire was a "strategic balancing act" since the government conceded some of their demands and showed gestures, for example, by annulling the red corner notices issued against some of their leaders (Prachanda's statement, quoted in Muni 2003: 115).[85] Importantly, the ceasefire had set in motion a fragile political process as both the government and the Maoists formed their respective negotiating team. At the same time, a section of the political class expressed fear that the Maoists would make use of ceasefire to regroup and launch renewed attacks on the army. The issue became embroiled in national politics when some political leaders wanted the Maoist not to engage the King in any political dialogue and, instead, urged them to negotiate with the democratically elected leaders. That the Maoist tilted their balance towards the democratic forces was evident from their decision to sign a 22-point code conduct with the government. At the same time, they used their leverage (earned through the possession of arms and their capacity to strike at the army) as a tool to bargain with the government. On 21 March 2003, they asked the government to release at least five of their leaders and withdraw cases against many of them including Prachanda and Baburam Bhattarai. The government accepted some of them, but increasing incidents of violation of the code conduct by the Maoists caused concerns in the army. There arose a situation eventually when the ceasefire broke down in August 2003, inciting the combatants to exchange coercion as a chosen strategy for the next two years.

---

[85] See S D Muni , 2003, p 115

At the end, in September 2005, the Maoists decided to declare unilateral ceasefire first for three months and then extended it for another one month. It was aimed at warding off the combined pressure from the army, the international community, human rights organizations and political parties and create a pro-peace image for themselves both in Nepal and abroad (Rajamohan 2007: 112).[86] But when King Gyanendra who held the state power refused to reciprocate, the Maoists decided to end their ceasefire on 2 January 2006. What followed this was the Maoists' fury, demonstrated in a number of armed attacks on the army, abduction of several officials and security personnel. The King unleashed repression not only against the Maoists but also on the political leaders. This brought both the Maoists and political closer to "strengthen their alliance against the King".[87] The popular political uprising had forced the King to restore at least partially the civilian control of the state: the House of Representatives was reinstated to make the way for Prime Minister Girija Prasad Koirala to take charge of resolving the Maoist insurgency. His appeal for peace was responded positively by the Maoists who announced a unilateral ceasefire for three months on 27 April 2006. The government reciprocated by its decision to remove the Maoists' terrorist label and engage them in a peace process, which resulted in an accord in November 2006.

Sri Lanka's ethnic war was paused many times before it ended in May 2009. Ceasefire had been a notable strategy pursued by both the government and militants under each other's military pressure. After the outbreak of the war in mid-1983, the combatants had agreed for a 12-week ceasefire, which preceded the two rounds of Thimpu peace talks in July-August 1985. The failure of talks led to resumption of hostilities. Next, even as the IPKF continued its military offensive against the LTTE, the Sri Lankan government sought to alienate the Indian government by declaring a truce and holding peace talks with the Tiger leaders in mid-1989—both continued almost for a year. But this tactical move on the part of both Colombo and the LTTE did not promote peace, but strengthened the conditions for violence. Yet, within six months of recommencing the war, the LTTE felt the need for a respite. It, therefore, declared unconditionally a unilateral ceasefire on the last day

[86] P G Rajamohan, "Nepal: Continuing Violence: 2006", In D. Suba Chandran, ed., *Armed Conflicts and Peace Processes in South Asia*, (New Delhi: Samskriti, 2007), p 112

of 1990 and expressed its willingness to hold peace talks. The government was urged to respond positively for an indefinite extension of the ceasefire. Given its bitter past experience that the LTTE used ceasefire to regroup and rearm to launch attacks on the military, the Premadasa government was initially quite wary of the LTTE's offer. At the same time, it did not want the opposition and the international community to blame it for its hard-line position and missing a chance for peacemaking. Therefore, after consulting the opposition leaders, the government declared a conditional seven-day ceasefire on 3 January 1991: It said that while there would be no offensive operations, security forces would conduct routine patrolling and administrative tasks including surveillance of waters. Furthermore, no one other than the security forces would be allowed to carry weapons, and measures would be taken to prevent militants from entering the communally sensitive areas and arousing communal discord or indulging in extortion.[88]

However, the government refused to extend the week-long ceasefire in the wake of its violations by the LTTE. Defence Minister Ranjan Wijeratne had attributed the Tigers' interest in ceasefire to their military weakness: the truce was "a ruse to gain as their forces were in disarray", he said. The LTTE blamed the government for breakdown of the ceasefire. However, after re-commencing the military operations, the government showed its interest in another ceasefire if the Tigers wanted serious negotiations. But it made two more conditions. One was that any future negotiations would have to be conducted with LTTE chief Prabhakaran himself and not with the People's Front of Liberation Tigers (PFLT). The PFLT was seen to be only a front organization of the LTTE conducting political negotiations while the military wing prepared for war. By negotiating directly with the LTTE leader, the government hoped to circumvent the problem it had faced in June 1990 when the PFLT did the talking while the LTTE armed itself. The second demand was that government, diluting its earlier condition—that the LTTE should lay down arms for any dialogue to begin—insisted that peace talks should be preceded by a declaration against the possession and use of arms by a group or person other than those who were legally authorized. Elucidating this point, Wijeratne conceded that the LTTE did not have to lay down arms immediately. But, as expected, the LTTE rejected the conditions for ceasefire.

---

[88] Ibid, p 221

Thus, for about four years (1990-94), many bitter battles were fought between the Sri Lankan army and the LTTE. The new regime under President Chandrika (since 1994) offered to talk peace without, at the same time, halting the military operations. But the LTTE put pressure for a ceasefire since it needed a respite (given that it was engaged continuously in the war since 1990). In order to convince the government it declared a week-long unilateral ceasefire on 12 November 1994. Prabhakaran corresponded with Kumaratunga and Deputy Minister of Defence Anuruddha Ratwatte. In response, the government wanted the LTTE chief to commit himself to the peace process, and not to make use of cessation of hostilities for respite and regrouping of its cadres aimed at launching fresh round of war, as happened during 1989-90, and carrying out killings of its Tamil opponents in North and East and the Sinhalese leaders in South. It also wanted the cessation of hostilities to promote serious and substantive negotiations to find a political solution to the conflict.

The government relented under the LTTE's unrelenting pressure. In January 1995, a formal declaration to cease hostilities was exchanged between President Kumaratunga and Prabhakaran. Both of them signed it simultaneously in Colombo and Jaffna on 5 January and implemented it in three days, on 8 January. The government maintained that it declared cessation of hostilities and not cease-fire. It considered the former to be less formal and binding, as a prelude to the latter. Under cessation of hostilities marking the absence of violence, both combatants could remain fully armed and alert. That the Sri Lankan President and the LTTE chief were the signatories to the agreement indicated the need felt most probably by the government to involve the top leaders directly in the peace process and enlist their commitment to a negotiated solution.

Importantly, ceasefires during 1983-94 were all brief in terms of operational duration and based on bilateral understanding (and not formal written agreements) or unilateral decisions. However, for the first time in January 1995, the government and the LTTE entered into a formal and written ceasefire agreement. It laid down some ground rules for the combatants. It sought to establish a direct communication link at the field level between the commanders of security forces and the LTTE and created a buffer zone of 600 metres between the bunker lines of both the combatants with their right of movement being restricted to within 100 metres of their respective bunkers. The rest of the area (covering 400 metres between the bunkers of the two parties) was declared "no man's land". While restraining the Sri Lankan navy and air force from launching operations against the LTTE, the agreement allowed them to perform their legitimate duties of safeguarding the country's sovereignty against any aggression. At the same time, it categorically demanded the LTTE to stop all its violent acts of sabotage, bomb explosions, assassinations and intimidation against any political group, party or individual. It proposed to set up peace monitoring committees with members drawn from various walks of life and four representatives from Canada, Norway and the Netherlands and the International Committee of Red Cross. It was their responsibility to take immediate action on complaints made by the parties and resolve the disputes. The agreement was valid for an indefinite period; either party could withdraw from it by giving a 72 hours advance notice of termination (Sahadevan 1995).[89] The truce declaration, though a victory for the LTTE since the government accepted it without preconditions, did not convince the LTTE leadership to start talks on the substantive political issues. By April 1995, it became clear that the LTTE was merely interested in gaining tactical advantages vis-à-vis the government. The resumption of war thus became inevitable; it continued for about six years without a ceasefire.

The Norwegian role in the peace process led to a comprehensive ceasefire agreement (CFA) in 2002. Valid for an 'indefinite period', the CFA provided a comprehensive framework for maintaining peace. Its provisions were grouped under two categories—cessation of military operations and confidence-building measures (CBMs). Some of the provisions under the former included: (i) stopping of offensive military operations by both combatants who were to maintain a zone of separation of a minimum of 600 metres, but each party enjoyed the right to movement within 100 metres of its defence localities, keeping an absolute minimum distance of 400 metres; (ii) Any movement of munitions, explosives and military equipment into areas controlled by each other was prohibited; (iii). Tamil paramilitary groups were to be disarmed in 30 days of the CFA coming into force and their members were to be given an opportunity to join the armed

[89] P Sahadevan, "Why the Cease-fire in Sri Lanka Failed", *Mainstream,* 29(20), 1991.

forces for duty outside the Northeast; and (iv) Unarmed soldiers were given unlimited passage between Jaffna and Vavuniya using the A9 Jaffna-Kandy road. In addition, unarmed combatants in plain clothes were allowed to visit their family and friends residing in areas under the control of their opponent. Such visits were limited to six days every six-month (the time taken to travel is excluded). In three phases, all unarmed LTTE members were to enjoy freedom of movement in the entire Northeast except certain specified military areas.

CBMs stipulated in the CFA were aimed at restoring normalcy in the entire country; they included: (i) Stopping of all hostile acts against civilians (torture, intimidation, abduction, extortion, etc.); (ii) prohibition of activities aimed at offending cultural or religious sensitivities of any community; (iii) Vacation of all places of worship held by both parties in 30 days and be made accessible to the public. Places of worship situated in high security zones were to be vacated by armed personnel and maintained in good order by civilian workers even when they were not made accessible to the public. School buildings should be vacated and returned to their intended use in 160 days; (iv) Permission for unimpeded flow of non-military goods to and from the LTTE-held areas; however, certain items used for military purposes were kept in the banned list; (v) review of security measures including checkpoints set up particularly in densely populated areas in order to prevent harassment of the civilian population; (vi) Both parties agreed to extend the rail service from Batticaloa to Welikanda, open the A9 Kandy-Jaffna highway to civilian traffic in 30 days and gradually ease fishing restrictions in 90 days; and (vii) stopping of search operations and arrests under the Prevention of Terrorism Act, and family members of the detainees were given access to the detainees.

An international committee—Sri Lanka Monitoring Mission (SLMM)—was set up to investigate the CFA violations through on-site verification. Headed by a Norwegian government representative, its members were drawn from various Nordic countries. It had headquarters both in Colombo and Wanni and maintained its presence throughout the Northeast by establishing six local monitoring committees—one each in Jaffna, Mannar, Vavuniya, Trincomalee, Batticaloa and Amparai. Each committee had five members—both the Sri Lankan government and LTTE appointed two members each and one international monitor was appointed by the head of the SLMM. On their part, both the government and LTTE were (i) to co-operate to rectify any matter of conflict caused by the respective sides; (ii) ensure the freedom of movement of the SLMM members in performing their task; (iii) give the SLMM immediate access to areas where CFA violations are taken place; and (iv) facilitate the widest possible access to such areas for the local committee members. A major responsibility of the SLMM was to take "immediate action on any complaints" made by either party to the CFA, and to "enquire into and assist the Parties in the settlement of any dispute" arising out of such complaint. With a view to resolving all disputes as expeditiously as possible at the lowest possible level, a communication link was established between the army commanders and the LTTE area leaders. Finally, it was stated that the CFA could be amended and modified by mutual consent of both parties. However, its termination required a 14-day advance notice by either party.

The 2002 ceasefire agreement was far more comprehensive and structured than the one which President Kumaratunga signed with Prabhakaran in 1995. One possible reason is that unlike the 1995 agreement negotiated and drafted bilaterally between the Sri Lankan government and the LTTE, the Norwegian facilitators, who played a significant behind the scene role in drafting the agreement, did not want to leave the issues ill-defined or ambiguous. They wanted to make the warring parties committed to and responsible for the deal that they had signed to cease their hostilities. In 1995, the ceasefire agreement resulted from the peace talks; it was agreed during the second round of talks held in January 1995. On the contrary, the 2002 CFA was a precursor to peace talks between the parties. The aim was to achieve military disengagement between the Sri Lankan army and the LTTE before commencing talks.

Implementation of the CFA began in earnest immediately after it was signed. But the process had encountered many difficulties to cause inordinate delays in commencing the talks. It took both the government and LTTE about six months to hold the first round of negotiations. The LTTE was particularly unhappy that the army did not vacate all public places and residential areas as per the government's commitment under the CFA. For the national security reasons, it maintained many high security zones mostly in the Jaffna peninsula, which uprooted a large number of people. The positive side of the CFA was that it enabled more than a half of the total (370,000) internally displaced persons to return to the areas of their original habitation during the first two years (2002-2004). One of the flaws in the CFA was that it had disarmed prematurely the non-LTTE groups. Neither the Sri Lankan government nor the Norwegian facilitators anticipated that the LTTE would threaten the existence of the disarmed groups and kill their leaders mercilessly. Related to this was the absence of a mechanism and commitment of both the parties to protect human rights. This gave the LTTE a free hand to violate human rights by engaging itself in political killings, intimidation and, above all, recruitment of children as combatants. By August 2005, the SLMM had recorded more than 3,000 cases of CFA violations by the LTTE, as against about 140 violations by the government. Many blamed the SLMM and the Norwegians for the ceasefire violations, without realizing the structural lacuna both in the CFA and status of mission agreement (SOMA). The SLMM had only a limited mandate and was faced with huge constraints in maintaining peace. It needed the full cooperation of both parties for its effective functioning by resolving disputes arising out of implementation of the CFA. This means that the SLMM could merely assist them in resolving their dispute, but was in a position to impose its decision if one or both parties refused to cooperate and comply with its ruling. Neither the CFA nor the SOMA specified the response of the SLMM if a party did not cooperate. By 2003, the CFA failed to work towards promoting peace negotiations and its eventual breakdown down paved the way for resumption of the fourth *eelam* war in 2006.

A principal strategy of the regime in Myanmar has been to combine military coercion with ceasefire agreements with the ethnic insurgent groups. Coercion is applied first to make the offers of ceasefire acceptable to the non-state armed groups. Their refusal to accept the ceasefire offers tends to intensify the state's determination to use military coercion. The military junta started implementing this strategy way back in 1988; one of the first ceasefire agreements was concluded with some breakaway groups from the Communist Party of Burma (CPB), which collapsed immediately in 1989 in the wake of "ethnic mutinies" (South 2012: 11).[90] The same strategy

---

[90] Ashley South, *Prospects for Peace in Myanmar: Opportunities and Threats*, (Oslo: Peace Research Institute Oslo, 2012).

has continued since then to cover a large number of armed groups so that there are about 25 ceasefire agreements; some of them have now lasted more than two decades. Many powerful armed groups including the United Wa State Army (UWSA), the Kachin Independent Organization (KIO), and New Mon State Party have been coerced to accept ceasefire. Many of the agreements are mere understanding to cease violence and military operations; they do not include commitments, particularly of the government, to begin peace negotiations to address the grievances of the ethnic communities. Therefore, ceasefire agreements have not created trust between the parties; it has been eroded further completely when the military junta proposed to convert the ceasefire groups into Border Guard Forces (BGF) under the direct control of *Tatmadaw* (the Royal Force) commanders. Some of the groups have accepted willingly or under coercion, and others resisted at the risking of earning the wrath of the junta, which launched military operations to disarm or defeat the defiant armed groups (ibid: 11-12). [91]

The above cases analyzed here reveal that the adversaries' objectives behind declaring or asking for a ceasefire have been different. Some insurgent groups have used it as a tactics to escape from military defeat, and others to negotiate peace. The fear of defeat however has not forced any government to declare a ceasefire, but the limitations of their coercion have formed a factor in some cases. Therefore, the governments have invariably accepted ceasefire to find a solution to their conflicts; they have done so in a situation of hurting or simple stalemate in the conflict process. But the outcomes are different: The ceasefire between the Nepali government and the Maoists led to peace, but the same outcome was not possible in the Sri Lankan war. Though the ceasefires have helped end many ethnic insurgencies in Myanmar, the resolution of conflicts has not taken place.

Ending or Seeking External Support

The importance of external patrol role in internal conflict has been underlined in the previous section. Identifiably, there are two different responses that parties make to a patron's intervention in conflict: both adversaries try to

[91] Ibid

end patrons' support to each other even while they seek to gain external support separately. In other words, ending and seeking external patron support have been the twin strategies that many parties in internal conflicts adopt. The notable exception has been the Indian government, which has merely sought to end the patron support of countries such as China, Bangladesh and Bhutan extended to the Naga and ULFA insurgents, and has never tried to secure external support for itself to counter the militants. In the earlier period of insurgency in the Northeast, India mainly target the Chinese who said to have armed and trained the Naga militants in guerrilla warfare and helped them in forging a nexus with the Karen insurgents— both of them had shared operational tactics, information, arms and ammunitions. Importantly, it was alleged that China offered to induct some People's Liberation Army (PLA) advisers into NNC combat units in Nagaland. However, the level of Chinese support varied: since the Chinese government merely used militants as its foreign-policy tool against India, it lacked commitment to their cause. As such, the issue attained greater bilateral dimension: India considered the Chinese support to militants as part of its proxy war strategy. Since bilateral interactions were frozen for long and contentious issues like the border question dominated the foreign policy agenda, the Chinese patron role in India's northeast was always a peripheral issue for the policymakers. India was convinced that improvement of its bilateral relations with China alone would stop the latter's patron support to the northeastern militants. But the process of normalization of their bilateral relations in the 1970s provided India an opportunity to raise the issue with the Chinese leadership. During his visit to Beijing in 1979, the then External Affairs Minister (and later Prime Minister) A. B. Vajpayee, secured an assurance from the Chinese leaders that they would stop all their support to Indian insurgents. They reiterated the same assurance in subsequent years.[92] Even though Beijing did not appear very serious about its assurances and continued to aid and abet insurgency,[93] there has been a noticeable decline in the level of Chinese involvement in the northeast over the years. This is partly due to the conscious decision of Beijing not to complicate its relations with New Delhi, and partly because the insurgents have not served Chinese interests in any significant way.

[92] *Sunday Standard*, 10 August 1980
[93] *Hindustan Times*, 11 January 1987

Pakistan had been a patron to the northeastern insurgents when Bangladesh remained its territory. Afterwards, in the post-liberation period, Bangladesh granted sanctuary to various insurgent groups, but denied any such patron role in India's internal war in the northeast.[94]

This seemed to have been a calculated but clandestine measure to deter the indirect support India had extended to the Shanti Bahini in its insurgency against the army in the Chittaong Hill Tracts (CHT). Many therefore had expected the repatriation of Chakma refugees from India to encourage Dhaka to curb the ISI activities, drive the insurgents out of their sanctuary in Sylhet and the CHT, and stop the flow of arms into India through its territory from Southeast Asian black markets. Some in unofficial quarters even felt that Bangladesh provided sanctuary to the insurgents mainly to win concessions from India on the Ganges water dispute. Although this linkage was not articulated in clear political terms, it was true that Bangladesh needed some pressure-exerting mechanisms to deal with India.

The sanctuary issue became a source of distrust between the two countries and figured in bilateral discussions at the political and official levels. But successive Bangladeshi regimes lacked political will to respond to India's demand for a crackdown on the insurgent groups such as the ULFA. While in power, the Bangladesh National Party (BNP) leader, Begum Khaleda Zia, repeatedly denied that her government extended any tactical support to the insurgents. But while in opposition, she came out openly in their support by calling them "freedom fighters".[95] A change of government in both countries in the mid-1990s has brought about a positive change in each other's attitudes and perceptions. A new bilateral equation grounded in positive understanding between the Awami League government of Sheikh Hasina and the United Front governments (of H. D. Deve Gowda and I. K. Gujral) paved the way for the resolution of some of the ticklish bilateral issues like the Ganges water sharing and cross-border support to insurgency.

---

[94] Nani Gopal Mahanta, "Changing Contours of Armed Violence in Northeast India", In V.R. Raghavan, ed. *Conflicts: A Four State Analysis (India, Nepal, Sri Lanka and Myanmar)*, (New Delhi: Vij Books India Pvt. Ltd, 2013) and Samir Kumar Das, "ULFA Indo-Bangladesh Relations and Beyond", In Sanjoy Hazarika and V.R. Raghavan, eds., *Conflicts in the Northeast: Internal and External Effects*, (New Delhi: Vij Books India Pvt. Ltd, 2011).

[95] *Frontline,* 30 May 1997: 57

India's flexible stand on the water issue that resulted in a landmark treaty made Bangladesh to give up some of its anti-India postures and activities. Encouraged by the spirit of good neighbourliness that reflected in the Ganges water treaty, both India and Bangladesh reached an understanding in January 1997 not to allow insurgents to operate from their soil. It ended the covert support that successive governments in Dhaka had extended to the Northeastern insurgents since 1978. The Bangladesh security forces soon started cracking down on various militant groups: they arrested several ULFA militants, destroyed their hideouts and also closed down their training camps, forcing them to seek alternate sanctuaries in Myanmar and Bhutan. India mounted pressure on Bangladesh to arrest and handover some of the top ULFA leaders like its Chairman, Arabinda Rajkhowa, to the Indian authorities who had subsequently arrested and then released them on bail to participate in peace talks. Earlier, in December 2003, India made Bhutan to drive the northeastern insurgents militarily away from its territory. The Indian army provided logistical support for the Royal Bhutan Army's military action, which resulted in destruction of the insurgents' camps and hideouts and killing and arrest of hundreds of them.[96] Thus, a major part of external dimensions to the northeast insurgency has been neutralized, if not ended totally.

Unlike India, Sri Lanka's strategy focused not only on ending the external support that the Tamil militants enjoyed but also securing support for itself to counter them. India had been the most targeted patron whom the Sri Lankan government wanted to wean away from the militants in the process of achieving their complete subjugation. India assumed such critical importance in Sri Lanka's war strategy because it demonstrably determined the militants' strength and weakness, and success and failure. Since 1983, several militants groups had depended upon India's politico-military support for their survival against the government's military onslaught. The support India had extended varied from mobilization of international opinion in favour of the Tamil cause and extension of military support in the form of training and supply of arms.[97] At the height of the war in June 1987, it resorted to direct military action by sending its air force to paradrop food and medicine

---

[96] See note 94

[97] S D Muni, *Pangs of Proximity: India and Sri Lanka's Ethnic Crisis*, (New Delhi: Sage Publications, 1993)

over the Jaffna Peninsula. Apparently, New Delhi's aim was to pressurize the Sri Lankan government to stop the onward movement of its army to capture Jaffna and save the Tamil militants from a humiliating defeat at the hands of their formidable adversary. This incident, and also India's overall pressure tactics during its mediation (1983-87), had developed a strong feeling among Sri Lanka's ruling elite that the Indian government would never accept the Tamil militants' defeat as long as it played a patron role in the *eelam* war. Thus, the Sri Lankan government's diplomatic efforts largely focused on winning India not really directly to its side in the war (at least in the 1980s) but to stop its patron support to the militants.

Since India's security concerns (arising mainly out of Sri Lanka's desire to involve external forces in the ethnic war) in the 1980s formed the principal factor behind its tough policy posture, the island's leadership sought to address them seriously as a part of the process of resolving the ethnic conflict. The 1987 India-Sri Lanka Agreement provided the context and framework for developing greater understanding between the two countries: it was a different matter that the Sri Lankan government benefited more than the Indian government out of this relationship. Both of them had peculiar strategic objectives to achieve in concluding the peace agreement: while India wanted to protect its strategic interests in the region, Sri Lanka was keen to make its national security free of threat from the former. It means that India would completely cease its support to the militants, which perceivably posed a threat to Sri Lanka's sovereignty and territorial integrity, and deport all those Sri Lankan citizens who were found to have engaged in terrorist activities or advocating separatism. Sri Lanka had extracted these assurances from India and, in return, accommodated its security concerns. This formed a significant diplomatic victory for Sri Lanka which, in the ultimate analysis, not only weaned India away from the militants but also turned it against them. India's war to disarm the LTTE under the 1987 Agreement was the most significant result of Sri Lanka's strategy of winning patrons. By making India one of the principal parties to enforce peace in the island, President Jayewardene carved out a participant role for it. His hidden objective was to use the same patron to neutralize its client (the LTTE) militarily so that the military would win the *eelam* war ultimately. However, winning the patron had not concomitantly resulted in winning the war in the 1980s and 1990s.

Once having withdrawn its support to the militants, India has never tried to replay the same patron role in the war. Successive governments in Delhi had chosen not to get involved in the *eelam* war in any direct manner that would either help the government in Colombo or the LTTE. India's internal opinion has also undergone a drastic change particularly after the assassination of Rajiv Gandhi; even the political pressure that the people of Tamil Nadu had exerted on the central government to intervene in the island waned until the mid-2000s. There was greater introspection on the gains and losses of India's role in Sri Lanka's ethnic war during the 1980s, and a growing realization that instructed India to desist from getting involved in the *eelam* war. As a significant step, the government banned the LTTE in 1992; the ban is being extended periodically ever since then. Sri Lanka has benefited greatly from the change in Indian policy; no where this is demonstrated except in the fourth *eelam* war. The Rajapaksa regime enjoyed an unhindered political and strategic space not just because it was backed by countries such as China, Pakistan and Russia, but also due to India's discreet endorsement of the war by refusing to intervene to stop it even as the human cost of its escalated beyond the acceptable level. Wining India's indirect support for the war and weaning it away from the Sri Lankan Tamil community have been the most significant achievement of Sri Lanka's conflict management strategies.

Since the 1980s, in the wake of the ending of India's patron support, the LTTE had to rely heavily on the Sri Lankan Tamil diaspora settled mostly in the West (Fair 2007). This necessitated Sri Lanka to focus on winning the host governments of the diaspora. Hence, the issue has occupied the agenda of Sri Lankan diplomacy more prominently since the mid-1990s. Every single visit of the Sri Lankan leaders had the objective of countering the LTTE's overseas activities. Their diplomatic efforts yielded significant results: some of the countries such as Canada, Australia, the UK put restrictions on its operations among the diaspora; the US went beyond to declare the LTTE a foreign terrorist organization in 1997.[98] Subsequently, after the September 11, 2001 terrorist attacks in the US, Sri Lanka capitalized maximum on the

---

[98] P Sahadevan, *Coping With Disorder: Strategies to End Internal Wars in South Asia*, RCSS Policy Studies 17, (Colombo: Regional Centre for Strategic Studies. 2000), pp 83-86.

international community's anti-terrorism policies and drew widespread support for its war against the LTTE. It made the world to accept its position that the LTTE was a terrorist organization and its offensive military operations were to defeat terrorism in the island. The international support for 'Sri Lanka's war on terror' was available until the world community realized the real nature and dimension of the war: the mounting civilian death caused by the massive and indiscriminate use of military power led the international community to rethink on its support to the war against the LTTE. By the time the West exerted pressure on Sri Lanka to stop the war, the assertive Rajapaksa regime achieved most of the strategic targets of the fourth *eelam* war and mobilized strong support of China, Russia, Pakistan, etc., which provided it with a much needed diplomatic shield against the Western intervention (tried through the United Nations) in the island and also a variety of military assistance particularly by the Chinese. As a matter of fact, the Chinese role in the conflict and *eelam* war has been a longstanding affair. Sri Lanka has consistently cultivated both China and Pakistan since the mid-1980s to protect its national interest from the perceived Indian threat. Thus, Sri Lanka's foreign policy behaviour during the *eelam* war period carried the twin objectives of not only ending the external role (in the Sri Lankan Tamils' support) but also seeking external support in its favour.

Unlike Sri Lanka, Nepal did not have to counter the external role but to maximize it to benefit the government's strategy. The influential external actors (including India and the US) were opposed to the Maoists even when they disapproved the King's autocratic decisions to undermine the democratic forces. At the same time, the Maoists did not have the wherewithal to oppose or resist the external influence and role, seen in terms of foreign military assistance to the government, support to its political negotiations with the Maoists and participation in peace-building. Nor did they try to cultivate any patron for advancing their radical cause and enhancing their power vis-à-vis the state. [99]

In Myanmar, the external interest is focused more on the pro-democracy movement than on the ethnic conflicts. Here, both the regime and NLD sought external support to promote their goals. Whereas the military junta

---

[99] See n.63

countered the Western intervention not just by its total defiance and rejection but also cultivating countries such as China, with whom Myanmar has forged strong strategic relations, the pro-democratic forces found in the international community the support for restoring democracy. In fact, the issue has occupied the agenda of the international community, which sought to isolate and penalize the military junta for its authoritarian policies. The US and the European Union pursued a policy of non-engagement and also imposed economic sanctions on the country. The United Nations is another external actor, which has exerted pressure on the regime to democratize Myanmar and establish peace through negotiations with all the ethnic groups. Cumulatively, the external pressure has played at least a partial role in bringing about the recent political change.

Divide and Engage

Dividing and then engaging a group is a much preferred strategy of every government involved in internal conflicts. However, no government admits that it seeks to divide a group. Certainly, since the top group leadership opposes such a strategy, governments tend to interpret the strategy as an opportunity for peace willingly extended by them. More than other governments dealt with in this chapter, both India and Sri Lanka have shown strong interest in the divide-and-engage strategy and earned dividends over the years. Breaking the unity of the Nagas was pursued as a major war-ending strategy of the government. In the 1950s, the focus was on strengthening the hands of the moderates to emerge as an alternate force to the militants. The government had encouraged the Naga People's Convention (NPC) to mobilize tribal opinion against the secessionist demand of the NNC and exert pressure on its leadership to accept a political settlement to the war. In its several resolutions during 1957–59, while urging the Indian government to satisfy the Naga people's territorial aspirations, the NPC leaders asked the NNC to join hands with them in negotiating a political settlement. In 1958, the NPC appointed a liaison committee to contact the militant leadership with a view to involving them in drafting a charter of demands. But when the Naga Federal Government insisted upon its recognition by the Indian government and sought to negotiate only around the issue of independence to Nagaland, the NPC went ahead alone to formulate its proposals. There always existed a line of communication between the NPC and the Indian leadership. Prime Minister Nehru met its leaders on several occasions, and in order to increase their credibility in Naga society, accepted their statehood demand in 1960. While these political gestures to the NPC drove a wedge between the moderates and militants, they did not isolate the NNC from the mainstream Naga society. But the very fact that a section of Naga opinion was ready to accept a solution within the Indian Union showed the emerging challenges to the NNC's claim as the sole representative organization of the Nagas. The government consciously cultivated the moderate forces further which, in 1963, had even objected to negotiations with the militant leadership except on the basis of surrender of arms and acceptance of the Indian Constitution [100]

Since the mid-1950s, efforts were also under way to create divisions in the ranks of the Naga Army. As early as in 1957, the government declared general amnesty and ordered the release of several convicts and under-trials. Yet, it could not penetrate into the militant outfit with the aim of splitting it until 1968, when a group proclaiming itself the Revolutionary Government of Nagaland emerged under the leadership of Scato Swu. It opposed the Federal Naga forces for "their intransigent and destructive pursuit of a hopeless cause", and praised the Indian government for its steps to resolve the war. Swu met Prime Minister Indira Gandhi before the surrender of his forces at a much-publicized function in Kohima in August 1973 and pledged to "live a life of [a] peace-loving and law-abiding citizen in the service of Nagaland and India". He backed the government's war to end militancy.[101] Interestingly, in his new life, Swu became a Member of Parliament and most of his men were inducted into the Border Security Force (BSF). Then the Shillong Accord came to disturb the cohesion of the Naga Federal Army. Responding to the amnesty offer, a number of insurgents surrendered with their arms and ammunition. The government set up peace camps for them to adjust with the new life, released under-trial prisoners and all those serving sentences in jails for their militant activities and extended financial support for their rehabilitation. In 1976–77, a sum of Rs. 33.40 lakh was spent for this purpose. The split of the NNC and the birth of the NSCN in 1980 were

---

[100] Neville Maxwell, *India and the Nagas,* Minority Group Report no.330, (London: MRG, 1973), p 14.

[101] Ibid, p 17

the results of the peace accord. Contrary to the expectation that the strength of the movement would dwindle after the split, the NSCN (I-M) emerged as a strong force to carry forward the war.

The government has allegedly been playing off one group or tribe against another. While putting obstructions to any move to unite the militant groups under a common platform, the centre seems to be according a dominant status to the NSCN (I-M). At the same time, former Chief Minister S. C. Jamir had patronized the NSCN (K, or Khaplang) faction: it was under his pressure that the central government had agreed to include it in the current peace process. Many in the government hoped that the NSCN (I-M) would split along tribal lines–Isaac Chishi Swu is from the Sema tribe and T. Muivah belongs to the Tangkhul tribal group. The Sema Nagas feel that the Tangkhul Nagas hold a disproportionately large share of top posts in the organization. This, however, has not become a source of rivalry in and division of the NSCN (I-M). Also, the Naga militants alleged that the government was using the Kuki tribals against the Nagas; they attributed the violent clashes between the two groups to the government's divide-and-engage strategy. Whatever be the truth, the government's desire to weaken the cohesion of the Naga rebels is not unknown.

It is in this context that the government's surrender-cum-rehabilitation package for the North-Eastern militants should be seen. Aimed at weaning away the militant youth, the scheme, launched in April 1999, offers a number of monetary incentives and benefits to the militants who are ready to bid farewell to arms. The idea is to ensure that the surrendered militants do not return to militancy. Although the scheme covers only those who surrender with at least one weapon, in exceptional and deserving cases, even militants without weapons could also be considered for rehabilitation. It was announced that each rocket rifle would fetch Rs. 25,000, an AK-47/56/74 assault rifle Rs. 15,000, each pistol or revolver Rs. 3,000, rockets Rs. 1,000 per piece, each grenade Rs. 500, every sophisticated remote control device Rs. 3,000, each improvised explosive device Rs. 3,000 and explosive material Rs. 1,000 per kg [102]. The amount for surrender would be put in a [bank] fixed deposit in the joint names of the surrendered militant and a nominee of

---

[102] *The Hindu*, 24 November 1999

an NGO or the state government. A militant gets deposit at the time of his leaving the rehabilitation camp. Once the modalities were completed, each surrendered militant would be paid a monthly stipend of Rs. 2,000 for a year. The scales of stipend for various categories of surrendered militants are decided by the state governments in consultation with the Home Ministry of the Central government of India. The latter provides 100 per cent reimbursement for expenditure incurred on rehabilitation of the surrendered militants, but the state governments implement the scheme directly. Amnesty is given to only those militants charged for minor offences, others are to face trial. The response of the Naga militants has been limited. Only a few of them availed the scheme. In a cumulative sense, the government's efforts to divide the Naga militant forces have not paid dividends to the extent of strengthening its war-ending strategy.

However, the scheme has evoked a more favourable response in Assam where about 500 ULFA militants surrendered by November 1999. It must be noted that the offer of amnesty and financial incentives has been the Indian government's dominant strategy to divide ULFA. It has been successful to some extent in weaning away a number of militants. As early as in July 1991, the government declared general amnesty to all those arrested during Operation Bajrang and 400 of them were released. The militants were offered handsome resettlement benefits amounting to Rs. 50,000; jobs for those qualified and soft loans up to Rs. 2 lakh for those interested in self-employment (Ministry of Home Affairs 1998). In 1992, soon after Operation Rhino, Chief Minister Hiteswar Saikia played a key role in creating a pro-peace group within ULFA, five leaders of which held a meeting with Prime Minister Narasimha Rao on 12 January 1992. He promised Rs. 110 crore as a rehabilitation package to those who surrendered.[103] This brought the division in the outfit to the fore, with one faction favouring peace talks and reconciliation with the government, and another opposing it. As a result, many activists and middle-level leaders surrendered along with their arms in exchange for the government's protection and rehabilitation assistance. This trend has continued ever since then. By encouraging surrenders, the government likes to see that ULFA is purged and only the hardliners remain.

---

[103] *India Today* 31 August 1992:p 65

It was felt that the intense military pressure and arrest of several leaders caused some demoralization on the ULFA cadres. It also created a vacuum of leadership on the ground as some of the top leaders have taken shelter outside India. This has forced many cadres to accept amnesty. Further, the government tried to play upon the rift between the top ULFA leaders– Paresh Barua (chief of the armed wing) and Arabinda Rajkhowa (chairman of the political wing)–who seemed to have competed for power in the group. The latter favoured talks with the government, and the former believed in continuing the insurgency. The army's operational strategy seemed to have taken this factor into consideration. For instance, it concentrated Operation Rhino in Upper Assam where Baruah was said to have a greater following than in Lower Assam. The army has also cultivated the SULFA (Surrendered ULFA) to its strategic advantage. This category of former insurgents has given valuable information to the intelligence agencies on the movement of the ULFA militants and helped the police and the army in liquidating them— these killings are mostly described as "encounter deaths".[104] For this reason, the army seemed to be unhappy when the state government decided in 1999 to disarm the SULFA; the plan was finally given up under pressure from the army and the police.

At the organizational level, only the Rajkhowa faction of ULFA has responded to the government's peace overtures; the Barua faction considers them as a dividing strategy. In 1999 the state Governor, Lt. Gen. S. K. Sinha (retd.), had announced one-week safe passage to enable the ULFA leaders and cadres to visit their families. He guaranteed security to Rajkhowa to visit his ailing parents in Upper Assam. Later, Chief Minister Prafulla Kumar Mahanta offered a 10-day 'safe passage' (21-31 December 1999) to coincide with the new millennium celebrations. There were no strings attached to the offer, but the rebels were not allowed to carry weapons with them while they visited their families. Further, the state government declared that those ULFA militants who had not committed heinous crimes would be granted general amnesty. The ULFA leadership rejected both offers, yet several cadres responded positively by even defying the orders of their top brass. As the response was huge, the government had extended the date of safe passage till 17 January 2000. Later, following the civil society's initiative for

---

[104] *The Hindu*, 24 October 1999

peace in Assam, the government in January 2007 offered a 'safe passage' to ULFA leaders provided they showed interest in peace talks. But the offer was not appealing to the Barua faction, which forced the government to continue the army operations. In ULFA's view, accepting the peace overtures of the government without a solution to their problem would amount to conceding its military weakness, thereby deepening the demoralization of its cadres caused by the military pressure and the surrender of many insurgents. For it, therefore, fighting a war seemed preferable to its complete surrender. Although it is a no-win fight for ULFA, some of its leaders like Barua like to continue violence. There is no doubt that the government's strategy has weakened ULFA both in terms of its military and organizational strength. It most notable achievement has been conversion of Rajkhowa into a potential peacemaker, if not really a peace-lover, who is interested in a negotiated political deal.

Encouraged by its experience in Northeast, the central Indian government has adopted a 'surrender-cum-rehabilitation policy' in the Maoist affected states. It has formed part of the government's "overall policy to build consensus and evolve an acceptable and peaceful solution to violence perpetrated by extremist groups, to usher in peace and development, especially in the disturbed regions".[105] In other words, according to the government, the policy is part of its "multi-pronged conflict management and resolution strategy", which is implemented "along with firm action" against those Maoists who "follow the path of violence." [106] Importantly, "the real and perceived neglect, deprivation and disaffection" is factored in the policy as it is intended to provide "gainful employment and entrepreneurial opportunities" to all the surrendered Maoists.[107] Thus, the aim is to encourage them to join the mainstream by making the movement unattractive for them. However, only hardcore underground Maoists are eligible for the government benefits, which include training in a trade or vacation of their liking or according to their aptitude, a monthly stipend of Rs.2000 for a maximum

---

[105] Ministry of Home Affairs "Guidelines for Surrender-cum-Rehabilitation of Naxalites in the Naxal Affected States", Government of India, 2011. available at www.mha.nic.in/uniquepage.asp?Id_PK=540

[106] Ibid

[107] Ibid

period of three years, and an immediate grant of Rs. 1.5 lakh to be fixed deposited for three years in a bank in the name of the surrendered Maoist. In addition, the government has provided monetary incentives for surrendering weapons and ammunition. In October 2012 the government announced a novel incentive: it has offered to do vasectomy reversal procedures at its expenses for all Maoist cadres who surrender or are arrested by security forces.[108] The policy is being implemented by the affected state governments, with whom the central government coordinates and reimburses all security-related expenditure. The Maoists' poor response indicates that their absolute and unbreakable commitment to their goal and ideology, particularly when the government is unable to neutralize or defeat them militarily. Thus, the surrender-cum-rehabilitation policy remains unattractive so far.

Sri Lanka is another state that has consistently used the divide-and-engage strategy to its advantages. The ethnic conflict there has had multiple parties as contestants against the government, and lack of structural cohesion has thus been its hallmark. There had been a sharp cleavage not only between the moderates and militants, but also among the militants owing to their competition for power and domination. The moderate Tamil United Liberation Front (TULF) could not see eye to eye with half-a-dozen militant groups, which dominated the *eelam* movement in the 1980s. The Sri Lankan government made use of the prevailing disunity to drive the wedge further between the moderates and the militants. Its decision to negotiate only with the TULF during 1983–85 should be seen in this context. Although it could not penetrate into different militant groups to divide them, in the 1980s, India had used its intelligence agency Research and Analysis Wing to prevent unity among the militants by favouring one group against another. Military training and arms were provided to some groups, and others were ignored or given less favourable treatment (Muni 1993: 72).[109] This created rivalry within the militant movement much to the satisfaction of Colombo, leading to the emergence of the LTTE as a formidable force. India's strategy of promoting militants in the movement resulted in the alienation of the TULF from the Sri Lankan Tamil society. Its political marginalization both at the

---

[108] *Hindustan Times*, 29 October 2012
[109] See SD Muni 2003

hands of the Indian government and the militants was the most undesirable outcome of the *eelam* war.

After the singing of the India-Sri Lanka peace accord (1987), India's focus was once again shifted to cultivation of the non–LTTE groups. Groups like the Eelam People's Revolutionary Liberation Front (EPRLF) became a favourite of India; it had received enormous political and military support when the IPKF was operating against the LTTE on the island. As a matter of fact, the EPRLF was promoted as a counterweight to the LTTE, which challenged India militarily. At the same time, the Sri Lankan government under Premadasa had befriended the LTTE against India and the EPRLF–led provincial government backed by New Delhi. The LTTE–Premadasa talks were to end India's military role in Sri Lanka and abandon the 1987 accord on which both the parties had a unanimous view. That they were successful in their attempts showed the way in which the divide-and-engage strategy worked. Since their tactical cooperation was directed against India's participation in the war, accomplishing the same in 1990 soon made them revert to becoming adversaries. When the war broke out in 1990, the Premadasa regime relied on the non–LTTE groups to alienate the Tigers by offering to negotiate a peace deal with them. The Parliamentary Select Committee (PSC) brought together a number of anti–LTTE forces, but the protracted negotiations did not lead to a peace package. Then, in 1994–95, came the Kumaratunga government's dialogue with the LTTE; this time the non–LTTE groups were not excluded. Once the talks broke down and the war resumed, the government did not have much option except engaging the moderate non–LTTE groups in political parleys to enlist their support to the 1995 devolution package. President Rajapaksa (since 2005) went a step further when he inducted some of them in his cabinet.

The attempts at dividing the militants produced complex results. While India and Sri Lanka managed to contain the non–LTTE groups and kept them divided, the LTTE's emergence as the predominant group was an unexpected development resulting from the strategy of divide-and-engage. Neither India nor Sri Lanka could ever infiltrate into the LTTE with the aim of creating an internal dissension or split. Even the 2004 split in the LTTE that led to the formation of a group led by Karuna primarily resulted from an internal power rivalry, rather than engineered by the external forces. But, of course, once the split occurred, the government allegedly extended political, security and material support and recognition to the splinter group. The offer of amnesty under the 1987 peace accord or periodically by the government and a huge financial reward offered by India in 1987 as an incentive to accept peace did not interest the LTTE at all. Thus, the limitations of the divide-and-engage strategy had been clearly exposed in the *eelam* war.

Development Work

The governments have pursued socioeconomic development in strife-torn regions as a conflict management strategy. This has been the Indian government's chosen strategy, implemented mostly in its conflict affected underdeveloped regions such as the north-east and tribal areas. It is undertaken simultaneously with its coercive strategy in the hope that redressing hardship to which the people have been subjected would not turn them against the government, but wean them away from the insurgents. In the north-east, the government's strategy of winning people has not only been evolved late, but was also centred more on giving economic sops to the region than addressing the core political aspirations of different ethnic groups. It reveals New Delhi's thinking that the conflicts are rooted in economic underdevelopment of the region and hence removing the economic backwardness would bring about peace. It is only recently that it has started recognizing implicitly that the problem is more political than mere economic in nature: it means that an economic package, in the absence of a political settlement, cannot achieve peace. Therefore, its present approach combines political process with a larger development strategy. It has a critical objective of creating a base for peace in the region.

For long, there has been greater involvement of the centre in the development work of the region: the objective is to achieve accelerated economic development with a view to ending the people's feeling of alienation from the national mainstream. It must be noted that for the sake of development planning, the whole of north-east is treated as a single entity: the government addresses the problem of underdevelopment collectively of the entire region and seeks to evolve an integrated regional solution. Of course, certain special economic measures are often unveiled for the war-torn societies of the north-east to achieve the immediate result of winning the people's support. Sometimes it is pursued in conjunction with political gestures to them. In this section, we first list out the government's specific politico-economic measures for Nagaland and Assam, and then analyze various development initiatives for the entire region of which these war-torn states form integral part.

In Nagaland, special attention to the development of the state began to be paid with the outbreak of insurgency. The centre declared its intention to "bring all the benefits of a welfare state to these hitherto neglected areas" so that they could be "abreast with the rest of the country in the shortest possible time".[110]

A measure of economic relief to the people has been the government's decision not to levy land tax in the Naga Hills. As early as in the late 1950s, it took steps to raise the standard of living of the people, improve communications, increase agricultural production and provide water supply and health and education facilities. There has been progressive increase in the expenditure on developmental works since then: in about 25 years, the centre has spent around Rs. 30,000 crore. Successive governments in the state, whether belonging to the Congress or regional parties, have joined hands with the central government in implementing its conflict management strategy. Sustaining the democratic process amidst violence in the state has enabled the government to keep an uninterrupted channel of communication with the people and to create a constituency for peace. Many central leaders have made periodic visits to the state in their attempt to end the Nagas' feeling of alienation.

Respect for human rights is included in the government's counter-insurgency strategy; the code of conduct for the soldiers has insisted on making a clear distinction between combatants and non-combatants. In June 1995, an Army Development Group (ADG) was formed to carry out some civic functions under Operation Good Samaritan. It was essentially to bridge the gap between the security forces and the people, and project the desire of the former to work for peace through development. Besides the ADG, many other army formations and units adopt villages, participate in cultural and sports competitions, and conduct health care camps and vocational

---

[110] Ministry of External Affairs , *The Naga Problem*, New Delhi: Government of India., 1962

training programmes. In 1996, the state government launched a "peace offensive" at a cost of Rs. 113 crore to motivate the non-governmental organizations, tribal Ho Hos (the traditional Naga tribal representative bodies) and church groups to work for peace. The NSCN leaders denounced the government's objective of pumping money into the Hills. They held the view that "the pouring in of Indian capital in our country for political reasons, has shattered the Naga people into a society of wild money", creating a parasitic, exploiting class of "reactionary traitors, bureaucrats, a handful of rich men, and Indian vermin".[111] It reflects their fear of losing the support of people who, lured by the welfare schemes, would turn to the government's side. This is what they want to prevent at any cost.

Although Assam did not figure as a high-priority state for central assistance earlier, there have now been efforts to remove the Assamese feeling of economic exploitation by New Delhi. A good chunk of central funds for the north-east under various five-year plans has always gone to Assam. It is mainly used for development of road and rail routes, inland navigation, power and airports. Deve Gowda's special economic package for the region had a specific agenda for Assam: it earmarked about Rs. 1,600 crore for construction of a road-cum-rail bridge across the Brahmaputra, up-gradation of the Guwahati airport into an international airport and flood control projects on the Brahmaputra.[112] As the issue of foreigners has been sensitive to the Assamese, the centre has undertaken projects for construction of roads and fences on the India–Bangladesh border to prevent infiltration of people. A scheme for issuing identity cards in some areas of Assam has been approved to stop illegal migration from Bangladesh. Since the payment of royalty for the crude oil extracted from the state has been the main grievance of Assam, the centre has revised the rate periodically, but not to the total satisfaction of the people. It forms a fertile ground for perpetuation of New Delhi's image of being an internal colonizer in economic terms.

The task of achieving integrated socio-economic development of the region has been entrusted to the North Eastern Council (NEC), a nodal

---

[111] B G Verghese, India's Northeast Resurgent: Ethnicity, Insurgency, Governance, Development, (New Delhi: Konark, 1996.), pp 98-99

[112] *Times of India*, 28 October 1996

regional development agency created under a Parliamentary Act (1971) and fully funded by the central government.

It is an advisory and planning body. The NEC–sponsored schemes run concurrently with the state and central government projects. Until 1998, the central government had spent about Rs. 3,200 crore for the development of transport, communications, health, manpower, agriculture, water resources, power and industries. It has evolved a mechanism to monitor the progress achieved by the NEC by constituting a committee consisting of Union ministers who recommend priority areas for development. In 1986, the committee decided to draw up time-bound development plans; for this, one more committee of higher officials was appointed. Suggestions made by the Chief Ministers of the region are followed up with the central ministries and departments. To strengthen the NEC and increase New Delhi's guidance and control over its functioning, the central government decided in 1997 to place it under the Deputy Chairman of the Planning Commission; until then, the states' governors used to be its heads.

In recent years, visits of the Prime Minister and central ministers to the region have become occasions for unveiling development plans. In October 1996, Prime Minister Deve Gowda undertook a six-day-long tour to all seven states and made wide-ranging promises and policy announcements. It included a special package of projects at a total cost of Rs. 6,100 crore (in addition to the allocation under the Ninth Plan) and a promise that all central ministries and departments would earmark at least 10 per cent of their budget for specific programmes in the north-eastern states. Seven months later, in May 1997, his successor, I. K. Gujral, spent five days touring six states: he announced another Rs. 900 crore to make the total package Rs. 7,000 crore and also promised a new industrial policy. This amount was stepped to Rs. 10,271 crore during the visit of Prime Minister A. B. Vajpayee to Shillong in January 2000. The package had diverse components, but power and infrastructure projects took the lion's share. Arrangements have been made by the Home Ministry to monitor the progress of the central government's new economic initiative; even a special cell was to be set up in the Prime Minister's Office for the purpose.

It seems that the government's development initiatives have not yielded the expected results. The people of the north-east seek development, but this in itself is not enough for lending their support to the central government. An honourable solution to redress their political grievances is also equally important. Many attractive promises made by successive governments have got bogged down at the stage of implementation by sheer political and bureaucratic bottlenecks, inefficiency and corruption. Many well-conceived schemes were not implemented according to schedule, and consequently, funds were allowed to lapse, leading to a proportionate reduction in subsequent fund allocations. There has been no proper utilization of funds, and in many cases, the state governments have diverted funds to meet other expenses. Above all, there is hardly any accountability for irregularities. It is said that the fruits of development initiatives have not reached the common people, who still find themselves alienated from the national mainstream. The strategy of winning the hearts and minds of the north-eastern people has, therefore, had only limited success.

The Indian government has pursued the development strategy in the Maoist infected tribal regions with much greater determination to marginalize or defeat the insurgents by weaning the tribal population (spread over nine states) away from them. This has been the single most important strategy of the government. The main aim is to end the sense of alienation that has gripped the tribal society over the years, by improving their socio-economic conditions. First, the central government has provided constitutional/ legal safeguards to protect tribal rights and interests particularly over land. Second, it has implemented an array of poverty alleviation programmes and taken measures to strengthen their 'livelihood security' under various legislation enacted in recent years. Third, in response to a large scale displacement of tribal population caused by land acquisition, a national rehabilitation and resettlement policy was formulated in 2007. Several welfare schemes have been undertaken to reduce hunger and malnutrition and improve literacy in throughout the tribal region. The government's tribal development plan has also included programmes for income generation.[113] All these steps forming a significant part of the government's conflict management strategy are undertaken even when it pursues coercion vigorously as the most preferred and dominant strategy to end the Maoist insurgency. Thus, there have been

---

[113] V R Raghavan, ed, *The Naxal Threat: Causes, State Responses and Consequences,* (New Delhi: Vij Books India Pvt. Ltd, 2011)

serious attempts to separate the tribal population from the Maoist insurgents and in the process, the existing discreet relationship for tactical reasons between the two is somewhat recognized.

The Sri Lankan government did not pursue this strategy systematically during the war period, except taking a few goodwill measures that largely coincided with peace talks with the militants. Successive governments seemed to have been convinced that any efforts to erode the Tamil militants' support base in north-eastern society and convert their constituency into a critical force that would work to the government's advantage would be futile. Except the Kumaratunga regime, which eased the economic pressure on the Sri Lankan Tamils to some extent, none of the other governments made a clear distinction between the Tamil militants and the non-combatant Tamil people. As such, the Sri Lankan army's high-handed behaviour of targeting both of them equally led to alienation of the non-combatants from the national mainstream and, at the same time, their identification with the militants. This effectively rendered the government's non-military measures prone to be suspicion and thus ineffective. Further, the tendency of clubbing both the combatants and non-combatants together in pure military terms had developed a perception that economic reconstruction or effective rehabilitation of the Tamils would eventually benefit the militants. It was thought that the non-combatants would never shift their loyalties to the government even if they ceased to support the militants who, in any case, would never let their constituency be won over by their adversary through political or military means. The army had always been reluctant to allow in certain essential commodities and medicines to the north on the ground that they would find their way to the LTTE. Thus, instead of using economic development as an effective strategy to wean the people away from the militants, the government in Colombo had invariably used economic coercion to cut of links between the two.[114]

Even after the government's decisive military victory in the *eelam* war, improving the welfare of people in the north and the east has not received any greater importance in the post-war agenda of the regime led by President

---

[114] P Sahadevan, *Coping With Disorder: Strategies to End Internal Wars in South Asia*, RCSS Policy Studies 17, (Colombo: Regional Centre for Strategic Studies, 2000).

Rajapaksa. Particularly, the socio-economic conditions of a large section of the Sri Lankan Tamil community have been pitiable. The government's half-hearted measures to resettle and rehabilitate internally displaced people (IDPs) have proved its detractors right: that the government is least interested in restoring the normal life of IDPs, if not empowering them in any manner. For about two years after the war ended in 2009, thousands of IDPs remained in the government-run internment camps and even after their release, they have been unable to return to their places of original habitation due mainly to the army's occupation of their areas under high security zones and establishment of many military cantonments.[115] The government's unwillingness to address the IDPs' problems in all seriousness has created an impression that it has not changed its war-time strategy even in the post-war period.

Both the Nepali and Myanmar governments have hardly used development as a major conflict management strategy. For the military junta in Myanmar whose sole interest lay in exercising tight control over the people, development has not found place in their agenda of (mis)governance. In Nepal, the government could not perhaps match with the Maoists' efforts to win over the people's support at least in those areas where they concentrated. Even the Integrated Security and Development Programme (ISDP), conceived and implemented by the army, was abandoned when the government found it difficult to shift the security forces from their primary duties of counter-insurgency operations. It helped the Maoists increase their support among people, who were told that their government had abandoned them and therefore they were the only 'available alternatives'.[116] However, the international efforts, even at the height of the Maoist insurgency to build peace, had focused on socio-economic development through which the people's support for peace was mobilized.

---

[115] Bhavani Fonseka, Commentary on Returns, Resettlement and Land Issues in the North of Sri Lanka, (Colombo: Centre for Policy Alternatives, 2010).

[116] Chiran Jung Thapa, "Nepal's Armed Conflict: A Narrative of Political Mismanagement", in V.R. Raghavan, ed. *Conflicts: A Four State Analysis (India, Nepal, Sri Lanka and Myanmar)*, (New Delhi: Vij Books India Pvt. Ltd, 2013).p 180.

Unilateral Political Measures

Not many governments have adopted this strategy, perhaps, because of its limitations in creating peace. Generally, conflict management is said to be a bilateral process in that both adversaries participate as stakeholders. If at all unilateral steps work to become a successful endeavour, they tend to establish hegemonic peace (of government) whose endurance in the absence of insurgents groups' total acceptance or endorsement is not certain. At best, they can merely privilege government over its insurgent adversary if it is able to generate some positive opinion or support among the latter's constituency members for its peace package, thereby putting pressure on the group to accept peace negotiations. At another level, if an insurgent group rejects its adversary's political package when its constituency welcomes the same, it tends to lead to alienation of the same group to the strategic advantage of the concerned government. Insurgents are not the ones to be blamed always for unilateral peacemaking. Governments find this strategy to be a viable one to ward off insurgents' pressure and offer a settlement from a position of their strength. Those government leaders who like to reject the demands of insurgents or refuse to recognize the latter as legitimate partners in peacemaking tend to show deep interest in unilateral measures either under political pressure from internal or external forces or under the military pressure of insurgents themselves. In government's understanding, peace established unilaterally is inexpensive because it does not entail a bargaining process that produces an outcome based on give and take or mutual compromise.

Sri Lanka under President Chandrika Kumaratunga had tried to win the Sri Lankan Tamils' support for the *eelam* war and isolate the LTTE from the rest of Tamil society by unveiling a devolution package in 1995. If implemented in their original form and content, the proposals would go a long way in bringing about drastic changes in the island's existing political structure. The preamble of the legal draft (of 1996) of the proposals (of 1995) assured all the communities that they [would] "enjoy and nurture their distinct culture, practice and profess their own religion and promote their own language, thus preserving the rich cultural and ethnic diversity typifying a plural society". This recognition of Sri Lanka's multi-ethnic character is a clear reference to the Sri Lankan Tamils' legitimate place in the society, of which they were always concerned and doubtful. Empowering the community has been the hallmark of the devolution package. It sought to convert Sri Lanka from a "unitary state" to a "Union of Regions" in order to satisfy the Sri Lankan Tamils' age old demand for a federal setup, create a Regional Council for every province, and end the absolute supremacy of Parliament in legislative matters. The fundamental purpose is to create autonomous units with substantial powers devolved to the regional level. As many as 75 subjects and functions listed under the Reserved List would be exercised solely by the central government, with 64 items enumerated under the Regional List. Some of the other novel features of the proposals included setting up of a High Court for every region, a Regional Public Service and a Regional Police Service with different recruitment terms, and a Regional Finance Commission. The regional governments were to be empowered to develop their fiscal competence through direct and indirect taxation and international borrowing and grants. Furthermore, they could exercise control over state land.[117] The devolution package was presented to the whole nation, with an eye on the susceptibilities of the Sri Lankan Tamils who, the government in Colombo hoped, would exert pressure on the LTTE to accept the peace process.

The euphoria that Kumaratunga's peace initiative generated was short-lived. Even though many in north and east found her more sincere than all her predecessors about resolving the ethnic conflict, the support they extended to the peace process in 1995 dwindled soon due to many reasons. First, there had been steady efforts on the part of the government to dilute the original peace proposals under the Sinhalese hard-liners' pressure. Second, long-drawn-out delay in giving constitutional status to the proposals owing to a lack of consensus among the Sinhalese had eroded the Sri Lankan Tamils' faith in the constitutional exercise. Third, the continuation of *eelam* war, the incidents of human rights violations, and the persistence of misery and hardship of the people in north and east after the re-imposition of the economic embargo all led to significant altering of the Sri Lankan Tamils' views on the Kumaratunga government. Moreover, the continued reliance of the people on the LTTE out of fear or lack of choice had in a way incapacitated them to play any role in the government's favour, so they did not want to identify themselves with the regime's efforts to isolate the LTTE. Clearly, the community was not willing to forget its collective sacrifice made

---

[117] International Centre for Ethnic Studies (ICES), *Sri Lanka: The Devolution Debate*, (Colombo: ICES, 1996)

at the behest of its leaders and sufferings at the hands of successive governments in Colombo. This made the government's task of winning the entire community over to its side through political and economic gestures exceedingly difficult.

In recent years, Myanmar has seen the military-backed government's unilateral steps to address albeit half-heartedly some of the issues related to restoration of democracy in the country. Partly under the growing internal pressure exerted by the NLD, which has mobilized a vast section of freedom-loving and democracy-hungry people against the military junta, and partly because of the constant international pressure that has sought the regime to restore democracy, a slow and unsteady democratization process began to unfold first in the early 2000s and then in the late 2000s. In 2003, a seven-step road map for democracy was announced, indicating the junta's inclination to seek an international political recognition for their rule. This paved the way for drafting a new constitution (2008) under the effective guidance of the military and its approval in a controversial referendum held in the same year. The government elected under the constitution is a 'quasi-civilian' authority as the Union Solidarity and Development Party (USDP), which won a huge majority in the 2010 elections (that were boycotted both by both the SNLD and the Shan Nationalities League), has been in reign with the military's open support and the massive mandate of the people. It has released most of the political prisoners including Aung San Suu Kyi (whose right to engage in political activities was restored), conducted the bye-elections to the parliament in April 2012, lifted media censorship and restrictions, legalized union activities, and moved towards creating a human rights commission.[118] Yet, the democratization process is tardy and incomplete. Though the State Peace and Development Council (SPDC) was dismantled on the day President Thein Sein assumed office on March 30, 2011, the military still retains a prime position under the constitution. It enjoys a wide range of emergency powers and special privileges, including that it heads some of the key ministries (such as defence, home affairs and border affairs) and is given one-quarter of the total seats in both houses of parliament.[119]

---

[118] Uday Bhanu Singh, "Do the Changes in Myanmar Signify a Real Transition?", *Strategic Analysis*, 37(1), January-February, 101-104, 2013.

[119] Ibid.

The process of democratization and reconciliation does not include peacemaking with the rebellious ethnic minorities. There is hardly any meaningful political initiative that the present 'quasi-civilian' regime or the military junta in the past has taken to redress their ethnic grievances. Yet, the government is not tired of making peace overtures or promises for a durable peace. The only notable structural change, brought unilaterally under the 2008 constitution, to benefit the ethnic minorities is the creation of regional legislatures (*hluttaws*). There are fourteen such legislatures—seven 'regional *hluttaws*' in Burman-dominated areas and the same number of 'state *hluttaws*' in predominantly minority areas. Besides, six ethnic communities have been given some kind of "self-government through subordinate *hluttaws*". Beyond these steps the government has not unveiled a comprehensive peace plan unilaterally or through its active engagement with various ethnic group leaders.

Negotiating Peace

Political negotiations are the democratic means of managing internal conflicts. But in reality, this is the most difficult strategy on which adversaries do not develop interest and commitment easily. The general tendency of the powerful party in a conflict viz. state is to rely excessively on the unconventional strategies discussed above until their limitations and weakness are exposed. Only if the unconventional strategies do not work to end conflicts, negotiations become an option for peacemaking. Here again, it can be said that governments do not in every case engage the militant leaders directly in negotiations even though they are the combatants who need to be pacified for any peace deal. Instead, in many cases, the moderate leaders are brought up to play a key role in a peace process with the view not only to reaching a political settlement, but also, in the process, to marginalizing the militant groups. By "moderate leaders", we mean only those who have adopted political means of agitation and have not resorted to or taken part in violence. We do not consider as a moderate leader someone who heads a political wing that control a military wing of a given group, and participate in internal war as a combatant. Negotiating with him means talking to a militant. Indeed, this approach to peace process appears to be guided by, or be an extension of a given government's divide-and-engage strategy analyzed above. Possibly, negotiations with moderates take place against a backdrop of the continuation of fighting, or even after defeating or weakening the targeted militants. Sometimes the governments' failure to strike a meaningful peace deal with their militant adversaries itself will find a role for moderates in a peace process.

Thus, negotiating with the militants seems to be the last option for any government. It may be done under their military pressure since governments are unable to weaken or defeat them even after sustained military operations. If the moderates are so weak that they cannot help the government in restoring peace, and the latter is convinced that the militants alone hold the key for the success of a peace process, negotiations with them are inevitable. Talks are held with or without the help of a mediator, preceded by a declaration of ceasefire in most cases. Putting preconditions (such as surrender of arms by the militants and the return of troops to their barracks) for talks by either of the parties shows its position of strength from where it seeks to negotiate a peace deal. It means that unconditional talks are between two equally strong or weak adversaries who need peace. It must also be noted that all negotiating processes are pursued with the stated objective of peace in mind. In some cases, the militants participate in peace talks to gain a respite for themselves or for regrouping and refurbishing. It means that they still enjoy strength to carry on their armed struggle and are uncompromising on their goal.

The search for a negotiated settlement is not an integral part of conflict management strategies in every case dealt with in this chapter. Some of the conflicts have seen this process with the governments talking peace either with the moderates, or militants, or both, in that order. Others have proceeded without any political dialogue between the respective government and militant organizations. Such cases are those in which the unconventional strategies have privileged the concerned government. It is possible to infer that governments do not easily hold talks with militarily weak militants, who are set to lose their conflict goal, if they maintain a tough position on their secessionist goal. This is demonstrated in the Assam conflict. In such cases, negotiating with the moderates and singing a peace accord with them will be a measure of reconciliation in a conflict-torn society. Even an offer of peace talks in a half-hearted manner without, at the same time, engaging the real adversary in any political dialogue is to convince the aggrieved ethnic group of the government having only a superficial interest in a democratic settlement. This leaves out some cases where substantive negotiations take place as a matter of conflict management policy under the mutual military pressure of both adversaries.

After the outbreak of the *eelam* war in 1983, successive Sri Lankan governments had negotiated with the moderates and militants alternately. The talks were held at regular intervals, either under external (India's) pressure or internal (military) pressure (of the LTTE) or whenever a new leader came to power. For about two years (August 1983-July 1985), the Sri Lankan government had refused to talk to various militant groups, but engaged the moderate TULF in peace talks held under India's mediation against the backdrop of intense fighting in the north and east of Sri Lanka. The exclusion of the militants was a conscious decision of the Jayewardene regime that sought to deny them political recognition and legitimacy as representatives of the Sri Lankan Tamils. An interested external party in the conflict,[120] India helped formulate a set of proposals, known as 'Annexure C'. It had essentially envisaged the creation of Regional Council through the merger of District Councils in each province and also recognition of Tamil as a national language. But the proposals were not acceptable to a large section of Sinhalese political forces, which insisted that the unit of devolution should not be larger than the district councils. In the wake of an impasse in the peace talks, India realized the need for engaging the militants in political negotiations. The Thimpu talks, held in 1985 (see below), resulted from such a realistic understanding of the dynamics of the armed conflict.

During the political process that led to the signing of the India-Sri Lanka peace accord in July 1983, India had brought the Sri Lankan government and the TULF together to formulate proposals and counter-proposals. The fragile TULF-Colombo peace parleys alienated the militants politically, but did not achieve a forward momentum to yield peace. This made India expand its role from being an indirect facilitator of peace talks to a direct formulator of proposals based on its talks with the moderate Tamil leaders and the Sri Lankan government. The role was expanded further in 1987 to make India a direct participant in the ethnic conflict, when Prime Minister Rajiv Gandhi signed a bilateral peace accord with President Jayewardene.[121] The entire

---

[120] See S D Muni 2003

[121] Ibid

process and pattern of negotiating the agreement were unique. Beginning as a mediator India ultimately became a key negotiator for the Sri Lankan Tamils. The Tamil moderate and militant opinions were subdued clearly: at the most, they were given some sort of consultative status. This showed the desperation of the Sri Lankan government to end the *eelam* war with direct Indian help. But neither India nor Sri Lanka ever thought that they would have to face such tremendous challenges from the Sinhalese and Sri Lankan Tamils while seeking legitimacy for the agreement. A larger Sinhalese opinion was critical of the peace deal: many hardliners believed that India coerced the small island nation to accept an unequal solution to the conflict. Even the Sri Lankan Tamil opinion was sharply divided. India managed to convince the TULF and non-LTTE Tamil groups to accept the accord by assuring them that it would try to rectify the shortcomings of the proposed framework to meet the legitimate aspirations of the Tamils. Even if such an assurance was not forthcoming, the non-LTTE Tamil groups, dependent on India, did not have sufficient power to restrain the determined Indian government from signing the accord. But it was the LTTE that became the single most powerful opponent of the agreement: every political effort of India to enlist the Tigers' support failed. In the end, the use of heavy military pressure on the LTTE became inevitable to save the peace agreement from total collapse.

Thus, it was ironical that instead of ending the conflict, the accord had created another phase of it. This showed how important the militants are in managing or ending armed conflict, and the limited role that the moderates can play in the whole process. If the militants are weak, they can be ignored for achieving a negotiated end of the conflict; in that case one or more of the unconventional strategies are sufficient to make them irrelevant to the conflict management process. At the same time, the moderates cannot play a critical role if the militants are strong: it means that direct negotiations with the latter will have to be pursued at some stage. This is what happened in Sri Lanka in 1990 when the Premadasa regime offered peace talks with the LTTE. But the failure of the militants-government peace parleys made it inevitable to resume talks with the moderate leaders. The assumption here is that while at internal war, governments like to search for peace continuously if the cost of their military engagement rises with every passing year. This explains the second round of peace talks (1991–92) between the Tamil moderates and Sinhalese leaders under the framework of a

Parliamentary Select Committee (PSC).

The PSC exercise had exposed the weak bargaining position of the moderate Tamils vis-à-vis the Sinhalese leaders. This, in turn, strengthened the argument of the LTTE that the Sri Lankan Tamils' rights could be won only through a sustained war. With the war continuing since 1990 and after the failure of the PSC process, there was no serious attempt at resuming the political dialogue until October 1994, when the new government led by President Chandrika Kumaratunga offered an olive branch to the Tamils. This time, displaying a sense of realism, she sought to negotiate with the LTTE for peace. But history repeated itself once again when the government-LTTE talks failed and the war resumed in 1995. Once again, the moderate groups suddenly assumed more importance in the peace process initiated by the People's Alliance (PA) government. It was now keen to secure the moderate Tamil leaders' support for the 1995 devolution package, through which the government sought to isolate the Tigers from the Tamil society and eventually defeat them. The exercise was conducted since 1995 in the PSC, but became an unproductive one by 2000. The Tamil moderates felt that the PA government was not taking them seriously on the devolution issue. Thus, marginalized by the government and threatened by the LTTE, the moderates became an ineffective political entity, incapable of influencing the government on the issue of autonomy to the Sri Lankan Tamils.

Political marginalization or sidelining of the Tamil moderate forces happened again as the Norwegian-facilitated peace process (2002-03) seemingly recognized the LTTE's primacy and status as the sole legitimate representative of the Sri Lankan Tamils. No other Tamil group than the LTTE was therefore involved in highly published political negotiations; but such an exclusionary peacemaking process did not create resentment among the moderates—both the TULF and former non-LTTE militants. However, the breakdown and eventual failure of the internationalized peace process did not restore the importance of the moderates until the *eelam* war ended in decisive military victory   against the LTTE in May 2009. The LTTE's extermination has ended the secessionist goal and brought the autonomy demand back in the agenda, and opened space for the moderate Tamil National Alliance (TNA) to emerge as the principal organization to spearhead the political movement and represent the Sri Lankan Tamil aspirations for a maximum autonomy solution. Recognizing the change of leadership in the post-war Sri Lankan Tamil society, the Rajapaksa regime has held several rounds of talks with the TNA since 2010. But these talks have not been substantive since the government has failed to place a set of proposals at the negotiating table and refused to respond to the proposals submitted by the TNA for maximum autonomy. Rather, it has asked the TNA to join the PSC to work out a solution to the conflict.

More than the Tamil moderates, successive governments in Colombo had engaged the LTTE, albeit intermittently, in structured political negotiations. If they held talks with the TULF simply for tactical reasons, their negotiations with the LTTE appeared to be an option exercised under the Tigers' military pressure. Importantly, both sets of talks were held separately and except in the 1985 Thimpu talks, the moderate and militant leaders never sat together at a negotiating table in opposite to the government leaders. It shows that Sri Lanka has followed an exclusionary conflict management process. Since 1983, the government and the LTTE held peace talks at least four times (1985- 86, 1989-90, 1994-95 and 2002-2003). None of the top leaders from either side ever participated in negotiations; nor did they insist on any preconditions for peace talks. The LTTE had always appeared to be slippery on the issue of peace; its unbreakable commitment to the *eelam* goal had cast serious doubts about its interest in negotiated settlement of the conflict.[122] The talks held in 1985-86 were brief: in July-August 1985, the LTTE joined the other Tamil groups in the Thimpu talks and insisted on four cardinal principles as the basis for any political solution: recognition of the Tamils as a national minority; both the northern and eastern provinces as the traditional Tamil homeland; the Tamils' right to self-determination; and fundamental rights for all Tamils.[123] The intransigent positions of both the Sri Lankan government delegation and Tamil groups made the failure of Thimpu talks inevitable. Subsequently, in 1986, the government unsuccessfully tried to engage the LTTE separately in peace talks, when India was actively involved in the island in finding a political solution.

---

[122] P Sahadevan , "Negotiating Peace With the LTTE", In P. Sahadevan and Neil DeVotta, *Politics of Conflict and Peace in Sri Lanka*, (New Delhi: Manak Publications Pvt. Ltd, 2006).

[123] *The Times of India*, 17 July 1985

For the second time, direct talks between the government and the LTTE were held in 1989-90, when the IPKF was embroiled in a war with the Tigers. Both parties showed their insincerity during negotiations; the point is that political solution to the conflict did not figure much in their agenda. Since they sought to use peace talks as tactics out of compulsions to create a temporary *detente* to pressure India to withdraw its forces from Sri Lanka, they chose to end their talks and resume hostilities once this common goal was attained. Likewise, government-LTTE peace talks during 1994-95 could not progress beyond the preliminary stage of merely discussing some confidence-building measures, but the substantive issue of devolution was not covered. Indeed, the LTTE's public pronouncements in favour of a negotiated solution were not accompanied by a commitment to the peace process. It became too clear that the LTTE's participation in four rounds of peace talks was merely to strengthen its military position in pursuit of the *eelam* goal (Weerakoon 1998; Rajanayagam 1998).[124] Further, it wanted to explore "what might lie down that road", but without making the fundamental decision for a successful negotiation process. The Tigers were keen to "enhance their political status and preserve both their military position and their quasi-state in Jaffna." The PA government's contribution to the failure of peace talks could be seen in the lack of professionalism it had shown in negotiations. Instead of involving the political leaders, it had merely entrusted the task of negotiations to its officials and some prominent citizens of the civil society. Not only was there a failure in evolving a mutually agreed framework for negotiations, but also all four rounds of talks appeared to have been ill-planned. To make things tough for the government, the military was opposed to giving any strategic concessions to the LTTE. The implementation process of some of the positive decisions such as lifting of the economic embargo was slow. All these provided the LTTE a chance to blame the government for the Sri Lankan Tamils' suffering. Thus, yet another opportunity for bilateral peacemaking was lost. However, President

---

[124] Bradman Weerakoon, "Government of Sri Lanka (President Premadasa) and LTTE Peace Negotiations 1989/90", In Kumar Rupesinghe, ed., *Negotiating Peace in Sri Lanka: Efforts, Failures and Lessons*, (London: International Alert, 1998) and P Rajanayagam, "Government of Sri Lanka-LTTE Negotiations (1994-95): Another Lost Opportunity", In Kumar Rupesinghe, ed., *Negotiating Peace in Sri Lanka: Efforts, Failures and Lessons*, (London: International Alert, 1998).

Kumaratunga adopted a unilateral approach to peace by declaring a devolution package, which the LTTE rejected.

It took another seven years for both the government and LTTE to re-engage in a peace process, facilitated by Norway and directly supported by the US, the European Union and Japan. Beginning with a ceasefire agreement signed by both adversaries in 2002, six rounds of negotiations were held in different countries (Thailand, Norway, Japan and Germany) in about six months. The talks had covered a host of issues related to the framework of political solution, humanitarian relief, reconstruction, human rights, military normalization, de-escalation, gender, child soldiers, etc. At the third round of talks in Oslo in December 2002, both parties agreed to explore a federal solution and also initiate discussions on substantive political issues. This was a significant decision that raised the hope for peace, but the LTTE's backtracking on its commitment caused a deep sense disappointment among the Sri Lanka's liberal peace constituency. Most of the other decisions were confidence-building measures. On many issues such as security, resettlement and reconstruction, sharp differences persisted between the two parties. There was a huge gap between what they had agreed and how much they had implemented. Herein lay the problem encountering the peace process. The LTTE had sought to link every issue with the other as a bargaining strategy. In the process, it had showed its willingness to sacrifice the cumulative gains of settling some issues on the ground that others remained unresolved. This bargaining strategy was not unusual in a negotiation process to end ethnic wars. Whatever may be the merit of the issues raised by the LTTE, its rigid position to impair the peace process cast serious doubts about its commitment to a political solution?[125] When the LTTE withdrew from the peace talks in April 2003, it became clear that the Tiger leadership had sought to use the peace process as political tactics rather than a conflict resolution or management strategy. On its part, the LTTE blamed the Sri Lankan government of hobnobbing with the international community to isolate and weaken its position and interests.

---

[125] P Sahadevan , "Negotiating Peace With the LTTE", In P. Sahadevan and Neil DeVotta, *Politics of Conflict and Peace in Sri Lanka*, (New Delhi: Manak Publications Pvt. Ltd, 2006).

The negotiating experience in India is different in India where peace processes have been sustained even if they have failed to produce quick solutions. Let us take first the Naga peace process, conducted briefly in the 1960s and 1970s and then since 1997 to make it a protracted event. Notably, the peace process in the 1960s had involved an intermediary structure, namely a three-member Peace Mission (PM) established at the initiative of the Baptist Church Council of Nagaland. This coalition of intermediaries–B. P. Chaliha (Chief Minister of Assam), Jaya Prakash Narayan (an active Gandhian) and Michael Scott (Anglican churchman and human rights activist)–carried forward the task of striking a peace deal. On other two occasions, the intermediary role has not been structured; some individuals have merely facilitated the talks indirectly.

The peace talks in the 1960s were not unconditional: the central government made it clear that it would not entertain Phizo for any negotiations if he espoused the cause of Nagaland's secession.[126] Phizo did not accept the conditional offer, but other leaders from the "Naga federal government" sought to utilize New Delhi's interest in peacemaking. But, at negotiations, the Naga leaders took consistently tough bargaining positions. The failure of three years (September 1964—October 1967) of talks was attributable to their intransigence. The difference between the two sides had emerged first on the nature of the government delegation: while the rebel leadership insisted on talks at a political level, the government sent a delegation led by Foreign Secretary Y. D. Gundevia. As regards the agenda for talks, the government delegation proposed to focus on the safeguards to the culture and autonomy of the Nagas within the Indian Constitution, whereas the Naga leaders had reiterated their core demand for independence. While the disagreement persisted on the maximum-minimum goal of both parties, the fourth round of talks (on 13 October 1964) yielded a positive result. An understanding was reached to demilitarize Nagaland even before they worked out a solution to the conflict. Accordingly, the rebel leaders agreed to renounce force for attaining their goal and give up arms; the Indian government was to withdraw its security forces except those needed for external defence. The PM was entrusted with the task of implementing this

---

[126] Y.D Gundevia, *War and Peace in Nagaland*, (Dehra Dun: Palit & Palit, 1975), p 105.

understanding; it urged the Naga leaders to submit the list of their arms and ammunition by 15 November and deposit them with the PM by 31 December 1964. Realizing that giving up weapons before achieving their goal was suicidal, the Naga leaders backtracked on their commitment, and thus the entire demilitarization plan fizzled out.

The other issue was that throughout the period of negotiations, the Naga delegation considered itself from a separate country, holding talks with India on a bilateral basis. The Naga federal government's "Peace Declaration" sought give a neutral country status for Nagaland. The Indian delegation took strong objection to this blatant attempt at internationalizing the conflict and was convinced that there would not be any meeting ground for negotiations if the rebel leadership refused to take a compromise position. At this juncture the PM intervened to break the deadlock. It made a proposal on 20 December 1964 which, while appreciating the divergent stands of both parties, appealed to them to show goodwill and understanding on each other's position and evolve a mutually agreeable meeting ground for negotiations. In this context, it suggested that the Naga federal government could, of its own volition, participate in the Indian Union and mutually settle the terms and conditions for that purpose. The Indian government, on its part, could decide to restructure and recast the pattern of its relations with Nagaland so as to satisfy the political aspirations of the Naga people.

The Indian government had by and large accepted the PM's proposals, but the Naga delegation rejected them. It insisted upon India's recognition of Nagas' right to self-determination and asked for a plebiscite in Nagaland to decide its independence. The talks held on 4–5 May 1965 and the PM's frantic efforts to narrow differences did not succeed. In this situation, the Naga federal government declared that it would not extend the truce unless the Indian government agreed for talks at the ministerial level and sent the PM to visit Phizo in London. New Delhi accepted the first demand and rejected the other. Now, the Naga leaders wanted a summit meeting with Prime Minister Indira Gandhi, which the government reluctantly accepted on the condition that they would hold discussions within the framework of the Indian Constitution. The first Delhi meeting between Indira Gandhi and a five-member delegation led by Kughato (the self-styled 'Prime Minister of the Naga Federal Government') was held on 16 February 1966. The PM played a limited role because. J. P. Narayan had kept himself away from the meeting. It was an exercise at reiterating each other's resolve to find a political solution and maintaining peace in the Hills. In this regard, it was decided to reconstitute the Observer Group to monitor cease-fire violations. No worthwhile political issues were discussed at the meeting. But the Naga delegation made its position clear to the media, viz. a commitment to achieve independence and sovereignty for Nagaland. Unperturbed by this pronouncement, the government kept the doors for negotiations. Prime Minister Indira Gandhi expected some real progress towards restoration of peace in Nagaland from the second round of talks in April (Gundevia 1975: 173–74).[127] It was held on 26 April without the intermediary role of the PM, which came to an end with the resignation of J. P. Narayan on 25 February 1966 over his differences with the Naga leaders. At the meeting, Indira Gandhi ruled out the separation of Nagaland from the Indian Union but agreed to consider proposals for autonomy. But, mostly in public platforms, the Naga leaders kept reiterating their goal of sovereignty.

These tactics were continued until the third round of talks on 10 August 1966, when the Naga delegation submitted a 14-point memorandum contesting India's claim over Nagaland (Mankekar 1967: 122–24).[128] This brought down the seriousness of the talks and thus the fourth round in October 1966 turned out to be an exercise in affirming each other's desire for peace. For about 18 months, there could not be any talks and the last round held on 6 June 1967 was a meeting involving the lower-rung Naga leaders and officials and ministers from the Indian side. The final breakdown came when Indira Gandhi had cancelled the talks scheduled for 5–6 October 1967 for an unforeseen reason after the Naga delegation came prepared to Delhi. Before leaving for Nagaland with disappointment, it issued a note accusing the Indian government of duplicity in enforcing the cease-fire and conducting peace talks. Thus, the protracted first phase of peace process ended on a discordant note. The peace talks failed due to the intransigence of the Naga leaders. It appeared that they wanted a respite in the war, so that the peace process would enable their cadres to consolidate their military

---

[127] Y.D Gundevia, *War and Peace in Nagaland*, (Dehra Dun: Palit & Palit, 1975), p 105.

[128] D.R Mankekar, *On the Slippery Slope in Nagaland*, (Bombay: Manaktalas, 1967).pp 122-24

position especially after the return of a number of Chinese-trained men. It is this group of Naga men who were violating the cease-fire agreement by resorting to sporadic violence in the Hills and preparing themselves for resuming the war. It was also found that the hardliners kept the Naga federal government leaders under pressure not to compromise on the sovereignty goal. The non-participation of Phizo in the talks was another major drawback for the peace process. A top leader who forged the militant movement towards secession, his role could have made the bargaining process more constructive. Of course, given the Nagas' commitment to their cause, it was any body's guess whether his participation would have led to a peace deal.

Continuing military pressure by the Indian forces and growing dissidence in the Naga movement had renewed the prospects for another round of peace talks in the early 1970s. In 1973, a breakaway faction (the Revolutionary Government of Nagaland) surrendered their arms and accepted the Indian Constitution. Subsequently, India made peace overtures to dissident elements in the movement and tried to co-opt them in its efforts to restore peace in the Hills. The Shillong Accord (1975) was the result of this sustained process. Disgruntled with the war approach of the front-line Naga leaders, a section of them came forward to hold four rounds of talks with the Indian government representatives. Unlike the 1964–67 peace talks, these were not directly with the central government; nor did they take place at the political level. The Governor of Nagaland, L. P. Singh, negotiated on behalf of the central government with a five-member delegation of rebels. Two state government officials and a Joint Secretary in the Union Home Ministry had assisted the Governor. A five-member Observers Group set up during the earlier peace talks also took part in the discussions. It turned out to be a productive exercise in the sense that it resulted in an agreement—a first of its kind in the Naga war. It was a somewhat unusual peace accord.

It was not intended to redress the grievances of the Nagas but to end the violence by accomplishing the rebels' surrender, which formed the precondition for formulating political issues for "discussion" aimed at final settlement. All three operative clauses of the main accord (of 11 November 1975) stated that the representatives of the underground organizations accepted without any condition the Indian Constitution and agreed to surrender their arms, the details of which were worked out under a supplementary agreement on 5 January 1976. Accordingly, the collection of arms was to be completed by 25 January 1976, and they would be handed over to Peace Council teams at the respective places of collection. The Peace Council would transport the arms to a peace camp at Chedema for safe custody. It was also decided that the surrendered militants would stay at peace camps set up at various places and the Peace Council would arrange their maintenance.[129] Later, many under-trials were released and the government assisted in setting up the peace camps. It was the government's mistake to expect that the Shillong Accord would end the conflict. As stated earlier, only a small section of the NNC leadership took part in the peace process, which was unequal both in terms of its exercise and outcome. The accord testified to the government's strong position from which it negotiated. Hence, it was an unequal deal to end the conflict. Several front-line Naga leaders including Phizo repudiated the accord; it also resultantly led to significant marginalization of Phizo's position as the anti-accord forces consolidated themselves under the NSCN (two factions) to carry on the fight. Thus, since the 1970s, the Indian government has had to deal with a more formidable force while trying to restore peace in the state.

For nearly 22 years after the Shillong Accord, Nagaland did not have a peace process. Neither the government nor the NSCN leaders tried to negotiate for peace. Prime Minister Rajiv Gandhi's efforts to hold secret talks with the rebel leaders did not materialize. So was the result of peace initiatives by the Narasimha Rao government. As such, the internal war remained their sole preoccupation. But a change happened in their response and attitude in 1997 due mostly to the growing war-weariness in the sta. Informal facilitation role by influential political leaders from Delhi and Kohima and the Baptist Church in Nagaland led to establishing contacts between the central government and the NSCN (I-M) leadership. The NSCN leaders met Prime Minister H. D. Deve Gowda in Zurich on 3 February 1997 and what followed was a series of initiatives to start unconditional talks to find a political solution. Its endorsement by both the Atlanta peace meet organized by the Baptist Church in July 1997 and the All-Naga Tribes Ho meeting in

---

[129] Ved Marwah, *Uncivil Wars: Pathology of Terrorism in India*, (New Delhi: Harper Collins. 1995), pp. 452-55

February 1997 gave further impetus to the initiative. As a measure of goodwill and confidence, the government withdrew the international arrest warrants issued against Isaac Swu and Muivah. With the ceasefire in operation since August 1997, a protracted peace process is underway. An immediate outcome of this has been suspension, by and large, of organized militancy and military operations by the security forces.

But the peace process lacks a forward momentum. Despite several rounds of talks in the last fifteen years, both parties are unable to agree on a framework of solution. The NSCN (I-M) leaders have often declared their commitment to the peace process, but have not been categorical in their position that they would renounce their secessionist goal and accept a political solution within the framework of the Indian Constitution. At the same time, the central government is vehemently opposed to even entertaining any discussion on the issue of independence for Nagaland. It is also unable to accept the Greater Nagaland demand (integration of Naga-predominant areas in other states), on which the Naga leaders have taken an unrelenting position. Furthermore, what ails the peace process is its exclusivity in the sense that it has included only the NSCN (I-M) and kept out other groups like the NSCN (K). For a durable peace, inclusion of all Naga groups in broad-based peace talks is essential. There is no fixed time-frame for concluding the entire negotiation process. Thus the parties' desire to establish peace is not accompanied by their demonstrated determination to work out a viable framework of solution in a time-bound manner.

Similarly, the peace-talks in Assam are also beset by the same kind of problems. They are 'fragile' and 'truncated' in the sense that both the central government and dissident ULFA leaders, branded as a 'pro-talk faction' led by chairman Arabinda Rajkhowa, are engaged in intermittent talks, rather than in any serious and sustained negotiations aimed at reaching a peace deal. Getting some of the ULFA leaders to talk peace has been the notable outcome of the government's use of military coercion and divide-and-engage strategy. The other faction led by the group's military commander, Paresh Baruah, is opposed to the political engagement with the government, and maintains its total commitment to the secessionist goal and armed struggle. For him, the peace talks are a political ploy of the government to disarm the group and also create rift among its leaders and cadres. Until recently, he was able to spearhead the 'anti-talk' sentiments and position within the

ULFA. But the recent split in the group as pro- and anti-peace talks has signaled a changing dynamics of the conflict.

It must be noted that the government invited the ULFA for peace parleys way back in 1990, at the time when its security forces were able to maintain high military pressure on the group. But New Delhi has insisted that its interest in peace talks does not mean that it is ready to discuss the ULFA's demand for sovereignty for Assam. Sovereignty was non-negotiable as far as both parties were concerned. They held uncompromising views on this issue, thereby making peace talks a non-starter. Thus, as long the ULFA leaders considered their sovereignty demand as supreme, the government refused to engage them directly in peace talks. It was only when they were prepared to alter their demand, from 'sovereignty of Assam' to 'sovereignty of the people of Assam', the government began to engage them for peace. Interestingly, much before the pro-talks faction came out openly to talk peace by renouncing its demand for sovereignty, the government held in 2005-06 three rounds of talks with an eleven-member Peoples' Consultative Group (PCG) nominated by the ULFA. Most of the PCG members were ULFA sympathizers from Assamese civil society. The main idea behind sending the PCG was to prepare the ground for direct negotiations between the government and the ULFA.[130] Finally, this turned out to be a futile exercise when the government asked the ULFA leaders to make a written pledge on their participation in direct talks. In protest, the PCG withdrew from the peace talks.[131]

The government's desire for direct peace talks was fulfilled when seven top pro-peace talk faction leaders of the ULFA led by Rajkhowa met the Home Minister and Home Secretary in New Delhi in August 2011. The delegation submitted a "framework" for political negotiations to resolve "the issues between Assam and India", and asked for "an honorable, meaningful and peaceful resolution" of all issues. As regards the issue of sovereignty, the ULFA's sought the government to take 'a fresh look at the issues of sovereignty, so as to ensure that the people of Assam can assert their

---

[130] Sanjib Baruah,"The Rise and Decline of a Separatist Insurgency: Contentious Politics in Assam, India", In Rajat Ganguly, ed., *Autonomy and Ethnic Conflict in South and South-East Asia*, (London: Routledge, 2012).

[131] Ibid.

inalienable rights to control their land and their resources therein".[132] No doubt, the meeting has set the stage for a long drawn political process, whose positive result is dependent upon both parties' serious commitment for a genuine political solution. But the path towards a permanent peace is unclear and the process is uncertain.

The peacemaking experience in Nepal has been unique in many respects. Unlike other insurgents groups, which resist military pressure to avoid political negotiations or use peace process as tactics to maximize their strategic interest vis-à-vis their adversary, the Maoists became the willing participants in negotiations and serious partners for a peace deal to end the violent movement. It reveals that they had used violence to exert pressure on the state to engage them in serious political negotiations and accept their demands, whereas the former sought to end the Maoist insurgency militarily and deny them a peace deal. Thus, the purpose of use of violence by the adversaries was reverse in Nepal. Another novel feature of the peace process is that it had entailed a coalition of democratic political parties and the Maoists as principal negotiating parties. At the final stage of insurgency, leading to the peace accord, negotiations were held between the Seven Party Alliance (SPA) leaders on behalf of the Nepali state and the Maoist leaders. This arose out of the political expediency created by the King's move to usurp powers of the parliament and undermine the functioning of the democratically elected parties. In return, the SPA sought to cut the King's powers and authority down to size and undermine his role in peacemaking. Needless to say, the peace process helped the democratic forces and the Maoists to consolidate their position and influence against the monarch.[133]

This does not mean that the King kept himself always away from the peace process. It must be noted that direct peace talks were first initiated under King Gyanendra's influence in 2001. The government of Prime Minister Sher Bahadur Deuba held talks, in that the main actors were the King, the CPN and the mainstream political forces represented in parliament. Instead of working together to end violence and establish peace, they tried to promote their respective political agenda and goals. While the King used

---

[132] Ibid.
[133] See Thapa 2013,

the peace talks to gain legitimacy and consolidate his position, the Maoists wanted to gain tactical advantages over all other protagonists. On their part, the political parties were keen to strengthen their political position vis-à-vis the monarchy. Then, there was an issue of compromise; both the government and Maoist leaders appeared unrelenting in their position. There were also spoilers within the government who wanted the peace talks to fail utterly.[134] In sum, "the peace process of 2001 was not a genuine attempt by the protagonists to resolve the conflict but rather a circumstances intersection of complimentary short-term interests".[135]

The failure of the 2001 peace talks led to escalation of violence between the security forces and the Maoists. Under their mutual military pressure, both parties agreed for a ceasefire in January 2003, which resulted in resumption of peace talks, for the second time, between the King's emissaries and some senior Maoist leaders. Importantly, the political parties were kept out of the peace parleys; once the King restored the elected parliament and executive authority to the elected leaders under severe pressure from the parties, they took immediate charge of the peace process and excluded the King now. Annoyed with King Gyanendra's approach to internal and external issues, India began to side with the democratic forces and sought to involve itself indirectly in the peace process in 2005. It not only worked towards bringing the SPA and the Maoists together but also contributed to a 12-point peace agreement reached between them in Delhi. In fact, the resentment against the Monarch had 'precipitated the momentum'[136] for a permanent peace. The comprehensive peace accord (CPA), signed on 6 January 2007 by the interim government (formed by the SPA) and the Maoists, has paved the way for ending insurgency and initiating a political process to restructure the political system including the state.

Peace negotiations are not a preferred conflict management strategy in Myanmar. The junta was only keen to disarm and integrate the ethnic insurgent groups into the state controlled military institutions. It did not go beyond negotiating ceasefires with them to address their grievances.

---

[134] Ibid

[135] Ibid

[136] Ibid.

However, the Sein regime has created a peace negotiation team under U Aung Min, which has proposed a three step peace plan: First, insurgent groups cease violence under separate agreement; Second, the government undertakes economic development and permit ethnic group leaders to establish political parties. They are required to commit themselves to promote national integration and preserve the state sovereignty; third, signing of peace agreements in the parliament. The whole process is said to be "one-sided". It is imposed on the ethnic non-state armed groups, rather than "developed with them trough negotiations". The government expects them to "give up arms, set up political parties to compete for a place in Parliament and only once they reach Parliament, discuss political settlement".[137] Thus, the term peace process has a different connotation in the context of the conflict in Myanmar. It must be noted that it is not only in responding to ethnic insurgencies but also to the movement for democracy that the government is extremely reluctant or unwilling to hold political negotiations. It even failed to live up to its promised offer of an open and unconditional peace and reconciliation dialogue with the NLD leaders.[138]

Outcomes of Strategies

The discussion in the preceding section shows that many governments have adopted multiple strategies simultaneously or singularly in pursuit of peace or to end conflicts. Their interest in a particular form of outcome has determined the nature and extent to which they have used one or more strategies. It is clear that a government desirous of achieving a negotiated settlement has always used coercion in conjunction with other strategies. However, coercion invariably remains the first and foremost strategy of all governments. Therefore, it is a common government strategy; the difference is that some governments have used it at a moderate level to push the rebels to accept a negotiated deal. Others have applied it excessively to achieve a military victory. From the time a government uses coercion till it is able to start negotiations, a shift in strategies is always possible. The

---

[137] Ramu Manivannan, "Conflict Resolution in Myanmar: An Evaluation of Opportunities and Challenges for Dialogue and Reconciliation", In V.R. Raghavan, ed. *Internal Conflicts in Myanmar: Transnational Consequences*, (New Delhi: Vij Books India Pvt. Ltd., 2011)

[138] Ibid.

purpose of each strategy is largely determined by the concerned government's conflict goals, response and strategies of rebel groups, and power relations between the adversaries. If the use of military coercion and other non-military strategies work to strengthen the governmental position vis-à-vis rebels, reflecting in the increase in power asymmetry in favour of the former, it can either try to take advantage of the ground reality to achieve a honourable settlement or suspend a negotiation process and deny negotiated peace or impose a settlement virtually from a position of strength. A fundamental proposition in the context of internal conflicts is that the viability of initiating a negotiation process and finding a negotiated settlement is largely conditioned by the adversaries' relative military capability, defined in terms of their ability to withstand and exert pressure on each other. The more they are able to ensure their survival in an armed conflict and threaten each other, the better are the prospects for a negotiated settlement.

A number of points emerge from the assessment of conflict management strategies in the previous section: First, identifiably there are two main clusters of strategies, which the governments analyzed in the chapter have adopted. One cluster includes multiple strategies that are much common to most of the governments. The strategies forming this cluster are military coercion, ceasefire agreement, ending or seeking external role, development work, divide and engage rebels and, finally, political negotiations. More than other governments, successive Indian governments have preferred to pursue the strategies in this cluster invariably in all the conflicts except in the case of the Maoist insurgency for the reasons mentioned below. It is important to note that in spite of the enormous strategic gains made from the consistent use of military and non-military strategies over the years, India has developed fundamentally a greater commitment to negotiated settlement than to military victory. Here again, the Maoist movement is an exception. Nepal and Sri Lanka have pursued the strategies from the same cluster, but the difference between the two and also in comparison with India is that cumulatively, Sri Lanka pursued all the strategies without, at the same time, committing itself to a negotiated settlement. Thus, its main objective in using the strategies has been to gain relative strategic advantages so that, in a situation marked by greater asymmetry of power relations between the government and the rebels, a negotiated settlement is considered as irrelevant or unnecessary. In Nepal, the government could not take a similar approach; it had to pursue political negotiations seriously as a preferred strategy mainly because the Maoists had denied it strategic advantages in the internal war.

The other cluster includes strategies such as coercion, ceasefire agreement, ending or seeking external support and finally, unilateral political measures. Strikingly, political negotiations do not figure in this cluster. Myanmar has largely followed the strategies listed in this cluster to demonstrate that both the military junta and military-controlled regime have not developed a preference for negotiated peace. This raises a question, linking the nature of the state and the pattern of conflict management. The question is: do democracies tend to show more interest and seriousness in a negotiated peace than autocracies? Do illiberal democracies make honourable or fair peace deal with rebels? Are liberal democracies more committed to peace process and negotiated settlement than illiberal democracies? Are autocracies interested only in military victory?

The different experiences of peacemaking in the conflict situations dealt with in this chapter underline the fact that the nature of the state system is a crucial factor in the conflict management process. Both the chosen strategies and their eventual outcomes are determined largely by the nature of state that participates in conflict as a principal adversary. Myanmar has laid more emphasis on ending conflicts militarily rather than resolving them through political negotiations, since the autocratic or semi-democratic regimes in the country are least bothered about national and international opinion and willing to defy even reasonable demands and positive suggestions. A national security state, it has no or less faith in the ethnic groups and the democratic leaders from the majority Burman community. If Myanmar has not produced peace because of absence of democracy or due to its illiberal nature, why has the democratic state in Sri Lanka been so evasive in its commitment to peace even after securing a decisive military victory? The answer lies in the illiberal nature of the state and the majoritarian framework within which its ethnic policies are decided. The basic point is that expecting an illiberal democracy to produce liberal or positive peace is a difficult proposition. This raises another relevant question: Does India, a liberal democracy, have a better track-record on peacemaking and if so, what is the nature of such peace?

India's peacemaking record is better than other countries. The government has shown deep interest in a negotiated peace and less determination to achieve a military end of any conflict. Better peacemaking record does not mean that the quality peace made in India is better than what other liberal democracies elsewhere have produced. Positive peace is hard to establish even in India. Out of three internal conflicts analyzed in this chapter, political negotiations mark two of them and coercion alone is employed as a dominant strategy in one conflict (the Maoist insurgency). Yet, there is no negotiated settlement or military end of any of these conflicts in India. As mentioned earlier, the Indian government has refused to enter into a ceasefire agreement with the Maoists or engage them in any peace talks. This is in spite of the fact that the Maoists have made occasional peace overtures and the security forces have suffered heavy casualties over the years. As a precondition, the government insisted that they should abjure violence and then come forward for talks.[139] Later, in order to appear flexible in its position, Union Home Minister P. Chidambaram clarified that he did not expect the Maoists to lay down their arms: "Only if they abjure violence, the government can hold talks with them".[140] It is important that the same flexible condition is not extended to other militant groups; this is evident from Chidambaram's contrasting statement in the Rajya Sabha in 2009: "We made it clear that we will not entertain any ceasefire from militant groups. Militant groups are most welcome to abjure the path of violence, lay down arms and come for talks".[141] It is evident from the conflicts dealt with in this chapter that as a general policy, the central government in India refuses to hold talks with militant groups if they continue to use violence and/or insist on raising the issue of sovereignty. Abjuring violence is a clear precondition; sovereignty is non-negotiable as far as the government is concerned. Its refusal to negotiate directly with the ULFA until recently and rejection of the Maoists' peace overtures must be seen in this framework of the government policy.

What have the conflict management strategies produced? Discernibly, there are three outcomes: negative peace; peace with disorder, and

[139] *Hindustan Times,* August 18, 2010
[140] *The Indian Express,* February 1, 2013
[141] *Hindustan Times,* July 10, 2009

persistence of violent conflict. By negative peace, we simply mean 'absence of direct violence'; it is a condition in which there is no active, organized violence. Further, negative peace can be categorized into stable and unstable conditions. Stable negative peace denotes a condition in that there are no immediate prospects for return of violence. Negative peace is stable in the ethnic conflicts in India's Nagaland and Sri Lanka, and the centralist conflict in Myanmar; it is unstable in the ethnic conflicts in Myanmar and India's Assam. Peace is restored in Nepal, but what marks the post-conflict situation is a durable disorder. The stakeholders are unable to agree on the process and mechanism to create new order in the country. There is bitter contest for power and in the process, the agenda of constitution-making has been politicized, denigrated and delayed. The Maoist conflict in India and some of the ethnic insurgencies in Myanmar persist without an end; even those conflicts where there are peace processes and prevailing negative peace conditions (such as the Naga and Assam ethnic conflicts, and the centralist conflict in Myanmar), post-conflict as a much desired condition appears to be a distant dream. In all these, there is missing category viz. positive peace. It denotes more than mere absence of violence; it is a condition in which diversity, human emancipation, dignity, equality, democracy, empowerment of people, non-exploitative social structures, etc. are established and sources of structural violence are eliminated.[142] It underlines the establishment of peace with justice. For the realists, however, positive peace is utopia at best; it is an unattainable goal. Whatever may be its prospects, the argument is that it is not unreasonable or too much to expect that some of the elements of positive peace are ingrained in any peace accord.

Conclusions

The chapter reveals that the strategies of managing conflicts have yielded unclear and mixed outcomes. Given the peculiar structure and processes in internal conflict, this is something not unexpected. From the comprehensive assessment, made in the chapter, of the conflict management strategies and their outcomes, a number of trends can be identified: First, use of coercion is intense and widespread; both adversaries willfully employ this

---

[142] Johan Galtung, "Violence, Peace, and Peace Research", *Journal of Peace Research.* 6(1):167-91. 1967.

strategy without worrying much about its consequences for the society and polity. It reflects their deep commitment to their mutually incompatible goals and the value they attach to them. Second, like the conflicts, some of the peace processes are also protracted in nature. They continue as normal events even when conflicts are seen to be persisting. Third, political negotiations, wherever or whenever take place, do not entail generally the higher political leadership, but are between the top or middle level rebel leaders and officials or second-rank political leaders from the government's side. Fourth, external influence or role is a factor in most of the internal conflicts, but the direct participation of influential states in peacemaking or conflict management is unusual. In other words, most of the parties do not entertain or even discourage any form of third party role in peacemaking. Even insider mediation or quasi-intermediary role by prominent people from the conflict parties is also rare.

There is no one best policy or strategy for managing internal conflicts. Each conflict is specific in nature although some of the characteristics are common to all conflicts. In the absence of any best policy or strategy, it is important to emulate the available best practices in conflict management. Such an approach should combine coercion with a set of non-coercive instruments and processes, including political negotiations. What should be the extent of use of coercion? On this, there can be different viewpoints: some would argue for an excessive application of military coercion, to such an extent that a rebel group is *forced* to end violence and exterminated or allowed to survive to negotiate or accept a peace deal. Others would emphasis on a minimal use of coercion, to such an extent that a militant group is *willing* to hold political negotiations and *accept* a reasonable peace deal based on mutual compromise. Coercion should just be used as an instrument of *facilitating* a peace process rather than a *means* to end a conflict or *impose* an unfair settlement. In this regard, credibility, commitment and sincerity of governments are of importance. A government seeking to use coercion should be equally committed to find a negotiated political settlement.

A peace process should be seen as a 'continuum' in engagement of all stakeholders. It does not just end with a political deal, but proceeds further to transform the society and polity. If it is so, there are possibilities for more than one deal in any internal conflict. Mini peace agreements or understanding on less contentious issues should be the base on which the final big deal can be built. The use of insider as mediator can be an effective tool to promote peace if both parties are serious in peace process. Trade-off (buying peace through economic development after making people to compromise on their identity-related issues) often tends to be a non-workable strategy in ethnic conflicts. It is said that ethnic groups accept development, but not at the cost of their basic needs, viz. identity and power. Finally, the truism that preventing a conflict is a better strategy for a state than managing it, needs to be underlined and reemphasized in the context of conflict and peacemaking in South Asia.

References

Agnew, John (1989), "Beyond Reason: Spatial and Temporal Sources of Ethnic Conflict", In Kriesberg, Louis, et.al. eds., *Intractable conflicts and their Transformation*, Syracuse: Syracuse University Press.

Baruah, Sanjib (1994), "The State and Separatist Militancy in Assam", *Asian Survey*, 34(10): 863-877.

Baruah, Sanjib (2012), "The Rise and Decline of a Separatist Insurgency: Contentious Politics in Assam, India", In Rajat Ganguly, ed., *Autonomy and Ethnic Conflict in South and South-East Asia*, London: Routledge.

Brass, Paul (1991), *Ethnicity and Nationalism: Theory and Comparison*, New Delhi: Sage Publications.

Brown, Michael E. and Ganguly, Sumit, eds. (1997), *Government Policies and Ethnic Relations in Asia and the Pacific*, Cambridge, Mass: The MIT Press.

Brown, Michael E. ed. (1996), *The International Dimensions of Internal Conflict*, Cambridge, Mass: The MIT Press.

Burma Partnership (2012), "We Have Seen This Before: Burma's Fragile Peace Process", Available at www.burmapartnership.org

Carment, David (1993), "The International Dimensions of Ethnic Conflict: Concepts, Indicators, and Theory", *Journal of Peace Research*, 30(2): 137-50

Collier, P. and Hoeffler, A. (1998), "On Economic Causes of Civil War", *Oxford Economic Papers*, 50: 563-73.

Das, Samir Kumar (2011), "ULFA Indo-Bangladesh Relations and Beyond", In Sanjoy Hazarika and V.R. Raghavan, eds., *Conflicts in the Northeast: Internal and External Effects,* New Delhi: Vij Books India Pvt. Ltd.

Das, Samir Kumar (2013), "India's Northeast: The Post 'Pacification' Era, In V.R. Raghavan, ed. *Conflicts: A Four State Analysis (India, Nepal, Sri Lanka and Myanmar)*, New Delhi: Vij Books India Pvt. Ltd.

Dasgupta, Jyotirindra (1990), "Ethnicity, Democracy and Development", In Atul Kohli, ed., *India's Democracy: An Analysis of Changing State-Society Relations*, 2nd Edition., Princeton: Princeton University Press.

de Silva, K.M. (1984), "University Admissions and Ethnic Tension in Sri Lanka, 1977-82" In Robert B. Goldman and A.J. Wilson, eds., *From Independence to Statehood: Managing Ethnic Conflicts in Five African and Asian States*, London: Frances Pinter.

de Silva, K.M. (1996), *Regional Power and Small State security: India and Sri Lanka 1977-90*, New Delhi: Vikas Publishing House.

Edmonds, Martin (1972), "Civil War, Internal War, and Intrasocietal Conflict: A Taxonomy and Typology", In Robin Higham, ed., Civil Wars in the Twentieth Century, Lexington: The University Press of Kentucky.

Esman, Milton (1991), "Political and Psychological Factors in Ethnic Conflict ", in Joseph V. Montville, ed., *Conflict and Peacemaking in Multiethnic Societies*, Lexington, Mass: Lexington Books.

Fair, C. Christine (2007), "The Sri Lankan Tamil Diaspora: Sustaining Conflict and Pushing for Peace", in Hazel Smith and Paul Stares, eds., *Diasporas in Conflict: Peace-makers or Peace-wreckers?*", Tokyo: United Nations University Press.

Fearon, James D. (1998), "Commitment Problem and the Spread of Ethnic Conflict", In David A. Lake and Donald Rothchild, eds., *The International*

Spread of Ethnic Conflict: Fear, Diffusion, and Escalation. Princeton: Princeton University Press.

Fonseka, Bhavani (2010), *Commentary on Returns, Resettlement and Land Issues in the North of Sri Lanka*, Colombo: Centre for Policy Alternatives.

Fortna, Virginia Page (2004), *Peace Time: Ceasefire Agreements and the Durability of Peace*, Princeton: Princeton University Press.

Galtung, Johan (1969), "Violence, Peace, and Peace Research", *Journal of Peace Research*. 6(1):167-91.

Goldstone, Jack A. (1980), "Theories of Revolution", *World Politics*, 32(3): 425-53.

Gundevia, Y.D (1975), *War and Peace in Nagaland*, Dehra Dun: Palit & Palit.

Gurr, Ted Robert (1990). "Terrorism in Democracies: Its Social and Political Bases", In Walter Reich, ed., *The Origins of Terrorism: Psychologies, Theologies, States of Mind*, Cambridge: Cambridge University Press.

Gurr, Ted Robert (1970), *Why Men Rebel*, Princeton, N.J.: Princeton University Press.

Gurr, Ted Robert (1993), "Why Minorities Rebel: A Global Analysis of Communal Mobilization and Conflict Since 1945", *International Political Science Review*, 14(2): 161-201

Hardin, Russel (1995), *One for All: The Logic of Group Conflict*, Princeton: Princeton University Press.

Hazarika, Sanjoy and Raghavan, V.R. Eds. (2011), *Conflicts in the Northeast: Internal and External Effects*, New Delhi: Vij Books India Pvt. Ltd.

Heraclides, Alexis (1990), "Secessionist Minorities and External Involvement", *International Organization*, 44(3): 341-378.

Horowitz, Donald L. (1985), *Ethnic Groups in Conflict*, Berkeley: University of California Press.

Huntington, Samuel P. (1968), *Political Order in Changing Societies*, New Haven: Yale University Press.

International Centre for Ethnic Studies (ICES) (1996), *Sri Lanka: The Devolution Debate*, Colombo: ICES.

Jackson, Richard (2001), "The State and Internal Conflict", *Australian Journal of International Affairs*, 55(1): 65-81.

Kaufman, Stuart J (1997), "Spiraling to Ethnic War: Elites, Masses and Moscow in Moldova's Civil War", In Michael E. Brown, ed., *Nationalism and Ethnic Conflict: An International Reader*, Cambridge, Mass: The MIT Press.

King, Charles (1997), *Ending Civil Wars*, Adelphi Paper 308, London: Oxford University Press.

King, Charles (2001), "The Benefits of Ethnic War: Understanding Eurasia's Unrecognized States", *World Politics*, 53: 524-52.

Lake, David A. and Rothchild, Donald.1997, "Containing Fear: The Origins and Management of Ethnic Conflict," In Michael Brown, ed., *Nationalism and Ethnic Conflict: An International Reader*. Cambridge, Mass: The MIT Press.

Licklider, Roy, ed. (1993), S*topping the Killing: How Civil Wars End*. New York: New York University Press.

Lijphart, Arend (1969), "Consociational Democracy", *World Politics*, vol.21, January, 207-25.

Lijphart, Arend (1977), *Democracy in Plural Societies,* New Haven: Yale University Press.

Lijphart, Arend (1984), *Democracies: Patterns of Majoritarian and Consensus Government in Twenty-One Countries,* New Haven: Yale University Press.

Mahanta, Nani Gopal (2012), "Changing Contours of Armed Violence in Northeast India", In V.R. Raghavan, ed. *Conflicts: A Four State Analysis (India, Nepal, Sri Lanka and Myanmar)*, New Delhi: Vij Books India Pvt. Ltd.

Manivannan, Ramu (2011), "Conflict Resolution in Myanmar: An Evaluation of Opportunities and Challenges for Dialogue and Reconciliation", In V.R. Raghavan, ed. *Internal Conflicts in Myanmar: Transnational Consequences*, New Delhi: Vij Books India Pvt. Ltd.

Mankekar, D.R (1967), *On the Slippery Slope in Nagaland*, Bombay: Manaktalas.

Manogaran, C. (1994), "Colonization as Politics: Political Use of Space in Sri Lanka's Ethnic Conflict", In Chelvadurai Manogaran and Bryan Pffaffenberger, eds., *The Sri Lankan Tamils: Ethnicity and identity*, Boulder: Westview Press.

Marwah, Ved (1995), *Uncivil Wars: Pathology of Terrorism in India*, New Delhi: Harper Collins.

Maxwell, Neville (1973), *India and the Nagas*, Minority Group Report no.330, London: MRG.

Mehta, Ashok K. (2005), *The Royal Nepal Army: Meeting the Maoist Challenge*, New Delhi: Rupa & Co.

Midlarsky, Manus I. (1975). *On War: Political Violence in the International System*, New York: Free Press.

Midlarsky, Manus I., ed. (1992), *The Internationalization of Communal Strife*, London: Routledge.

Ministry of External Affairs (1962), *The Naga Problem*, New Delhi: Government of India.

Ministry of Home Affairs (2011), "Guidelines for Surrender-cum-Rehabilitation of Naxalites in the Naxal Affected States". Available at www.mha.nic.in/uniquepage.asp?Id_PK=540

Mitchell, C.R. (1970), "Civil Strife and the Involvement of External Parties", *International Studies Quarterly*, 14(2): 166-194.

Mueller, John (2000), "The Banality of 'Ethnic Wars'", *International Security*, 25(1): 42-70.

Muni, S.D (1993), *Pangs of Proximity: India and Sri Lanka's Ethnic Crisis*, New Delhi: Sage Publications.

Muni, S.D. (2003), *Maoist Insurgency in Nepal: The Challenge and the Response*, New Delhi: Rupa & Co.

Nayak, Nihar (2011), "International Impact of Conflict in Nepal", In V.R. Raghavan, ed. *Internal Conflict in Nepal: Transnational Consequences*, Delhi: Vij Books India Pvt. Ltd.

Oberst, Robert C. (1988), "Federalism and Ethnic Conflict in Sri Lanka", *Publius,* 18(3): 175-94.

Perera, Jehan (1998), "An Analysis of the Breakdown of Negotiations in the Sri Lankan Ethnic Conflict", In Kumar Rupesinghe, ed., *Negotiating Peace in Sri Lanka: Efforts, Failures and Lessons*, London: International Alert.

Phadnis, Urmila (1989), *Ethnicity and Nation-building in South Asia*, New Delhi: Sage Publications.

Posen, Barry R. (1993). "The Security Dilemma and Ethnic Conflict", *Survival*, vol. 35, no. 1, pp. 27-47.

Pyakurel, Uddhab (2013), "Changing Patterns of Nepal's Ethnic Movement", In V.R. Raghavan, ed. *Conflicts: A Four State Analysis (India, Nepal, Sri Lanka and Myanmar)*, New Delhi: Vij Books India Pvt. Ltd.

Pye, Lucian W. (1964), "The Roots of Insurgency and the Commencement of Rebellions", in Harry Eckstein, ed., *Internal War: Problems and Approaches,* New York: The Free Press.

Raghavan, V.R., ed. (2011), *The Naxal Threat: Causes, State Responses and Consequences*, New Delhi: Vij Books India Pvt. Ltd.

Raghavan, V.R., ed. (2011a), *Internal Conflict in Nepal: Transnational Consequences*, Delhi: Vij Books India Pvt. Ltd.

Raghavan, V.R., ed. (2011b), *Internal Conflicts in Myanmar: Transnational Consequences*, New Delhi: Vij Books India Pvt. Ltd.

Raghavan, V.R., ed. (2013), *Internal Conflicts: A Four State Analysis (India, Nepal, Sri Lanka and Myanmar)*, New Delhi: Vij Books India Pvt. Ltd.

Rajamohan, P.G (2007), "Nepal: Continuing Violence: 2006", In D. Suba Chandran, ed., *Armed Conflicts and Peace Processes in South Asia*, New Delhi: Samskriti.

Rajamohan, P.G. (2008), "Nepal: State in Dilemma", In D. Suba Chandran and P.R. Chari, eds., *Armed Conflicts in South Asia: 2008*, New Delhi: Routledge.

Rajanayagam, P. (1998), "Government of Sri Lanka-LTTE Negotiations (1994-95): Another Lost Opportunity", In Kumar Rupesinghe, ed., *Negotiating Peace in Sri Lanka: Efforts, Failures and Lessons*, London: International Alert.

Ramachandran, Sudha (2011), "The Maoist Conflict in Dandakaranya", In Sanjoy Hazarika and V.R. Raghavan, eds. *Conflicts in the Northeast: Internal and External Effects*, New Delhi: Vij Books India Pvt. Ltd.

Ramana, P.V. (2011), State Response to the Maoist Challenge: An Overview", In Sanjoy Hazarika and V.R. Raghavan, eds. *Conflicts in the Northeast: Internal and External Effects*, New Delhi: Vij Books India Pvt. Ltd.

Regan, Patrick M. (1998), "Choosing to Intervene: Outside Interventions in Internal Conflicts", *The Journal of Politics*, 60(3): 754-79.

Rosenau, James N., ed. (1964), *International Aspects of Civil Strife*, Princeton, NJ: Princeton University Press.

Rotberg, ed., *Creating Peace in Sri Lanka: Civil War and Reconciliation*, Washington, D.C: Brookings

Rothschild, Joseph (1981), *Ethnopolitics: A Conceptual Framework*, New York:

Columbia University Press.

Rothchild, Donald and Lake, David A. (1998), "Containing Fear: The Management of Transnational Ethnic Conflict," in David A. Lake and Donald Rothchild, eds., *The International Spread of Ethnic Conflict: Fear, Diffusion, and Escalation.* Princeton: Princeton University Press.

Sahadevan, P. (1991), "Why the Cease-fire in Sri Lanka Failed",

Mainstream, 29(20).

Sahadevan, P. (1995), "The Internalized Peace Process in Sri Lanka", *BIISS Journal,* 16 (3): 343-45.

Sahadevan, P. (1995), "On Not Becoming a Democrat: The LTTE's Commitment to Armed Struggle", *International Studies,* vol. 32, no. 3: 249-82.

Sahadevan, P. (2000), *Coping With Disorder: Strategies to End Internal Wars in South Asia,* RCSS Policy Studies 17, Colombo: Regional Centre for Strategic Studies.

Sahadevan , P. (2006), "Negotiating Peace With the LTTE", In P. Sahadevan and Neil DeVotta, *Politics of Conflict and Peace in Sri Lanka,* Neew Delhi: Manak Publications Pvt. Ltd.

Sahadevan, P. (1991), "Why the Ceasefire in Sri Lanka Failed", *Mainstream,* 29 (20), 9 March

Saideman, Stephen M. (1997), "Explaining the International Relations of Secessionist Conflicts: Vulnerability Versus Ethnic Ties", *International Organization,* 51(4): 721-53.

Sakhong, Lian H. (2013), "Ethnic Conflict in Burma", In V.R. Raghavan, ed. *Conflicts: A Four State Analysis (India, Nepal, Sri Lanka and Myanmar*), New Delhi: Vij Books India Pvt. Ltd.

Samarasinghe, S.W.R.D. (1984), "Ethnic Representation in Central Government Employment and Sinhala-Tamil Relations in Sri Lanka: 1948-1981", In Robert B. Goldman and A.J. Wilson, eds., *From Independence to Statehood: Managing Ethnic Conflicts in Five African and Asian States,* London: Frances Pinter.

Sartori, Giovanni (1966), "European Political Parties: The Case of Polarized Pluralism", In Joseph LaPalombara and Myron Weiner, eds., *Political Parties and Political Development,* Princeton: Princeton University Press.

Schaffer, Teresita C. (1999), "Peacemaking in Sri Lanka: The Kumaratunga Initiative", in Robert I.

Silverstein, Josef (1997), "Fifty Years of Failure in Burma", In Michael E. Brown and Sumit Ganguly, eds. (1997), *Government Policies and Ethnic Relations in Asia and the Pacific*, Cambridge, Mass: The MIT Press.

Singh, Uday Bhanu (2013), "Do the Changes in Myanmar Signify a Real Transition?", *Strategic Analysis*, 37(1), January-February, 101-104.

Small, Melvin and Singer, J. David (1982), *Resort to Arms: International and Civil Wars, 1816-1980*, Beverley Hils: Sage Publications.

Snodderly, Dan, ed., (2011), *Peace Terms*: Glossary of Terms for Conflict Management and Peacebuilding, Washington, D.C.: USIP.

South, Ashley (2012), *Prospects for Peace in Myanmar: Opportunities and Threats*, Oslo: Peace Research Institute Oslo.

Stavenhagen, Rodolfo (1990), *The Ethnic Question: Conflicts, Development, and Human Rights*, Tokyo: UN University Press.

Stedman, Stephen John (1991), *Peacemaking in Civil War: International Mediation in Zimbabwe, 1974-1980,* Boulder: Lynne Rienner Publishers.

Steinberg, David I. (2011), *Myanmar's Perpetual Dilemma: Ethnicity in a "Discipline-Flourishing Democracy"*, Politics, Governance, and Security Series No.22, Washington D.C.: East-West Center.

Tanter, Raymond and Midlarsky, Manus (1967), "A Theory of revolution", *Journal of Conflict Resolution*, 11(3): 264-280.

Thapa, Chiran Jung (2013), "Nepal's Armed Conflict: A Narrative of Political Mismanagement", In V.R. Raghavan, ed. *Conflicts: A Four State Analysis (India, Nepal, Sri Lanka and Myanmar)*, New Delhi: Vij Books India Pvt. Ltd.

Tiruchelvam, Neelan (1984) " Ethnicity and Resource Allocation" In Robert B. Goldman and A.J. Wilson, eds., *From Independence to Statehood: Managing Ethnic Conflicts in Five African and Asian States*, London: Frances Pinter.

Toland, Judith D. (1993), *Ethnicity and the State*, New Brunswick:

Transaction Publishers.

Varshney, Ashutosh (2002), *Ethnic Conflict and Civic Life: Hindus and Muslims in India*, New Delhi: Oxford University Press.

Verghese, B.G (1996), *India's Northeast Resurgent: Ethnicity, Insurgency, Governance, Development*, New Delhi: Konark.

Weerakoon, Bradman (1992), *Premadasa of Sri Lanka: A Political Biography*, New Delhi: Vikas Publishing House.

Weerakoon, Bradman (1998), "Government of Sri Lanka (President Premadasa) and LTTE Peace Negotiations 1989/90", In Kumar Rupesinghe, ed., *Negotiating Peace in Sri Lanka: Efforts, Failures and Lessons*, London: International Alert.

Zartman, I. William (1989), *Ripe for Resolution: Conflict and Intervention in Africa,* 2nd edition, New York: Oxford university Press.

Zartman, I. William (1995), *Elusive Peace: Negotiating an End to Civil Wars,* Washington, DC: Brookings Institution.

Zartman, I. William (1998), "Putting Humpty-Dumpty Together Again", in David A. Lake and Donald Rothchild, eds., *The International Spread of Ethnic Conflict: Fear, Diffusion, and Escalation,* Princeton: Princeton University Press.

Legal Regimes in Conflict Situations

Geeta Madhavan

Introduction

Law and the judicial machinery, in whatever form they may exist, have a crucial role in the political process of nations caught in internal conflict situations. The causes for the conflict are peculiar to each country and are the result of the social, ethnic or religious divides in the society. Conflicts are a serious threat to peace and security and an armed internal conflict of warring factions within a State has far reaching consequences on its stability, economy and international relations. The state, which is responsible for maintaining its territorial integrity and the safety of its citizens, is often required to use its armed forces against those endangering peace and security. The use of armed forces is subjected to the rule of law, therefore states formulate special laws for armed action in special circumstances.

Marginalization, real or perceived, has led to those victimized rising up against the establishment which has imposed such policies upon them. Laws and legislations which have created and caused the conflicts are justified by those establishments and regimes. More laws are enacted to contain and suppress the uprisings which demand basic rights to the affected sections of that particular society. Often the rule of law is violated and the criminal justice systems are ignored leading to arbitrary arrests, disappearances, and summary trials ending in extended detentions and executions. The judiciary is often influenced, stifled or controlled leading to graver violations of basic rights to the citizens. Legal regimes that violate the basic principles of law play a role in the escalation of conflicts and contribute to the severity and the duration of the conflict.

Internal conflicts are complex, they are manifestations of human aspirations and needs and their denial, of human emergencies created within the society by those in power and of the need of the people to secure basic rights that have been long denied to them. In this complex scenario the first victim is human rights. Suffering, displacement and devastation is caused by the indiscriminate attack on civilians by both the State and the insurgents and the armed groups opposing the governments. The State's reaction to armed internal conflict is always forceful and often repressive and results in innumerable deaths both in the actual conflict and in its ruthless response. Mass expulsions, forcible relocations, deprivation of property and lifetime incarcerations are used by the States to create fear and bring order. These actions, however, have shown that after the initial quelling of the uprisings; there are resurgences that have lead to more deaths, more killing and more ruthlessness by both the State and the actors of the conflict.

This paper attempts to understand and analyze the legal regimes adopted by the countries subject to internal conflicts and the role of the judiciary in those countries. A case study has been made of Myanmar, Sri Lanka, Nepal and India. The causes of the conflict situations in these countries differ greatly from each other as do the responses of the governments through the legal regimes that they have adopted. This paper, therefore, is an analysis of the legal systems which have been put into place to deal with the conflict situations and the application of those laws by the judiciary. The paper also highlights how the judiciary, in some cases, has been made subject to the directions of the executive and thereby rendered inept and that such actions have led to the complete loss of confidence by the people.

Myanmar

The conflict in Myanmar dates back to the time Burma gained independence from Britain in 1948. The three major ethnic groups: the Shan, Kachin and Chin signed the historic Panglong Agreement in 1947 with Burma, as separate political entities, and gained independence simultaneously along with the Burmans from the British. Conflict broke out between these various ethnic groups on one side and the Burmese government on the other as a result of the policies of the Burmese government which did not take into consideration the ethnic diversities of the population of Burma. As the military seized power by a coup in 1962, the situation worsened and ethnic conflict escalated. Human rights violations under the military regime increased and in turn intensified the conflict. Successive military regimes have consistently dealt with the ongoing insurgencies with ruthlessness. The uprising in 1988 resulted in a military coup which not only resulted in the death of thousands of protestors comprising of students, professionals and Buddhist monks but also led to the establishment of the military regime which called itself the State Law and Order Restoration Council (SLORC). The SLORC with Order No. 2/1988, abolished all organs of state that had been created under the 1974 Constitution viz. the Legislature (Pyithu Hluttaw), the Council of Ministers, the Judiciary, the office of the Attorney-General and the Auditor-General. Other town and village level offices, which were the institutions which dealt with the local problems and situations, were also abolished. The State Peace and Development Council (SPDC) replaced the SLORC and enforced martial law till 1997. In 2003 a "Seven Step" plan to restoring democracy in Myanmar was announced by the military regime and as a move towards that, the military junta held a referendum in 2008 for the adoption of a new Constitution and subsequently published it. The Constitution had been suspended by the SLORC in 1974 and till 2008 Myanmar had no Constitution. In accordance with the 2008 referendum, as the Fifth Step in the road to democracy, the military regime held general elections in 2010 and in the restrictive political climate the military backed party – Union Solidarity Development Party (USDP) won the elections. After the elections former General Thein Sein was sworn in as President thereby launching a formally civilian government. However, the cabinet of ministers consisted of ex-military men, many of whom had held ministerial positions under the earlier totally military regime. Although the new Constitution was to be an instrument to restore democracy and install a civilian government in Myanmar subsequent actions by the military regime belied the intention. Therefore, Myanmar is still a military backed regime that has not secured for its people the basic rights of free expression or the right to choose their own political leaders.

The legal system that existed during the monarch's reign was of absolute power of the king (*thet oo san pine*). Burma also inherited the Common

Law system from the British colonial masters. Under the monarchy the executive power and the judicial powers were vested in the King. The King was the highest judicial authority and judicial powers flowed down from the King to the Supreme Queen, Crown Prince, Member Princes of the Parliament, Member Ministers of the Parliament to the Mayors, town chiefs and the village headmen. All the legislative powers also belonged to the King and the laws were not subject to review by any other authority. All civil suits were subject to trial by ordeal by way of water, rice, lead and fire. Criminal law suits were conducted according to the Buddhist principles and fines were imposed and death sentences were carried out in cases of murder, rebellion, insurgency and rape.

The 1950 Emergency Provisions Act was passed by the parliamentary government that came to power after independence to stifle all opposition by curtailing the freedom of speech. Journalists and writers were arrested under Section 5 of this Act which made it a criminal offence *to spread false news, knowing, or having reason to believe that it is not true,* and anyone who was considered to have contributed towards the diminishment of respect or disloyalty among members of the civil service or the military towards the government, either of which resulted in seven years imprisonment. Also any act that may *affect the morality or conduct of the public or a group of people in a way that would undermine the security of the Union or the restoration of law and order* was punishable with equal severity. In May 2003 the Depayin massacre took place against members and supporters of the National League for Democracy and 70 people were killed. The massacre has been widely regarded as the action of government organized thugs and which took place with the connivance of the military. Instead it was called an act against the government and many opposition members were arrested as political prisoners in accordance with the aforementioned Act.

The 1957 Penal Code of Burma was used to suppress freedom of expression under various sections and to prosecute persons on charges of treason against the government. Section 122 of the Code was notably severe as the prison sentences ranged from a maximum of 25 years imprisonment to the death penalty. The Printers and Publishers Registration Act placed further emphasis on curtailment of freedom of expression.

The 1962 Revolutionary Council abolished the Supreme Court and the High Courts and replaced them with a single Chief Court of Burma. In 1972 the Chief Court was renamed as Supreme Court and after the 1974 Constitution it is called the Supreme People's Court. The State Protection Act of 1975, the Unlawful Association Act 1908, Habitual Offender's Act, Act for Protection of National Solidarity 1964 and the Video Law of 1985 are laws that have all served to ensure that no opposition to the military regime would be tolerated. Under the military rule the SLORC's chief role was to ensure that all citizens "obey law and order"; but it placed itself above the law. After seizing power, the SLORC by a judicial decree: Judicial Law No. 2/88 established the Supreme Court and provided for the creation of civilian courts at the trial level. However, the Martial law Order 1/89 of 1989 empowered military tribunals to conduct summary trials of civilians. The courts confined themselves to according only three forms of sentences: three years imprisonment with hard labour, life imprisonment and death sentences. There has been no reported instance of acquittal by these tribunals. There was also no right of appeal from the sentences handed down by the military tribunals. These tribunals were abolished in 1992 but not before they had sent many civilians to suffering and deaths.

The death blow to the judiciary was by the adoption of the new Constitution in 1974 which merged the judicial and legislative arms. Senior judges were chosen from members of the parliament. Although the judiciary did not apply the martial law yet the military mindset of the judges was apparent from their use of military uniform in court. The judiciary was also kept under the executive as it fell within the control of the Ministry of Home Affairs. Thus any law passed by the executive could not be tested for arbitrariness and therefore there was no accountability of the government. The restrictive legal system which is in continuance despite the adoption of subsequent Constitutions, underlines the fact that the judiciary serves as an arm of the military rule.

Article 11 of the 1974 Constitution stated that the State shall adopt a single party system and that the Burma Socialist Program party is the sole political party and it shall lead the State. The military junta by law criminalized criticism and prevented any discussion or debate. The military junta's control of the judiciary is underlined by the fact that it controls the outcome of all trials. The judges hold no tenure and are appointed by the military. The judges are also ordered to follow the instructions of the military and read prepared judgments. Lawyers in Myanmar cannot challenge any law in court. Extra judicial, summary and arbitrary executions have been common especially of the ethnic minority. Although the Penal Code provides for rigorous imprisonment with hard labour and simple imprisonment, all convicted persons are handed over to the military and forced to rigorous labour irrespective of the sentence handed down by the courts. In all cases wherein a private citizen appears against a state agent of whatever rank in whatever matter, the court's compliance with the military regime ensures that he or she does not get a fair trial. Therefore the courts are ruled by the executive council which in turn is ruled by the military junta.

The Constitution of 2008 did not improve the legal systems or empower the judicial machinery. Article 20 (b) states that the Defence Services has the right to "independently administer and adjudicate all affairs of the armed forces". This places the armed forces above the law and leaves them unquestionably powerful. The provision is so broad that any activity can be brought under it as the military junta sees fit. Article 20 (c) gives the power to the executive administration, which is primarily in the hands of the military, to do all such acts that are required in "safeguarding the non disintegration of the Union, the non disintegration of the national solidarity and the perpetuation of the sovereignty". Therefore the military junta is given unlimited power to decide what it seeks to protect and from whom. Under Article 20 (f) the Tatmadaw is given the power to safeguard the Constitution. Article 46 is a confirmation of stance of the military junta that the military is the ultimate authority to determine what is to be protected. While Article 46 confers authority on the Constitutional Tribunal to declare legislative and executive actions as unconstitutional, it omits to confer similar power to declare military actions as unconstitutional thereby affirming even under the Constitution the supreme power of the military in Myanmar.

Article 232 (b) (ii) gives the power to the Commander-in-Chief to appoint Ministers of Defence, Home Affairs and Border affairs thereby confirming the broad powers of the military in civilian affairs and over civilian offices. Although the state governments have chief ministers, by Article

262 (l) (i) the President may remove a Chief Minister at will, making it apparent that they serve not by the will of the people but are local agents of the President. Article 20 states "Defence services have the right to administer for participation of the entire people in Union security and Defence". The imposition of military discipline over the entire population and the authority to enlist all the civilian population into the military for internal security is apparent. Under Chapter XI dealing with the declaration of Emergency, by which the military is allowed to assume all powers of the government albeit with Presidential agreement and Legislative ratification, total power is given to the military regime to rule at will.

Chapter I on the Basic Principles states that under Article 40 (c) the Commander in Chief can "If there arises a state of emergency that could cause disintegration of the Union, disintegration of national solidarity, and loss of sovereign power or attempts thereof by wrongful forcible means such as insurgency or violence, the Commander-in-chief of the Defence Services has the right to take over and exercise State power in accordance with the provisions of this Constitution". However, it is important to remember that only the military is in a position to assess whether any threat exists and there is no system that requires the military to obtain the approval of anyone.

Arrests and pre trial detention are common in Myanmar. The arrests are arbitrary and are by the military intelligence and they lead to prolonged interrogation, torture, denial of access to lawyer or family and adequate medical care. Ms Aung San Suu Kyi house arrest that stretched from 1989 to 1995 was under the State Protection Act of 1975. Various laws have been used to control the population by preventing freedom of speech and thought and all political opposition has been stifled by the use of these laws. Some of them are:

1. Unlawful Association Act 1908

2. Habitual Offender's Act 1961

3. Act for Protection of National Solidarity 1964

4. State Protection Act 1975

5. The Video law 1985.

The State Protection Act allows people to be detained without charge or trial up to 5 years with no right of appeal to any authority. Under the Unlawful Association Act any association can be declared unlawful based solely on the opinion of the head of the State. All political prisoners suffer due to the overly all encompassing laws and the chances of fair trial are nil. Besides, the interpretation of these laws is done according to the dictates of the military and often during trials evidences are fabricated to support the laws. Therefore, the manipulation of the law by the military regime has led to denial of fair trials and gross violations of human rights.

Special Rapporteur reporting in the 2nd session of the Human Rights Council stated

> *"The capacity of law enforcement institutions and the independence and impartiality of the judiciary [in Myanmar] have been hampered by sustained practices of impunity. I am also very concerned by the continued misuse of the legal system, which denies the rule of law and represents a major obstacle for securing the effective and meaningful exercise of fundamental freedoms by citizens.*

> *"Grave human rights violations are indulged not only with impunity but authorized by the sanction of laws. In that respect, I consider especially as a matter of grave concern the criminalization of the exercise of fundamental freedoms by political opponents, human rights defenders and victims of human rights abuses."*

The Chief Justice of Myanmar signed the 1995 Beijing Principle which was an initiative to ensure the independency of the judiciary leading to the Judiciary Law of 2000. According to the Judiciary Law 2000 the administration of justice was to be based upon the following principles;

(a) administering justice independently according to law;

(b) protecting and safeguarding the interests of the people and aiding in the restoration of law and order and regional peace and tranquility;

(c) educating the people to understand and abide by the law and cultivating in the people the habit of abiding by the law;

(d) working within the framework of law for the settlement of cases;

(e) dispensing justice in open court unless otherwise prohibited by law;

(f) guaranteeing in all cases the right of defence and the right of appeal under the law;

(g) aiming at reforming moral character in meting out punishment to offenders.

It becomes clear that while "administering justice independently according to law", "protecting and safeguarding the interests of the people", "working within the framework of law for the settlement of cases", guaranteeing in all cases the right of defence and the right of appeal under the law are in resonance with the rule of law principles as followed by most nations in their judicial regimes. However these principles are qualified by other guidelines that underline the fact that the military regime does not intend to follow the rule of law. For instance, protecting and safeguarding the interests of the people is connected to restoration of law and order and is justified as being part of the effort by the government of Myanmar to ensure regional peace and tranquility. This is apparently connected to the fleeing of people across the border to the neighbouring countries creating demographic problems there especially in countries like Thailand. Aiding the restoration would therefore be the attempt to restrain and arrest such persons with the greater purpose of establishing regional peace. Aiding in the restoration of law and order and regional peace and tranquility, transparency of the judiciary which is stated in dispensing justice in open court are obstructed by the clause "unless otherwise prohibited by law". Similarly, there is room for all forms of violation of basic human rights in the process of "aiming at reforming moral character in meting out punishment to offenders". The abuse of the legal system has been a consistent fact in Myanmar.

The ethnic diversity of Myanmar is the most complex factor in the prevailing conflict situation. The ethnic problem in Myanamr relates to the existence within the geographical territory of several ethnic communities who are non Burmans viz. Shan, Kachin, Chin, Arakanese, Mon, Karen and Kareneni. These minorities have been controlled and suppressed by the military leaders to ensure the union remains intact. The Burmans have exhibited intolerance for these ethnic minorities and the military regime exhibits racial supremacy when dealing with them. In an open letter to the KOI (Kachin Independence Organisation) Karen national Union (KNU) New Mon State Party (NMSP) Shan State Army (SSA) , Ms Aung San Suu Kyi expressed her anguish that conflicts within the non Burman ethnic areas has created human tragedy, suffering, loss of lives, economic deterioration and destruction of costly physical structures. There are misconceptions of the majority and minority configurations which do not consider the fact that in the non Burman areas the Burmans are in minority. The Constitution adopted in 2008 does not consider the diversity and gives the military clear monopoly and supremacy in every aspect of governance. The 2010 elections which were held as the Fifth Step toward democratization resulted in very few positive changes in the structures of the government although it did not empower these structures to act beyond the military bidding. The elections were assessed as having been held in a climate of fear and suspicion. Independent election observers and foreign media were not allowed to cover the elections. Ahead of the elections 11 political parties were dissolved and, three ethnic minority parties were denied registration. The military backed party the Union Solidarity Development (USDP) party emerged victorious. After these elections a range of new institutions have been created: a presidential system; two houses of parliament and 14 regional governments and assemblies. The new parliaments and assemblies, in which the military was automatically allocated 25 per cent of seats ensures that the military retained its powerful hold on the country. Although the Parliament consists of serving and retired military officials, yet as a step away from militriasation was the dissolution of the State Peace and Development Council (SPDC). This has, however, been viewed as a placating move to ensure foreign investment in the country that had suffered deep economic setback since the 1962 coup and throughout the military regime. Members of the junta have as always retained their prominent roles as president, vice-president, parliament speakers, cabinet ministers and regional chief ministers. A shift from highly centralized policies of the military regime so far is expected to assuage the advocates of human rights, the military government announced the release of political prisoners although the actual figures vary about the number of persons released. The nominally civilian new government has declared its intention to liberalize the hard-line policies of the military junta that preceded it. Easing censorship, legalizing labor unions, suspending an unpopular China-backed dam project and beginning talks with Aung San Suu Kyi and her pro-democracy movement to bring the leader into the political mainstream, are being viewed as positive developments. However, until the legal regimes are established in accordance with the principles of rule of law and the independence of the judiciary secured, the civilian population of Myanmar will be unable to secure their right to select the government they desire.

Since March 2011 the Myanmar government led by President U Thein Sein has displayed an earnest desire to reducing the military image of the government and projecting itself as a regime that is committed to restoration of democracy in phases. The release of Aung San Suu Kyi in November, 2010 after her 15 years of house arrest signals a change of policy which many deem to be a move to placate those nations that have been severe critics of Myanmar's military regime. The highly centralized and inclusive policy of the regime also seems to be shifting. The release of 651 prominent political prisoners and the cease fire agreement with the ethnic Karen are welcomed as positive political moves by the "civilianized" government of Myanmar. The result of this shift has resulted in the restoration of diplomatic relations of the United States with Myanmar. However, there is a great degree of skepticism prevalent whether these apparent overtures to democracy are more about attracting foreign investments in a bid to spur economic growth and fending off criticisms from the international community and less about securing rights to its people.

Military operations have persisted against armed ethnic groups which continued to demand their political rights. This is an absence of legal or statutory limits on military operations otherwise than as determined by the military.

Nepal

The legal system in Nepal in the early days was pluralistic law: elements of civil law, common law, customary law and religious dictums. This mixed legal system in Nepal was the result of the British colonial power overlaying some of its own legal systems on the law of the land while it retained the elements of Nepal's existing Hindu legal concepts. The Muluki Ain of 1854 which was introduced by the first Rana Prime Minister, Jang Bahadur Rana, was a compendium of ancient Hindu sanctions and customary laws along with customary law modeled on British and Indian codes. The Muluk Ain which was amended several times and blended with royal edicts and proclamations was completely revised in 1963. Over a period of time, more royal edicts and proclamations were added to it and some piecemeal legislation was also incorporated to create a corpus of laws termed as Ain Sangraha. The Muluki Ain was the family law that was uniformly applicable to all religious communities.

In the absence of provision of law or judicial procedures, local customs were applied to decide matters. Theoretically, law was applied equally to all persons with no discrimination of caste, sex or creed. The Code granted the right to divorce, permitted inter caste marriages and all laws that sanctioned untouchability were abolished. The Code drafted at the behest of the King remained substantive law till 1991. Major political events occurred in Nepal, which underlined the existing confusion in its political system. After the assassination of King Birendra and his family in June 2001 allegedly by the Crown Prince Dipendra who succumbed to supposedly self-inflicted injuries, King Gyanendra came to power on Jun 4, 2001. King Gyanendra was sworn in as the King of Nepal but the relationship between the people and the monarchy was exceedingly uneasy. It did not help relationship between the monarch and the masses when the king, by his consequent conduct in political affairs, did not show any inclination to be a constitutional monarch. In twelve years, parliamentary elections were called four times and the government changed thirteen times. Nepal had no Parliament after May 2002, when the King dissolved it and ordered fresh election and since October 2002, the monarchy's confrontations with major political partied did not improve the situation. On Feb 1, 2005 King Gyanendra dismissed the coalition government of four parties nominated by him and sacked the Prime Minister Sher Bahadur Deuba. The King declared a state of emergency and assumed all executive powers for the next three years. Many politicians were placed under house arrest. Security was beefed up and all channels of communications shut down. All links with the outside world were severed and Nepal went into political and regional isolation. Ostensibly the reason cited was that the Deuba government had failed to hold talks with the Maoist "rebels" and conduct parliamentary elections by April. Backed by the 78,000 strong Nepalese Royal Army of which the King was the Supreme

Commander, the King declared Emergency. The suspension of fundamental rights and the severe curtailments of civil liberties did not augur well for the political stability of Nepal. The King suspended several provisions of the Constitution including the freedom of speech and expression and the right to privacy. The right to preventive detention was revoked along with the freedom of the press. In 2006, King Gyanendra in response to the democracy movements that wanted to end monarchy in the country, relinquished his sovereign power to the people and reinstated the dissolved House of Representatives. The House unanimously voted to declare Nepal a secular state and ended monarchy in the country and moved from being a Hindu Kingdom to a Federal Republic. In 2007, Article 159 of the Constitution was amended replacing "provisions regarding the King" with the words "provision regarding the Head of the State" and the Bill came into force in 2008 and the nation changed its official name to Federal Democratic Republic of Nepal. Nepal has been for a long time plagued by political tensions and power-sharing jousts. The Communist party of Nepal won a large number of seats in the elections held in 2008 but was soon thereafter toppled. In May 2009 a coalition government was formed with all major parties barring the Maoists. Four years after the ceasefire between the Maoist rebels and the State under the 2006 Comprehensive Peace Agreement that ended 10 years of conflict, politicians pledged to write a new constitution by May 28, 2010. However, this deadline was extended by one year after it became clear that many key constitutional issues had not been resolved. Despite this extension, power struggles both within and between the three main political parties have meant that little progress has been made. Politicians have still to agree on what system of government to adopt and how many provinces the country will have. Although last minute talks continue, it is still unclear whether Nepal's squabbling political parties will be able to agree on the terms for another extension. In August 2011, the Interim Constituent Assembly elected the Maoist leader Baburam Bhattarai as the 4th republican Prime Minister. The New Prime Minister's priority is to complete the peace process with the Maoists, make concerted efforts to draft a forward-looking constitution, good governance and social economic development of Nepal.

The most pressing problem facing Nepal is the adoption of a new Constitution. On the Constitution making process, an extension of the Constituent Assembly by six months has been sought. There is an urge to ensure that the new Constitution will enshrine the independence of the judiciary. The past experiences of the people of Nepal were with a judiciary that was influenced by the autocratic regime and manipulated and corrupted by the system. Therefore, the top priority is acquiring for the people of Nepal, a judicial system that assures inclusiveness, accountability and accessibility. The current problems with the judiciary in Nepal are: the pendency of cases before various courts, the prolonged time frame for trials and the inordinate delays in delivering judgments. During the state of emergency declared by the King in February 2005, the judicial system became subordinate to the King and its powers were altered. An anti corruption body which had no credible legal status was created by the King and given wide powers. The six member Royal Commission on Corruption Control (RCCC) could investigate and indict suspects and conduct investigations at its own discretions. The RCCC could order persons to appear before it within 24 hours and detain them up to 30 days on suspicion and persons could be jailed for 6 months for contempt. The RCCC could investigate charges against heads of any constitutional agency and recommend necessary action to the King against such persons.

In the bid to tackle the Maoist rebels the Royal Nepalese Army was invested with wide ranging powers and the lack of accountability of the military led to abuse of power for personal gains. Numerous instances of abuse of human rights with cases of enforced disappearances, State sanctioned killings and torture have been reported. Protracted insurgency with associated state of abuse of laws between 1996 and 2006 led to the criminal justice system being severely undermined. When King Gyanendra seized control and absolute power in 2005 and declared a state of emergency, it led to a period of total suppression of civil and political rights. Subsequent to the peoples' uprising, the Jan Andolan in 2006 and the Comprehensive Peace Agreement, the House of Representatives was restored. Some of the major changes sought to be carried out by the Interim Parliament in 2008 in the administrative and legal systems were: the protection of individual rights, transparency and communication to the people of the intention and working of the government, reviews and accountability to restore the confidence of the people, reform and transformation of institutions and enhancement of powers of the constitutional institutions.

Defining the new Constitution and adapting to a new legal system under it would be major challenge for the political leadership of Nepal. The present hierarchy of the Court system has also been questioned;   jurists and law makers and practitioners in Nepal have called for an integrated system of the judiciary. Although the severity of the conflict situation may have abated, the damage it has caused to the judicial system will require purposeful restoration of the institution. The failure of the judiciary in Nepal to deliver equitable justice and without inordinate delay has left the people of Nepal with no recourse to basic rights. Controversies in appointment of judges, charges of widespread corruption, dismissals and promotions of judges in arbitrary manner has underlined the unfairness in the system and questioned the credibility of the legal structures. A monitoring system has to be adopted that not only manages the resources and deals with issues and controversies; there is also an urgent need for a mechanism that ensures that the judiciary enjoys the support of the executive branch of the government to function independent of the executive and legislative bodies. The distressing truth is that the political instability that still seems to haunt Nepal has done untenable damage to the legal system and the judiciary in Nepal and it is necessary to create to a stable Nepal that the legal and judicial structures are strengthened.

Sri Lanka

The religious and ethnic diversity of Sri Lanka and its colonial history had played a major role on its legal history. The Portuguese were the first colonizers of Ceylon, as it was known then, arriving in the 1500s. The Portuguese were replaced by the Dutch in the 1600s and they introduced the Roman-Dutch legal system in Ceylon. This was a well organized legal system which had three seats for the courts in the west, north and south of Ceylon. The Dutch attempted to codify the different customary laws of the diverse ethnic groups but applied the Roman-Dutch laws to the population in the coastal regions. In 1707, the laws and customs of the Tamils of the Northern Jaffna province, was codified as the *Thesawalamai* and with the consent of the Muslim elders, a code of Muslim laws as made applicable to the Muslim population. In the 1700s the British replaced the Dutch and set up unitary administrative and judicial units and extended the prevailing law to the rest of the island. Till gaining independence in1948, the prevailing Roman- Dutch law and the customary laws were applicable in Ceylon.

An authority on Sri Lankan law, H.W.Tambiah, in his writing about Sri Lanka in *Encyclopedia of Comparative Law: National Reports* describe the complex and diverse nature of Sri Lankan law:

> *In Sri Lanka, there are five systems of private law. The Roman-Dutch law, as modified by statutes, and interpreted by the courts, is the general law of the land. English common law applies to commercial contracts and commercial property and has been tacitly accepted in many matters. English law was also introduced by statute and as such forms the statutory law of the land. The Thesawalamai is both a personal and local law.... Similarly, Kandyan Law applies to the Kandyan Sinhalese, and the Muslim laws, to the Muslims, in [matters relating to] marriage,divorce, [alimony] and inheritance. Private law governs issues between individuals....*

The conflict in Sri Lanka is dated in history as having begun in 1983 although the ethnic problems started long before the specific year. The ethnic conflict which continued for nearly three decades, culminated in the defeat of the LTTE by the Sri Lankan forces and the killing of the LTTE leader Prabhakaran in May 2009. The long and bloody conflict not only tore apart the social fabric of the nation creating rifts that would be very difficult to heal for a long time and resulting in mutual distrust between the Sinhala majority and the Tamil minority; but also damaged permanently many of the structures of the government including the judiciary and the legal systems which were severely eroded by the onslaught of the conflict.

Two sets of laws were used by the government to tackle the violent activities that took place during the early days of insurgency and the subsequent civil wars in Sri Lanka: the regulations issued under Public Security Ordinance No.25 of 1947 and the Prevention of Terrorism Act of 1979. The Public Security Ordinance (PSO) of 1947 was passed by the colonial government to take security measures in the "interests of the public security and the preservation of public order". The power to the President to issue emergency regulations under the PSO is discretionary. Under Part I of the PSO the President is empowered to declare a state of emergency and by Rule 1 (2A) (b) the supreme authority is given to the President to issue any emergency regulation under Part II. During the self-declared state of emergency in the country, under the law several actions were allowed such as detention of persons, acquisition of private property, including land, on behalf of the government and search and seizure of any property. Section 5 of the PSO grants the power of authority to make emergency regulations (ERs) as they 'appear to [the President] to be necessary or expedient.' Any amendment, suspension and/or application of 'any law' was permitted and supreme legal authority was granted to the emergency regulations issued by the President over all other laws of the land (including those defined in the Constitution). The power to grant compensation to any persons affected by an emergency regulation vested solely in the President. Apprehension and punishment of offenders of any of the emergency regulation vested in the authoritative body's discretion. The President could also bestow upon any person of authority, military or not, the power to make any rules or orders pursuant to any emergency regulation. The provisions of Sections 16, 17, and 18 deal with curfew restrictions on residents and related penalties. Under these sections essential services during states of emergency could be demanded and any attempt to obstruct or hinder the progress of such service, physically, verbally, or via publication was subject to punishment and arrests for such acts could be made without warrant.

The Prevention of Terrorism Act (PTA) 1979 was passed to deal with the threat to public security posed by the insurgency of the LTTE by providing ways by which the government could issue emergency regulations for containment of terrorist activity. Under the act murder and detention of person was considered terrorist activity, the government security forces and the military being exempt from similar acts. Normal criminal procedures were not followed and the provisions provided for the arrest of any person, to enter and search any premises, to stop and search any vehicle and seize any document suspected of violating any law. Although the time for holding a person in custody was specified as 72 hours under Section 9 the period could be extended. A person could be held in detention on unspecified grounds for three months which could be further extended to another three months to a maximum period of 18 months and such order of detention could not be questioned in a court of law. Besides, such arrested person could be taken to any place for the purpose of interrogation. All suspected persons were subject to trial without preliminary hearing and without the presence of jury.

Both the emergency laws severely limited the jurisdiction of the courts in Sri Lankan. It also took away from the courts the power to prevent abusive detention and torture. Neither local magistrates nor did the provincial high courts provide any remedies for person in illegal and abusive detention. Habeas corpus petitions and applications for securing fundamental rights in the Supreme Court seldom provided relief to those who approached it. This was seen as a failure of the Supreme Court to protect constitutional and human rights in Sri Lanka. The Supreme Court did not play any role in constraining the powers of the security forces nor was it seen as pro active in protecting the rights of the minorities. The ability of the Sri Lankan judiciary to adjudicate in a fair and free manner in sensitive matters and secure political and basic civil rights within the rule of law was severely compromised. The judiciary also failed to protect minority rights and social and cultural rights. Gross violation of natural justice was exhibited in the Singarasa case, which is considered as the case that underlined the fact that the judiciary served the executive to the detriment of basic rights. The petitioner, Singarasa, was arrested and tortured for alleged links with the LTTE. He was convicted in the High Court based on the confessions obtained under torture and he was sentenced to 50 years of imprisonment. The Court of Appeal upheld the conviction but reduced the sentence to 35 years. He was denied a fair trial and his right to review without delay was violated. The Supreme Court refused leave to appeal. Singarasa then appealed to the UN Human Rights Committee. However, when the matter came up in the Supreme Court, it was held that Sri Lanka's obligations under international law extended only to those that have been incorporated into the laws of Sri Lanka. It was apparent that the Supreme Court was politically motivated in the judgment. By this judgment, Sri Lankan judiciary displayed that it was unwilling and unable to protect and promote human rights and the Court acted against natural justice and rule of law, and that it was not adequately mindful of the political consequences of legal decisions, particularly in the arena of minority rights. By placing the burden of proof on Singarasa that his confession was made under duress, his rights were further violated. The judiciary was under obligation to provide Singarasa with an effective and appropriate remedy, including release or retrial, and compensation, and to ensure that the sections of the Prevention of Terrorism Act (PTA) that allowed such treatment are made compatible with the International Convention for Civil and Political

Rights to which Sri Lanka is a signatory. One of the most fundamental issues concerning the effective implementation of international human rights conventions is the aspect of giving adequate domestic recognition to those human rights contained in international conventions. The State should ensure that international law is part of domestic law. Those rights contained in international conventions to which a State is Party are also rights under domestic law especially of civil and political rights of citizens. In the Singarasa case, the Supreme Court, however, held that the rights contained in the International Covenant on Civil and Political Rights were not rights under the domestic law of Sri Lanka as nothing had been done to transform international law into domestic law; therefore, rights under the Convention were not rights under Sri Lankan law and that as long as a government of Sri Lanka had not enacted implementing legislation which transformed the rights under the International Covenant on Civil and Political Rights into rights under Sri Lankan law, a citizen of Sri Lanka could not in any meaningful way argue in a domestic court that those rights had been violated. The Singarasa case is considered by jurists to be a certain case of political manipulation of the judiciary.

By the 1972 Constitution, unfettered control of the judiciary was placed in the hands of the President. The Parliament and the Cabinet Ministers were ranked over the judiciary. All judicial review of executive and administrative actions was terminated thereby curtailing judicial independence. Constitutional review was assigned to a Constitutional Court which was appointed by the President; it was not only clearly an arm of the executive but it also lacked the power to review any legislation after its enactment. The judiciary was, therefore, superseded by the executive and legislative branches of the government. Although the 1978 Constitution (now in force) strengthened judicial independence, Chapter III of the Constitution dealing with the eight Fundamental Rights viz. equality, free speech, association and conscience, freedom from torture and illegal detention, makes no mention of civil and political rights. By the 13th Amendment of 1987, a state of emergency was made immune from judicial challenge. The 1989 Regulation No. 17 allowed the Defence Secretary to detain persons to prevent them from "engaging in acts inimical to national security in future" other regulations dispensed with the need for search warrants and allowed the police to dispose the corpses without notifying the families. Regulation from the 1990s further extended detention powers. Emergency (Misc. Provisions and Powers) Regulation No. 1 of 2005 and Emergency (Prevention and Prohibition of Specified Terrorist Activities) and Regulation No. 7 of 2006 stated that a person can be detained up to 1 year by military or police forces to prevent acts "prejudicial to the national security or the maintenance of public order". By the Regulation of August 2008, detention powers were extended to further six months and broader search and seizure powers were given to the security forces.

Seventeen sets of regulations have been passed on divergent topics dealing with terrorist activities, high security zones, special administrative arrangements etc. The 17th Amendment of 2001 detailed the formation of the Constitutional Council to limit the presidential power over the judiciary but successive presidents have consistently ignored the constitutional control and by the powers vested by the emergency regulations have kept the judicial powers under check. By intermittent interventions into decisions on political questions, the judiciary has been deprived of its ability to function independently.

The freedom of expression is guaranteed under Article 14 of the Constitution of Sri Lanka. In May 2000, the President of Sri Lanka, acting under section 5 of the Public Security Ordinance (Chapter 40), promulgated the Emergency (Miscellaneous Provisions and Powers) Regulation (No. 1 of 2000). Under this, Regulation 14 imposed a number of restrictions on publishing and broadcasting, including for the protection of national security and public order. Regulation 14 also provides for the appointment of a Competent Authority and gives him the power to implement these restrictions, including requiring the media to submit material in advance of dissemination (prior censorship), as well as the power to ban publications which breach the Regulation and to place a sealing order on their premises. Therefore the prohibition on publishing or broadcasting matters prejudicial to national security or public order, found in Regulation 14 of the Emergency (Miscellaneous Provisions and Powers) Regulation, No. 1 of 2000, as well as the system established in the Regulation for implementing this prohibition, represent a substantial limitation on freedom of expression.

From the period 1983 to 2001 (except for a five month period) an uninterrupted state of emergency has existed in Sri Lanka. This period is seen as the period when there have been no guarantees of personal security. It has also been seen to be a period when no redress had been provided against arbitrary state violence. In August 2011, the President of Sri Lanka stated in the Parliament that the reasons for the stringent emergency regulations, which had been in force since 2005, no longer existed and that he was repealing the laws. The regulations were mainly intended to deal with the security predicament of the insurgency waged by the Liberation Tigers of Tamil Eelam (LTTE). With the war having ended in May 2009, and no terrorist activity recorded since then, the President expressed that there was no longer any need for the provisions. However, the situation does not change wholly in Sri Lanka as the government and the security forces enjoy far reaching powers under the Prevention of Terrorism (Temporary Provisions) Act of 1979 and other laws and regulations permitting long detention periods. The repeal of the emergency law does not have any effect for those already in detention, as it does not change the detention practices. Besides, the Supreme Court rulings have been often ignored by the Sri Lankan government indicating that despite repealing the emergency laws, the government and the security forces will continue to operate as before and without legal authorization. Therefore, although the conflict has ended, instead of a sense of freedom with the repeal of the emergency laws, there lurks an air of suspicion that the independence and the powers off the judiciary will not be restored and that the legal machinery is still not in a position to secure to all the people in Sri Lanka fair and equitable justice.

India

India has been grappling with the phenomenon of domestic terrorism and separatist insurgencies for more than three decades and often the two have over lapped. The country has witnessed the most proliferation of separatist organizations compared to areas of conflict in other countries of the world. The militant activities and separatist movements and insurgencies in several parts of India have led to different legislations to deal with them over a period of time. Internal conflicts in India are not confined to specific geographical locations or shared purposes; on the contrary there have been several insurgent groups acting in various parts of the country, each espousing their own ideological cause based on diverse factors like religion, ethnicity, language etc and indulging in varied violent acts. Therefore, India has always felt the need to formulate and pursue its own policy to deal with these insurgent activities.

The earliest perpetrators of violent activity in India were the left wing groups in the state of West Bengal. Informally termed as Naxalites, as the violent uprising and opposing movement was started in a village called Naxalbari in 1967 as a response to killing of peasants by the landlords, the movement spread to other states in the country. Although it fragmented in the period following 1970, it was estimated that by 1980 there were 30 odd groups sharing similar ideologies and having a membership of almost 30,000. The growing insurgency is still a major problem for the Indian government and it is estimated that at present the insurgent groups have a membership running beyond 20,000 and are suspected to have spread their influence over nine states in India viz. Andhra Pradesh, Maharashtra, Madhya Pradesh, Orissa, Chhattisgarh, Jharkhand, Uttar Pradesh, West Bengal and Bihar, where the guerrillas have control and run quasi-government structures in 160 administrative districts. In some states, Naxalites have been active for a number of years continuously. Initially, the Naxalites were treated as a law and order problem and, therefore, the responsibility of the state governments. The police in some states, particularly Andhra Pradesh, Bihar and Jharkhand, have been blamed for human rights violations. In Andhra Pradesh, local human rights groups say that a special police squad deployed against Naxalites and known as the Greyhounds was responsible for hundreds of faked "encounter killings." Large numbers of civilians have been internally displaced by armed clashes between the Naxalites and government-backed vigilante groups. In some areas, civilians have also been trapped, not just between security forces and the Naxalites, but also armed vigilante groups like the Salwa Judum in Chattisgarh state or the Green Tigers of Andhra Pradesh. While thousands are living in temporary shelters provided by the government, others are hiding in camps run by the Naxalites in the forest. Naxalism typifies a particular kind of militant and violent armed struggle by the peasants and tribals led by a leadership drawing doctrinal support from Marxism-Leninism and strategic inspiration from Mao. The contemporary Maoists draw heavily upon the iniquitous land tenure system and exploitation of the peasantry by landlords in framing their ideological aim.

The earliest legislation to deal with the uprising in the nascent stage was The West Bengal (Prevention of Violent Activities) Act of 1970 passed by the West Bengal government. In Jharkhand state, the Prevention of Terrorism Act, now repealed, was used for the arbitrary detention of hundreds of persons. The Special Public Protection Act, which came into force in March 2006, is a vague and overly broad law that allows detention of up to three years for "unlawful activities." The term is so loosely defined in the law that it threatens fundamental freedoms set out by the Indian constitution and international human rights law, and could severely restrict the peaceful activities of individuals and civil society organizations. The law also criminalizes any support given to Naxalites, with no defense given for acting under duress. Thus, persons whom the Naxalites force to provide assistance are subject to detention under the ordinance.

In the north eastern state of Assam, militant activity evolved as a reaction to the large-scale migration of refugees from East Pakistan – what is now Bangladesh – since India's Partition in 1947. The local demography of the state was eroded by the continuous flow of refugees and in 1977 agitations were launched for detection of illegal immigrants and their deletion from the voters list. The United Liberation Front of Assam (ULFA), the prominent militant organization in Assam along with their anti foreigner agenda included secession from the Indian Union as its chief goal. As the situation deteriorated and the local government failed to control the escalating violence, the army was deployed and the state was brought under the Assam Disturbed Areas Act, 1955 and the Armed Forces (Special Powers) Act 1958. The Assam government promulgated the Assam Maintenance of Public Order (Autonomous Districts) Act, 1953 (Act XVI of 1953). This act received the Assam governor's approval and was published in the Assam Gazette on June 3, 1953. It was the first of a series of successive legislations that were set out to govern the Naga Hills and then other parts of the Northeast, where other groups rose in revolt and espoused secessionist policies. The Disturbed Areas Act harks back to 1947 when the Government of India, facing communal violence at the time of Partition, enacted four ordinances to tackle the crisis: the Bengal Disturbed Areas Ordinance (Special Powers of Armed Forces); the Assam Disturbed Areas Ordinance (Special Powers of Armed Forces); the East Punjab and Delhi Disturbed Areas Ordinance (Special Powers of Armed Forces); and the United Provinces

Disturbed Areas Ordinance (Special Powers of Armed Forces). These were designed to confront the Hindu-Muslim riots during the time of independence when India and Pakistan were partitioned.

ULFA did not cease its violent activities proclaiming constantly its goal to liberate itself from the rule of the Indian government. Its activities consistently escalated and in 1990 it turned extremely violent. Counter-insurgency operations in Assam continued and in 1997, a Unified Command structure was set up to co-ordinate the functioning of the various forces carrying out operations against the terrorists in Assam. There have been continuous military and para-military operations in the area and although this has considerably weakened the ULFA, its activities have not ceased. Similar insurgent activities have also been occurring in the other parts of North Eastern region of the country- in the states of Manipur, Meghalaya, Mizoram, Nagaland and Tripura.

The Armed Forces (Special Powers) Act (AFSPA) was passed by the Parliament of India in 1958. Under this Act, security forces are given wide ranging powers to conduct operations after an area is declared disturbed. While AFSPA gives the armed forces wide powers to shoot, arrest and search for "aiding civil powers" requires that individuals apprehended in operations along with equipment should be handed over by security forces to the nearest civilian authorities. It was first applied to the North Eastern states of Assam and Manipur and was amended in 1972 to extend to all the seven states in the north- eastern region of India viz., Assam, Manipur, Tripura, Meghalaya, Arunachal Pradesh, Mizoram and Nagaland. It was withdrawn by the Manipur government in some of the constituencies in August 2004, although the Government of India was not in favour of its withdrawal. The Act has been employed in the state of Jammu and Kashmir since 1990.

According to the Armed Forces Special Powers Act (AFSPA), in an area that is proclaimed as "disturbed", an officer of the armed forces has powers to:

- Fire upon or use other kinds of force even if it causes death

- To arrest without a warrant and with the use of "necessary" force anyone who has committed certain offences or is suspected of having done so

- To enter and search any premise in order to make such arrests.

Army officers have legal immunity for their actions. There can be no prosecution, suit or any other legal proceeding against anyone acting under that law, unless permitted by the Central Government. Nor is the government's judgment on why an area is found to be disturbed subject to judicial review.

The 1972 amendments to the AFSPA extended the power to declare an area disturbed to the Central Government. In the 1958 version of the AFSPA the authority and power to apply and extend the Act vested in the states. Continued violence in these states led to the extension of this power to the Central Government. Therefore, the Central Government was given the ability to overrule the opinion of a state governor and declare an area disturbed. For instance in Tripura, the Central Government declared Tripura a disturbed area, over the opposition of the State Government.

Under the AFSPA, Section 4 sets out the powers granted to the military stationed in a disturbed area. These powers are granted to the commissioned officer, warrant officer, or non-commissioned officer, only a jawan (private) does not have these powers. The Section allows the armed forces personnel to use force for a variety of reasons.

The army can shoot to kill, under the powers of section 4(a) for the commission or suspicion of the commission of the following offenses: acting in contravention of any law or order for the time being in force in the disturbed area prohibiting the assembly of five or more persons, carrying weapons, or carrying anything which is capable of being used as a fire-arm or ammunition. To justify the invocation of this provision, the officer need only be "of the opinion that it is necessary to do so for the maintenance of public order" and only give "such due warning as he may consider necessary".

The army can destroy property under section 4(b) if it is an arms dump, a fortified position or shelter from where armed attacks are made or are suspected of being made, if the structure is used as a training camp or as a hide-out by armed gangs or absconders.

The army can arrest anyone without a warrant under section 4(c), who has committed, is suspected of having committed or of being about to commit, a cognizable offense and use any amount of force "necessary to effect the arrest".

Under section 4(d) the army can enter and search without a warrant to make an arrest or to recover any property, arms, ammunition or explosives which are believed to be unlawfully kept on the premises. This section also allows the use of force necessary for the search.

It is often argued that under Article 355 of the Indian Constitution, it the duty of the Central Government to protect the states from internal disturbance and that there is no duty under international law to allow secession. Although the enforcement of the AFSPA has resulted in allegations of incidents of arbitrary detention, torture, rape, and looting by security personnel, the legislation is justified by the Indian government on the plea that it is required to stop the Northeast states from seceding from the Indian Union. The law has also been declared by human rights organizations as draconian and as a violation of the fundamental freedoms of the citizens of the state. The security forces enjoy virtual impunity for any excesses while exercising these unrestrained powers as no one can be prosecuted without the prior permission of the Central government. The Jeevan Reddy Committee constituted by the government produced a Report that called for the repeal of the act, describing it as "too sketchy, too bald and quite inadequate." It went on to say "The Act, for whatever reason, has become a symbol of oppression, an object of hate and an instrument of discrimination and highhandedness. It is highly desirable and advisable to repeal this Act altogether, without, of course, losing sight of the overwhelming desire of the majority of the region that the Army should remain although the application of the Act should be removed." For that purpose, an appropriate legal mechanism has to be devised. The committee's report also felt that the removal of the application of the AFSPA could create political space for negotiations, dialogue, and peace in the Northeast. In December 2006, responding to the 'legitimate' grievances of the people of Manipur, Prime Minister Manmohan Singh declared that the Act would be amended to ensure it was 'humane' on the basis of the Jeevan Reddy Commission's report.

In 1961, the central government passed the Nagaland Security Regulation Act to deal with the secessionist groups active in Nagaland. This Act along with the Disturbed Areas Act was used to bring the situation under control. Along with the AFSPA, the Nagaland Security Regulations

Act was enacted to put more sweeping powers in the hands of police and civilian authorities. Between the 1960s and 2004 several laws were enacted to deal with the problems of internal security, which the police were viewed as incapable of handling because the acts constituted armed insurrection against the entire state, not just a part of it, and hence justified the use of the army or paramilitary forces.

AFSPA under both Indian and international law is in violation of the right to life which specifies that means no situation, or state of emergency, or internal disturbance, can justify the suspension of this right, the powers to kill as in the case of the offences under Section 4(a) by which the soldier may shoot even if there is no deadly force to threaten the soldier. The Code of Conduct for Law Enforcement Officials only foresees the use of deadly force by an officer when he is threatened with force. Under Section 4(a) of the AFSPA, the officer can shoot when there is an unlawful assembly, not defined as threatening, or when the person has or is suspected of having a weapon. Since "weapon" is defined as anything "capable of being used as a weapon", there is a lack of proportionality between the offence and the use of force. Therefore, to continue the use of AFSPA if required, it is essential that it must comply with the basic requirements under international law and the rule of law as set up by the Indian legal standards. This means the powers to shoot to kill under section 4(a) must be unequivocally revoked. Arrests must be made with warrants and no force should be allowed in the search and seizure procedures. Section 5 should clearly state that persons arrested under the Act are to be handed over to the police within twenty-four hours. Section 6 should be completely repealed so that individuals who suffer abuses at the hands of the security forces may prosecute their abusers. Not only should the definition of key phrases, especially "disturbed area" be clarified, the declaration that an area is disturbed should not be left to the subjective opinion of the Central or State Government. It should have an objective standard which is judicially reviewable. It is imperative that the declaration that an area is disturbed should be for a specified time, for instance, no longer than six months and such a declaration should not continue without legislative review.

On the other hand, AFSPA comes into effect after an area is declared 'Disturbed'. It is condition in which the state apparatus including its police, armed police and civil society is not in a position to control the situation or to restore law and order to levels in which the state can carry out its functions, and in which only military action can be useful. The use of military against armed actions of insurgents is thus a last resort. In other words, military action under AFSPA should remain an exceptional measure to deal with an exceptional circumstance. Notwithstanding this, state and central governments have kept the AFSPA into use for long periods extending to decades. The antagonism of the populace against such misuse of the 'Disturbed Area' has turned into a call for the repeal of AFSPA. The conundrum of use of 'Disturbed Area' and military action in circumstances where a ceasefire prevails between the government and militant groups needs to resolved.

The Disturbed Areas (Special Courts) Act, 1976, however, provides a clearer definition. Under the Disturbed Areas (Special Courts) Act of 1976, an area may be declared disturbed when "a State Government is satisfied that (i) there was, or (ii) there is, in any area within a State extensive disturbance of the public peace and tranquility, by reason of differences or disputes between members of different religions, racial, language, or regional groups or castes or communities, it may declare such area to be a disturbed area."

In the original version of the Armed Forces Special Powers Act of 1958, only the state governments had the power to declare an area as disturbed. This was consistent with Article 246 of the Constitution of India to be read with the 7th Schedule of the Constitution of India which places "law and order" under the State's list. The 1972 amendments to the AFSPA took away the power from the State government and its legislative Assembly and handed it over to an appointee of the Central Government. After the alleged extrajudicial execution of 32-year-old, Ms Thangjam Manorama Devi following her arrest as a suspected member of the Peoples Liberation Army (PLA) by the Assam Rifles personnel in 2004, Manipur faced unprecedented civil disobedience over the demand for removal of the AFSPA.

The period between 1978 and 1993 was a period of great turmoil in the state of Punjab with Sikh separatist movements demanding Khalistan – a sovereign Sikh nation. The organizations indulged in a frenzy of unabated violence. The organizations received financial support from the Sikh community in UK, USA and Canada. The militant activity brought to halt normal life in the state and hindered economic investment in Punjab plunging it into a state of total anarchy with high levels of violence. Finally, in June 1984, the army was deployed and in a major operation – *Operation Blue Star* the army flushed out the armed militants who had amassed weapons inside the holy Golden Temple of the Sikhs in Amritsar. Successive operations by the police against the militants weakened them and after the bombing of the Air India Flight 182 in June 1985 over the Irish Sea which claimed the lives of 329 Canadian civilians, considered the worst aviation disaster till the September 11, 2001 attacks, support for Khalistan dwindled. Eventually the separatist movement died out and normalcy returned to the state.

Internal conflicts situations in India have been complicated and there is sufficient evidence that the organizations in the Northeast and the Maoists have been receiving logistic support, weapons and training from foreign sources. Moser and Clark define political violence, as "the commission of violent acts motivated by a desire, conscious or unconscious, to obtain or maintain political power". Political violence is further explained as being about the acquisition of power through violent acts. It is driven by desires for power that lead people to transgress others' private domains. This phenomenon can be seen among guerrillas, paramilitary groups, tyrannical regimes, extremist religious and ethnic groups and others, aiming to undermine the other in order to achieve hegemony over a region, state or a group. The destruction and chaos provoked by the means used by perpetrators of political violence have their origins in diverse motivations that fluctuate from the desire to defeat a government to the desire to control a region or a land. Likewise, opposite motivations such as religious beliefs and economic interests coincide in the use of violence to achieve power".

India has introduced numerous legislations over a period of time but these have been confined to the specific areas where the activities have occurred. The last three decades, therefore, witnessed the enactment of numerous legislations to tackle various specific contingencies: Jammu and Kashmir Public Safety Act (1978); Assam Preventive Detention Act (1980); National Security Act (1980, amended 1984 and 1987); Anti-Hijacking Act (1982); Armed Forces (Punjab and Chandigarh) Special Powers Act (1983); Punjab Disturbed Areas Act (1983); Chandigarh Disturbed Areas Act (1983);

Suppression of Unlawful Acts Against Safety of Civil Aviation Act (1982); Terrorist Affected Areas (Special Courts) Act (1984); National Security (Second Amendment) Ordinance (1984); Terrorist and Disruptive Activities (Prevention) Act (1985, amended 1987); National Security Guard Act (1986); Criminal Courts and Security Guard Courts Rules (1987) and the Special Protection Group Act (1988). However, these legislations were enacted to tackle specific situations only.

There has been no all encompassing legislation to deal with internal conflict situations throughout the territory of India which could be applied uniformly and interpreted by courts consistently. The Preventive Detention Act was passed by Parliament in 1950 in the bloody aftermath of Independence and Partition to curb activity that was perceived as a threat to national unity. This Act expired in 1969 and was quickly replaced by the Maintenance of Internal security Act (MISA) in 1971, primarily used to curb the Naxalbari uprisings. MISA was a controversial Act giving the government and Indian law enforcement agencies super powers - indefinite "preventive" detention of individuals, search and seizure of property without warrants, and wiretapping to quell the civil and political disorder within the country and to counter foreign backed terrorist activities which were threats to national security. The legislation gained infamy for its disregard of legal and constitutional and the arbitrary arrest and torture. The 39th Amendment to the Constitution of India placed MISA in the 9th Schedule to the Constitution, thereby making it totally immune from any judicial review; even though it contravened the Fundamental Rights which are guaranteed by the Constitution. The law was repealed in 1977 and by the 42nd Amendment Act of 1978; MISA was removed from the 9th Schedule. When insurgencies and militancy became synonymous with domestic terrorism and the internal conflict situations came to be used by suspected terrorist outfits, the AFSPA and MISA were followed by Terrorist and Disruptive Activities Act (TADA) in 1985 and the Prevention of Terrorism Act (POTA) in 2002. Both the laws were criticized for authorizing excessive powers for the aim of fighting internal and cross-border terrorism and political violence, without safeguards for civil freedoms.

A serious situation has developed in India in the aftermath of the Khalistan movement and the never ending conflict in Kashmir. There is enough evidence that most, if not all, insurgent groups and those organizations with secessionist agendas are funded, trained and provided with weapons and other logistics by countries that seek to destabilize the unity and integrity of India. Therefore, all acts of secessionist activities are now deemed to be acts as terrorism. Acknowledging the fact that the existing situation in the country is peculiar, the Supreme Court of India in *Kartar Singh v. State of Punjab* observed that:

> *deplorably, determined youths lured by hardcore criminals and underground extremists and attracted by the ideology of terrorism are indulging in committing serious crimes against humanity. In spite of the drastic actions taken and intense vigilance activated, the terrorists and the militants do not desist from triggering lawlessness if it suits their purpose.[1]*

Two laws in India that were enacted at different times to deal with terrorism specifically were the Terrorists and Disruptive Activities (Prevention) Act (TADA) of 1985 (amended 1987) and repealed in 1995 and the Prevention of Terrorism Act 2002 (POTA) repealed in 2004. The Indian government had introduced the Prevention of Terrorism Ordinance (POTO) on October 2001 and the legislature passed The Prevention of Terrorism Act (POTA) in March of 2002. Both the laws resulted in gross abuse of human rights during implementation and there is sufficient evidence to uphold these allegations. The laws had abhorrent features that violated fundamental freedoms enshrined in the Constitution of India. Both these laws were severely criticized as they violated human rights and vitiated the due process of law. There was uproar in all sections of society and they were consequently repealed. That they flouted the basic concepts of the legal system is irrefutable.

Briefly, the inherent flaws were as follows: 180 days detention was permitted without charges being framed, there was a presumption of guilt of those subject to the law, there were clauses for summary trials, and trials in absentia - all of which violated all norms of equitable justice. The sketchy review procedure came under severe criticism. The gross abuse of the

---

[1] (1994) 3 SCC 569, p. 621.

laws occurred due to several factors. The texts of these laws were too broad and the term terrorism included everything. The generalized term covered ordinary criminal activities covered by the penal laws of the country like theft and murder. The interlocutory orders of the Special Courts set up under the new laws could not be reviewed. Since the state governments had powers equal to the Central government under these laws there was gross misuse by the state machinery especially in the states of Tamil Nadu, Gujarat, Maharashtra where the laws were used to quell political opposition or to settle personal scores and all this is supported by statistics. The erratic application of the laws at various times also varied from state to state.

Questions were also raised regarding the violation of the Fundamental Rights enshrined in the Constitution of India. These laws violate the right of equality. Establishing special courts and special procedures was challenged on the grounds that terrorists were being treated differently from ordinary criminals, and that this was discriminatory. In 1994, the Supreme Court in the landmark judgment of *Kartar Singh vs. State of Punjab* dealt with various provisions of the Terrorist and Disruptive Activities (Prevention) Act, 1987 and upheld the constitutional validity of the Act. The Supreme Court held that

> *...the rule of differentiation is that in enacting laws differentiating between different persons or things in different circumstances which govern one set of persons or objects such laws may not necessarily be the same as those governing another set of persons or objects so that the question of unequal treatment does not really arise between persons governed by different conditions and different set of circumstances.*[2]

Further

> *the persons who are to be tried for offences specified under the provisions of TADA Act are a distinct class of persons and the procedure prescribed for trying them*

---

[2] Kartar, p. 672.

for the aggravated and incensed nature of offences are under different classification distinguishable from ordinary criminals and procedure[3]

The procedure to record confessions was streamlined by the Supreme Court in the *Kartar Singh* case wherein six safeguards which were to be employed while recording a confession were defined. POTA incorporated these safeguards in its Section 32, which required that,

- A police officer shall, before recording any confession made by an accused under sub-section (1) of Section 32, explain to such person in writing that he is not bound to make a confession and that if he does so; it may be used against him.

- Further, provided that, where such person prefers to remain silent, the police officer shall not compel or induce him to make any confession.

- Under clause (3) of the same section it is laid down that the confession shall be recorded in an atmosphere free from threat or inducement and shall be in the same language in which the person makes it.

- Under clause (4) the person from whom a confession has been recorded under sub-section (1), shall be produced before the Court of a Chief Metropolitan Magistrate or the Court of a Chief Judicial Magistrate along with the original statement of confession, written or recorded on mechanical or electronic device within forty-eight hours.

- Further, under clause (5), the Chief Metropolitan Magistrate or the Chief Judicial Magistrate, shall, record the statement, if any, made by the person so produced and get his signature or thumb impression and if there is any complaint of torture, such person shall be directed to be produced for medical examination before a Medical Officer not lower in rank than an Assistant Civil Surgeon and thereafter, he shall be sent to judicial custody.

---

[3] Ibid, p. 673.

- Another significant departure from TADA is that if the detainee's confession is not recorded before a magistrate within 48 hours, such confession fails to carry credence.

These substantial changes with regard to the admissibility of and safeguards relating to confessions under POTA were incorporated to remove the lacunae that had existed in TADA.

Stating the severity of the earlier laws and their misuse only serves to underline the need to reframe the laws; it does not raise the question whether a new counter terrorism law is required are not.

In *State of Rajasthan vs. Union of India*, the Supreme Court noted:

> *It must be remembered that merely because power may sometimes be abused, it is no ground for denying the existence of power. The wisdom of man has not yet been able to conceive of a government with power sufficient to answer all its legitimate needs and at the same time incapable of mischief* [4]

Counter terrorist laws which are now used to deal with insurgencies and militant organizations due to their connections with terrorist groups, are an absolute necessity for society and it should not be treated as political issues even if the implementation is questioned by human rights forums. Counter terrorist law should be viewed as an efficient response *within the rule of law.* It has been seen that the policy of military response to terrorism is short lived and does not have long term legal effect. To stymie terrorist organizations and weaken the capabilities of terrorist organizations there is an urgent need to strengthen counter terrorist laws. The state machinery has to be empowered by law to prevent recruitment of cadres, raising of funds and other forms of support by propaganda and to scrutinize and freeze funds and assets. Vigil of terrorist organisations and of other such organisations with the potential to become terrorist organisations irrespective of whether terrorist acts are committed by them or not has to be sanctioned by law. Constant surveillance of its leaders, members and supporters is

---

[4] 1978 1 SCR, p. 77

required. A wait-and-see policy would endanger the liberty of society and lead to grave consequences.

Counter terrorist laws should be viewed as safeguards for collective safety and there should have no partisan or parochial considerations. It should be understood that *measured infringement of individual freedom* is not violation of fundamental right. It is the duty of the state to prevent the existence of destructive forces within its territorial jurisdiction which endanger the life and liberty of its citizens and the safety and security of other states.

The Indian government, in the aftermath of the terrorist attacks in Mumbai on 26th November 2008 that lasted till 29th and left 173 people dead, succeeded in getting two Bills — the Unlawful Activities (Prevention) Amendment Bill, 2008 and the other Bill to set up a National Investigation Agency passed in the Parliament. That there has been a need for a special law to deal with the growing terrorist activity in the country and that the existing laws were insufficient to deal with the extraordinary nature of these violent act was not questionable, but how far the new Bills have really addressed the issues and concerns are subject to some deliberation.

Prior to the attacks in Mumbai in November 2008, numerous attacks had occurred in several major cities in India, blasts had taken place in Delhi, in Bangalore, in Jaipur and serial bomb blasts had shaken Ahmedabad. The Indian government after each of these incidents stated that there was no need for special laws and that the existing laws were adequate to tackle the terrorist threats as well as their activities. Emerging from lassitude subsequent to the cunningly executed Mumbai attacks and pummeled into action by the angst of the citizens, the Indian government changed its previous stance and plunged into activity hastily tabling two Bills in the Parliament – an amendment to the Unlawful Activities (Prevention) Act of 1967 and another to set up a National Investigative Agency. It has been evident that the government did indeed have serious reservations to enact any law that contained provisions that could in any manner resemble the draconian measures that had existed in the repealed terrorist legislations: the Prevention of Terrorism Act (POTA) and Terrorist and Disruptive Activities Prevention Act (TADA). The abuse of several provisions of TADA and the gross misuse by some states to stymie opposition to the ruling political forces had been the underlying reason for repealing the extremely harsh

Act. Past experiences under such laws, therefore, underlined the need for caution in enacting laws to counter terrorism. The raison d'être for newer and specific legislation to deal with the growing threat of terrorism and the spate of attacks on civilian targets, certain caveats were necessary. However, on perusal of the Amendment to the Unlawful Activities (Prevention) Amendment Bill 2008, the hope that finally a forceful and comprehensive law has come into effect to counter terrorism in India is followed by a sense of trepidation. No doubt alarmed by the intensity and the ferocity of the Mumbai attacks the political establishments of the country seem to have spoken with one voice against terrorism, yet the haste with which the Bills went through Parliament raises reasonable questions about the abandonment of detailed debates and proper scrutiny on the distinctions and the implications of the two Bills. Any law that comes into force must be within the rule of law; it is therefore, disconcerting to note that the grimmest provision in the amending Bill is the one that sanctions the special courts to presume that the accused is guilty under certain circumstances. For instance, if it is proved that weapons and explosives used in a terror attack are seized from an accused or if his or her fingerprints are found on the site of the attack, then the court "shall presume, unless the contrary is shown, that the accused has committed such offence." The presumption of innocence, the primary bulwark of criminal jurisprudence and the basis of equitable justice placed for the fundamental protection for the person so accused, has been negated. Thus reversing the burden of proof undermines the credibility of the criminal justice system and raises serious questions of the inviolability of individual rights as affirmed by the Constitution.

The increase of the period for detention without charges from 90 to 180 days at the discretion of the court does not conceptually raise the possibility of conviction. The same provision under POTA was found to be abhorrent. If the period of enhanced detention is meant to act as a deterrent for perpetrators of violent terrorist activity it rests on the presumption that such persons have acted without thought to their actions. On the other hand, increased detention period presumes that the interrogating agencies will be able to gather more information and evidence with the passage of time. However, the increase in the period without charges lends itself to overall abuse as has been reported in innumerable instances under the earlier laws

- here, as well as in other in other countries where such laws are or have been in use.

The provisions for bail under the amending Bill have been made rigid; the courts may deny bail when they feel the charges against the accused are prima facie true – thus the entire issue of bail which was within the purview of ordinary criminal law has been made rigorous. The amending Bill to this extent seems to have duplicated the provisions that existed under POTA. Further bail can also be denied if the court feels that the charges against the accused are prima facie true. Besides, foreign nationals who have entered the country illegally and are being accused under this law shall be denied bail. There are some provisions that are not only noteworthy but also desirable. The provision denying bail: "except in very exceptional circumstances and for reasons to be recorded in writing" is significant as it allows indefinite detention of those who perpetrate terror attacks as the one in Mumbai. It must be noted that the schedule of banned outfits can also be expanded under the Act to include all organizations proscribed from time to time by the UN under the UN Prevention and Suppression of Terrorism Order, 2007. Also under the Act the entry or transit through India of proscribed individual can be banned. The Unlawful Activities (Prevention) Amendment Bill has certain other features that have to be deliberated. First, the definition of terrorism has been adopted from the resolution passed by the United Nations which has now been universally accepted. The working definition is broadly the adaptation of the description of the UN panel in 2005: any act "intended to cause death or serious bodily harm to civilians or non-combatants with the purpose of intimidating a population or compelling a government or an international organization to do or abstain from doing any act." The Act extends the definition of a terror act to include attacks on a public functionary and kidnapping or abduction of a person with a view to compelling the state to do or abstain from any act. The definition of a "terrorist act" has been further expanded in the Bill to include terror funding, organization of terrorist camps and recruitment of people for committing terrorist acts. The Bill also provides the power to freeze, seize or attach funds and other financial assets of individuals or entities listed as terrorists and those who are suspected to be involved in terrorism. The investigating officer has been authorized under the Act to seize credit cards and debit cards if he is satisfied that they are being used to fund terror. Widening the ambit thus allows for dealing with the financial and logistic aspects of terrorism and does not confine the term to merely the actual violent acts of terror. These significant changes are acceptable and there is a broadening of the definition to include in the definition of terrorism militancy, insurgency and Naxal extremism. Secondly, a redeeming feature that has been incorporated is the check placed on the power of the police to misuse the law: after the investigation is complete, an agency set up by the Centre or the State Government would decide whether the accused should be prosecuted. The law also provides for an independent judicial review board before the commencement of prosecution for the purpose of scrutiny. The question, however, remains open whether this will really lead to uniform and consistent application of such law by the enforcement authority and consistent application and interpretation of the law throughout the territory. Thirdly, it is stated that it would be punishable for anyone either in India or abroad to directly or indirectly raise or collect funds for commission of terrorist acts. The amendment to Section 17 says that such a person would be punishable with imprisonment for a minimum of five years and maximum of a life term. This should effectively deal with the illegal financial activities but there are terrorist organizations that through legitimate business generate and raise funds for their activities. To what extent such legitimate business activities can be brought under the scope of this provision is to be seen. Fourthly, despite pressures from other parties, the Bill has not acceded to the demand that confessions to the police be admissible as evidence. This has allayed the fears that the enforcement machinery would use all impermissible means to obtain confessions. The organization to be set up under the new Bill, the National Investigation Agency has been given the power to investigate and prosecute offences affecting the sovereignty, security and integrity of India. How far have the investigative agencies been empowered to monitor organizations suspected of or capable of terrorist activities and whether the leaders and other leading members of such organizations will be placed under constant or intermittent surveillance as they already pose threats or are capable of doing so, is also not clear. There is a need to permit admissibility of electronic and other evidence obtained during such surveillances. Whether this can be permitted is also a matter for discussion.

This Bill also envisages the setting up of special courts to fast track the criminal justice delivery system. This is a measure that needed to be taken to set aside interminable delay in the existing system of protracted judicial procedures. The hope is that the counter terrorism measures taken will strengthen the police, the interrogation agencies and the intelligence agencies sufficiently without creating any fear that there will be misuse of powers invested in them. However, certain features that would have complemented the tenability of new laws seem to have been overlooked viz. witness protection, transparency and review procedures and central judicial agency for even application and uniform interpretation of laws. Galvanized laws cannot eliminate terrorism but without a legal system to pre-empt and counter the threat of terrorism and laws to deal with persons who commit terrorist acts or seek to do so and those who instigate, provoke and support such acts the security of society and the nation will be constantly threatened. The Bills have been passed by the Parliament more to appease those who have accused the state of being soft on terrorism and to placate those who have exhibited anger towards the entire political establishment of the country after the Mumbai attacks in Nov 2008 than as a positive step to curbing terrorism and in that perhaps lies the inherent weakness of the legislation which aspires to address the new threats and yet imitates to some extent the earlier ones. There are no minor forms of terrorism and if there has been concrete evidence of earlier abuses of counter terrorism laws, it is the implementation of the law that should be scrutinized and rectified; the need for terrorism laws should not be questioned.

The 173rd Report on "Prevention of Terrorism Bill, 2000" states: "An extraordinary situation calls for an extraordinary law, designed to meet and check such extraordinary situations. It is one thing to say we must create and provide internal structures and safeguards against possible use and abuse of the act and altogether a different thing to say that because a law is liable to be misused, we should not have an act at all." They submitted that Indian Penal Code was not conceived and was not meant for fighting organized crime; that it was designed only to check individual crimes and occasional riots at local level. Organized crime perpetrated by highly trained and armed fanatical elements or mercenaries who are trained financed, armed and supported by hostile foreign countries and agencies had to be fought at a different level than as an ordinary law and order crime. They pointed out that the anti-terrorism laws of the U.K. and U.S.A. were far more stringent than the provisions of the proposed legislation. They submitted that the plea that police was likely to misuse or abuse the provisions of the new legislation could not be a ground for opposing the very legislation to fight terrorism. It is one thing to say, they submitted, that the provisions of the legislation must be so designed as to prevent or minimize its abuse and misuse and quite another thing to say that because of the possibility of abuse, no such law should not be enacted at all. They submitted that one must realize the extraordinary, alarming and dangerous situation in which the country was placed today because of the activities of the hostile neighbour and the fundamentalist Islamic terrorism which have made India their prime target. They pointed out that foreign terrorists now far outnumbered the local militants in Jammu and Kashmir and that thousands more were waiting to enter J&K with a view to carrying on Jihad. In such a situation, any delay or inaction on the part of the country to take measures to fight these elements would be a grave dereliction of duty on the part of the State. The present enactment was one of the means of fighting terrorism and therefore its enactment could not validly be opposed. The experience under TADA suggested that investing powers under the Act in higher authorities was an effective means of preventing its misuse.

Legal systems of countries must not only deliver justice efficiently within the acceptable norms of law and the framework of rule of law but they must also strengthen the legal regimes in their country to assure to their people the existence of a just system. To be effective not only do laws have to exist but they have to applied uniformly to all and the courts must be seen to dispense justice without influence or political pressure. Every country imposes restrictions on freedom of expression to safeguard national security and public order. However, such restrictions are only legitimate if they are clearly and narrowly drawn, if they are applied by bodies which are independent of governmental or political influence, and if there is a sufficient nexus between the proscribed expression and the risk of harm to national security or public order. In addition, the guarantee of freedom of expression means that sanctions for breach of these should be by the rule of law and not arbitrary. The state should also ensure that it is economically possible for all to approach the courts for redress and that all the structures are in place to permit a person to approach the courts easily and without fear. A safe and secure environment should be created for the persons approaching court for fear of life or liberty will defeat the purpose of the judicial system.

Conclusion

It is the duty of a State to protect its territorial integrity and ensure the safety and security of its citizens, creating and assuring conditions for growth and prosperity. Therefore, the state is constrained to use military force to fight groups and organizations which endanger national interests or aim at secession. This results in a paradoxical situation wherein, on the one hand, the State uses force against those acting against its interests; and on the other, has to abide by national and international laws. However, the armed secessionist groups, terrorist organizations or militant forces are under no compulsion or obligation to adopt such norms. The four states analyzed in this paper are placed in almost similar situations but their responses are influenced by their governing systems viz. democracy, monarchy and military dictatorship. It is therefore interesting to see the legal measures adopted by the four states for their military forces. While India, as a democracy, has used maximum restraint; Myanmar has not placed such pressures upon itself. Nepal, whose army was loyal to the King, did not have specific laws enacted to meet the Maoist challenge. Sri Lanka continues to be critiqued for human rights excesses by its army during its fight against the LTTE. The use of AFSPA in India, despite the enabling clauses which were enacted to limit excesses by the military, is criticized for its extended application.

The conclusion on the issue of legal safeguards against such laws is clear enough. Internal conflicts will continue to be dealt with military force. Application of military force cannot be with the objective of the destruction or elimination of anti-state elements. The use of military force needs essentially to be aimed for obtaining conditions in which a negotiated resolution of the conflict can take place. Legal restrictions for conducting military operations and safeguards for the protection citizens of the country from excesses have to be ensured. Internal conflicts should be dealt within this major policy cluster.

Internal Conflicts: Linkages and Consequences for Maritime and Littoral Security in South Asia

W.Lawrence S.Prabhakar

Internal conflicts in Peninsular South Asia and its adjoining regions have been the primary determinant of social, political, civic and economic instability. The region is essentially post-colonial and has experienced a wide spectrum of border and boundary changes and the resultant cartographic changes that has led to enduring internal conflict with external inputs. The scope of internal conflicts has been spilling from external sources and has been 'exported' to external points in the region through porous borders and boundaries. Conflict in this region is superimposed on primordial identities of ethnic, communal, lingual and sub-regional dimensions and it has been fanned by various social, political and communal forces. Studying and analyzing the various internal conflicts in South Asia from a hinterland perspective yields varied results and inferences with regard to their causal and consequential impacts. One of the novel dimensions of examining internal conflicts is to use the maritime contours of the region and analyse as to how maritime connectivity and maritime security of the coastal regions could shape and influence the discourse of aggravation of conflicts.

Two propositions are thus valid for consideration with regard to the idea of how maritime and coastal entities feed and influence conflict in the hinterland: One, in the age of maritime connectivity, globalization and trade, the inflow of maritime commerce and outflow could carry various contents of human, material and arms are clandestinely transmitted across maritime domains and porous coastal regions. The clandestine transmissions are endeavored and catalyzed by the various agencies of internal conflicts whose entrepreneurship is sustained by various means. Two, coastal regions are regarded to be "poorly secured" in view of the varying levels of poverty and relative deprivation of the communities and the denial of development. Given the relative neglect of the coastal regions and the communities and the lax security evident, the agencies and entrepreneurs of conflicts use these regions to access, store and transmit the illegal and the clandestine cargo of small arms and light weapons that fuel the dynamics of internal conflicts in the region.

Thus the linkages between internal conflicts and maritime and littoral (coastal) security are an interesting dimension to study while analyzing the 'structure of internal conflicts' in any regional setting. The paper endeavours to analyse: a) South Asia's internal security challenges and the maritime-littoral nexus 'securitizing' the persistent challenges and perils in the Maritime-littorals and the Exclusive Economic Zone, the implications of the dense sea-lanes of communication running adjacent to the region's maritime-littorals; the illegal infiltration in to the region's littoral-maritime space and in the vast EEZ; the conflation between organized crime in the hinterland with terror groups and the maritime based groups; b) the impact of globalization and maritime security and assess their impact on coastal communities that are stakeholders of security in the domain; c) Assess the various challenges that the maritime security agencies contend and responses generated by them in countering the challenges; d) Map the consequences and responses of the stakeholders in addressing this nexus.

Theoretical significance

Internal Conflicts, littorals (coastal) and the influence of the maritime domain has vital implications to the generic study of conflict. The conventional understanding of conflict and security in the maritime and littoral domains always considered the inter-state factors of maritime borders and boundaries. In its essence, this was viewed as traditional and symmetric conflict since the sanctity of the state's borders and boundaries were threatened. The implications of hostile alien activities in a country are Exclusive Economic Zone and the use of naval and coast guard forces to prevent such adversarial activities and enforce order and tranquility in the region. Essentially, all foreign adversarial activities were viewed as hostile to the state and their impact related only to the extent of the maritime and coastal regions. But the pervasiveness of this threat has expanded in the form of asymmetric conflict that has resulted in the adoption of terrorism and insurgency using the maritime domain to launch attacks on the land and facilitating the clandestine process of smuggling of human, narcotics and arms as auxiliary means that catalysis the conflicts. In its analytical framework, the nature of conflicts could be evident from the causal factor of: a) Low Intensity Maritime Operations and the resultant outcome; b) Chaos in the Littorals.

Low Intensity Maritime Operations could be defined as the sum total of all asymmetric conflicts and operations by the violent non-state actors. Low Intensity Maritime Operations are non-linear styles of operations that account for the waging of protracted conflict by maritime terrorists, pirates and other groups using the maritime medium to attack the state and its infrastructure either at sea or using the sea to conduct asymmetric attacks on the land. Violent non-state actors are terrorist groups and insurgents/ militants are now challenging national security forces. These groups have modified their strategy from low intensity conventional terrorism to total destruction. The violent non-state actors have their strengths focused on the exploitation of cheap, improvised and easy to obtain weapons to carry out destruction/damage to high value military targets in a mass spectacular way. These groups also seek to target naval ships and establishments and other targets in the coastal areas.

Violent asymmetric actors would use man-portable missiles, explosive-laden boats, and improvised submersibles with trained divers capable of planting mines and explosives on ships. Besides the intensity of clandestine activities like smuggling, poaching, gun-running along the coast and distant island territories presents a stealthy environment in which security forces with their traditional training and focus find it hugely challenging. Contemporary naval doctrines and operations are focused on Low Intensity Maritime Operations with emphasis on large numbers of low value patrol ships for reconnaissance surveillance and interception/interdiction of the asymmetric forces and countering threats covering a wide spectrum of threats. Navies are thus re-balancing in terms of their platforms that are now tuned for the entire spectrum from high intensity warfare to asymmetric warfare.

Low Intensity Maritime Operations suggests application of force, in the maritime domain, against actors that engage in maritime terrorism, piracy, gun-running, drug smuggling, illegal fishing, poaching, marine pollution and criminal activities at sea that have the potential to disrupt order at sea. The application of Low Intensity Maritime Operations involves use of force to an extent that it is short of conventional war against targets at sea. Violent non-state actors are compensating the absence of technological superiority over a stronger military asymmetric strategies and options to challenge maritime forces and inflict unacceptable costs.

The resultant outcome of the hostile operations in the littorals has resulted in the gradual corrosion of the coastal areas with unending conflicts and collapse of order in the coastal areas. In the age of globalization and the post-globalization phases of economic development and growth, the "maritime-littoral" have emerged to be hubs of development and transportation linking the seas with the hinterland. In its conceptual definition, the "maritime" refers to the "brown waters" or "green waters" from the coastal shelf. The "littoral" refers to the coastal strip of land 100 km from the shore into the hinterland that's hosts 60 percent of world's population and the next 350km hosts the world's 75 percent of the world's population; cities with population exceeding 1 million are all littoral cities and 50 percent of global cities with populations exceeding 500,000 are all littoral cities (ports).

The global maritime supply chains are the "principal drivers" of the maritime-based economic interdependence, while they constitute the maritime nations access to sea and trade are all located in the coastal regions; the maritime domain also has emerged as an arena of opportunity for various acts of violence at sea and on shore. In its physical and terrain geography the "littoral" connotes a continuum of the territorial maritime boundary and its seamless interface with the sea. In its social demographic salience, the littoral denotes the matrices of how the density of human demographics and the maritime-territorial geography are configured.

In its political and governance salience, the littoral is the fulcrum of how governance, maritime domain awareness and the operations of the agencies converge determining the security calculus and the development index of the region. Therefore the polyhedral importance of the littorals cannot be underestimated.

Maritime Regional Security Complex of South Asia

South Asia sits astride the Indian Ocean flanked by the Arabian Sea and Bay of Bengal. The maritime contiguity of the region is with West Asia, East Africa to the west and with Southeast Asia to the east. The Maritime Regional Security Complex of South Asia envisages the geographical and the political interdependence of the region with the adjoining regions. The concept of regional security complexes covers how security is clustered in geographically shaped regions[1]. The concepts of "amity/enmity" is affected by things such as ideology, territory, ethnic line and historical precedent, and it leads to what is called a "security complex" which is a "group of states whose primary security concerns link together sufficiently closely that their national securities cannot realistically be considered apart from one another". The Security Complex Framework could be conceptualized and applied to a multitude of international environments, including the post cold war manifestation of the same[2]. The Regional Security Complex Theory provides the basis for the analysis of the different levels of securitization in current international affairs. The maritime dimension of the Regional Security Complex provides the geographical and the conflict interdependence of the South Asian region with that of West Asia and Southeast Asia. Various issues of non-traditional security in its human and non-human factors affect the maritime security complex of South Asia. The analysis of the maritime regional security complex enables to assess the sources and roots of the various non-traditional challenges and threats and how internal conflicts are catalyzed by the challenges that come from the adjoining regions and through the maritime domain. Four types of non-traditional challenges in the maritime domain critically impacts on South Asia: i) Piracy and Maritime terrorism; ii) Human trafficking on the high seas; iii) Maritime Trafficking of small arms and light weapons and iv) Trafficking of narcotics.

The sources of these challenges and threats are located within South Asia and they feed into the adjoining regions and are also reinforced by the reverse flow of these challenges and threats from West Asia and Southeast

---

[1] Barry Buzan, People, States and Fear: An Agenda for International Security Studies in the post Cold War Era, ECPR Classic Series, 1991, p 187.

[2] Barry Buzan and Ole Waever, Regions and Power: The Structure of International Security, (Cambridge; Cambridge University Press, 2002), p 14

Asia. While the traditional lanes of sea provide for the traditional shipping and sea lanes of communication, there are parallel networks of sea lanes that are used by pirates, smugglers and they use the nodes of South Asia's coastal cities to perpetuate violence and terror on the land and the sea. Karachi, Mumbai, Jaffna, Chittagong, Maldives have all been sources and recipients of the four types of maritime based non-traditional challenges and threats.

The following are brief profiles of Karachi in Pakistan, Maldives in the Indian Ocean, Mumbai in India, Sri Lanka and Chittagong in Bangladesh that portray how events on the land and the sea and the successful exploitation of the maritime medium has resulted in the perpetuation of various crimes and terror activities that emanate from the land and are sustained in the sea.

Karachi, Pakistan

Karachi in Pakistan is the primary gateway of Pakistan to the sea. It enjoys the reputation of being the major port city for the port call for shipping from West Asia and South Asia. Karachi also enjoys a strategic position on the air route from west to east featuring growing volumes of traffic. Mohammed Ali Jinnah stressed that given the strategic location of Karachi, the eyes of the world were constantly on the way. To Jinnah, Karachi presented itself as the ambassador of the newly independent country. But the 1980s have been the decade of the infamy that Karachi has emerged as a paradise for terrorists, gunrunners, drug smugglers and now terrorists. Karachi's complex social and ethic fabric had always catalyzed ethnic strife, as it emerged as the hub to innumerable crime syndicates with the burgeoning terror connections. From a small fishing village, the city of Karachi has come a long way to be identified as the terror capital of Pakistan.[3]

Karachi is home to a very large number of drug cartels and syndicates. Drugs, essentially hashish, reach Karachi from Balochistan and the North Western Frontier Provinces (NWFP) via Khuzdar, Jacobabad and Dera Ghazi.[4] Al Qaeda and its associated organizations are known to use this route for smuggling. On reaching Karachi, part of the consignment is shipped

---

[3] Wilson John, *Karachi: A Terror Capital in the Making* (New Delhi: Rupa, 2003), p.1.
[4] ibid

out by the air route while bulk consignment are loaded onboard ships, dhows and smaller boats and transported through the port. The drugs trade is a key source of finance in al Qaeda's operations. One of the primary reasons of the deployment of the Combined Task Forces 150,151 has been for the maritime surveillance and reconnaissance of the region, monitoring the traffic that radiates from the region into the Arabian Sea.

In an incident that involved the vessel *Sara*, a crew of seven Romanians and 15 Pakistanis was detained in Italy. Investigation revealed that identification documents of the 15 persons were false. They were in possession of phone numbers of suspected terrorists and arms merchants, addresses of individuals connected with the Al Qaeda terror network, $30,000 in cash and air tickets from Casablanca to Karachi. Similarly, the *Twilling* was detained on February 19, 2002 at Trieste with 8 Al Qaeda operatives posing as Pakistani crewmen.[5] Reportedly, some 150 men belonging to Taliban and *al-Qaeda* from Afghanistan had entered Bangladesh in December 2001 through Chittagong.[6] These arrived by *M V Mecca* that was hired at Karachi to facilitate escape of Ayman al –Zawahari. Karachi has been an important port of clandestine transshipment operations of men and material that involved the al-Qaeda along with Pakistanis.

Al Qaeda operatives posing as seamen are flown in from Karachi, they embark vessels to destinations to support cells, collect/disburse/ disseminate cash, addresses, instructions and identity papers.[7] The strategy involves using small, weather beaten, and rusty cargo vessels that change names and flag at sea. Prior to arriving at a port, the vessel rendezvous with another ship offload the operatives and they masquerade as stowaway/ distressed immigrants.

Karachi had been the dire city that had involved in the killings of foreigners. Daniel Pearl, Wall Street Journal reporter was killed in Karachi

---

[5] *Cristi. Sara* and *Twillinger* are sister ships of the *Karine-A* that was captured by the Israeli navy while carrying 50 tons of arms and ammunition from Iran for the Palestine Authority.

[6] Alex Perry " Bangladesh: Al-Qaeda's New Safe Haven?" available online at <http://www.hvk.org/articles/1002/128.html.31990.VINCLUDEFIX>

[7] Vijay Sakhuja , "Who steers al Qaeda's Fleet" #975, 4 March 200 3 available online at http://www.ipcs.org/article/terrorism/who-steers-al-qaedas-fleet-975.html

while researching a story on Pakistani militants.[8] The videotape confirming his death was delivered to US officials in February 2002. In May 2002, 14 persons including 11 French naval engineers were killed and 23 others including 10 Frenchmen and Pakistanis were injured when an unidentified man blew himself up with his car after ramming it into a 46-seater Pakistan Navy bus outside the Karachi Sheraton Hotel.[9] In June 2002, a suicide bomber blew up a truck at the US consulate in Karachi, killing 14 Pakistanis.[10] These reflect the consequence of accumulated small arms and light weapons that had fuelled the ongoing sectarian strife in Karachi.

In 2011, the Pakistani naval base in PNS Mehran was attacked by the heavily armed militants of the Taliban. In a coordinated assault, the insurgents succeeded in destroying two of the just three P-3 series Orion anti-submarine and maritime surveillance aircrafts that Pakistan had acquired from the United States. These have been the consequence of the sustained inflow of small and light arms in and out of Karachi that had fuelled the ongoing conflict between the militants and the Pakistani armed forces. Karachi has thus seen terrorism and sectarian ethnic strife in many faces. The scourge remains a continuing plague and there is very little hope it will end through the process of law enforcement. Despite assurances by the Pakistan President, Karachi continues to remain the terror capital of South Asia. Karachi had served as the hub that had shipped arms as well as RDX explosives that led to the various bomb blasts in Mumbai in 1983. It had also played host to the underworld don Dawood Ibrahim who was key in the various terrorist assaults in Mumbai in 1983 and the 2008 attacks. Dawood Ibrahim's activities had used the Karachi underworld for his various nefarious activities that included drugs and arms and explosives smuggling into India; money laundering activities that aided terror activities and his base of operations in Karachi. Karachi as a port has emerged to be a vital maritime

---

[8] Emily Pennink, "Al Qaida - A Campaign of Terror", November 21, 2003 available online at <http://www.scotman.com>

[9] "11 French Engineers Among 14 Killed in Karachi Suicide Attack" available online at < http://www.karachipage.com/news/May_02/050902.html>

[10] See Emily Pennink, n.8.

hub that has its maritime trade and economic linkages along with its numerous groups that are headquartered in the city as a means to export terror and violence through the export of small arms and light weapons. On the other, the clandestine activities of money laundering and drugs have enriched the various sectarian groups that sustain the insurgency in Afghanistan as well export them into Mumbai, targeting India's economic infrastructure.

Maldives

Maldives in its historic existence had always been conservative and largely insulated from direct foreign domination despite its strategic location in the Indian Ocean astride the sea route from the Persian Gulf towards the port of Malacca. The islanders have been quite independent and were able to repulse attempts by the Portuguese colonialists and the Malabar potentates and others to control their atoll.

In November 1988, a week before President Gayoom was to assume his third term in office, two Colombo-based dissident businessmen from the Maldives, along with about 80 Tamil mercenaries belonging to the left-wing People's Liberation Organisation of Tamil Eelam (PLOTE), attempted to overthrow the Gayoom regime.[11] The President sought urgent assistance from Colombo and New Delhi. Sri Lanka's preparations to fly 150 elite force had to be called off after it was learnt that Indian forces were already on their way to Male. Some 1600 Indian commandos reached Male by air and sea and ended the coup. The mercenaries were captured while fleeing with hostages.[12] The threat of mercenaries has plagued the Maldivian security system ever since. It is evident that the small island territories are particularly vulnerable to aggression by mercenaries, terrorists and even

---

[11] Ravinatha Aryasinha, " Maldives, Sri Lanka and the India Factor", available online at <http://www.himalmag.com/97mar/cov-mal.htm.>

[12] 20 were killed in the coup attempt, and 68, including four Maldivians, were captured. Of them, 16, the Maldivians included, received death sentences, which were later commuted to life imprisonment. Prime Minister Rajiv Gandhi told the Indian Parliament that he saw the event as having "provided an opportunity for India to assist a friendly country and frustrate an attempt to overthrow a democratically elected government." While the big powers, including the United States, endorsed India's intervention, the world media interpreted the action as indicative of "the scale of its ambitions in South Asia", as *Time* magazine observed, a confirmation of India's growing role as a regional superpower cum policeman.

pirates. The arms dealers and the mercenaries could still occupy some of the islands for some time, complete their transactions and then move on. The farther most islands hold these kinds of threat scenario unabated.

Maldives is a nation of 270,000 Sunni Muslims and the political class is quite liberal in its outlook.[13] Despite the visits of an increasing number of Maldives students to Pakistan madrasas for studying Islam, there is, as yet, no evidence of 'sprouting of religious fundamentalism in the country'. Although there is no indication of any 'radicalisation of the Maldives youth in a direction favourable to pan-Islamist organisations such as Al Qaeda, the Jemaah Islamiah of South East Asia and the various jihadi terrorist organisations of Pakistan',[14] there exists a possibility of these groups attempting to influence events in Maldives. Importantly, these groups have maritime capability that has been demonstrated in Singapore and in Bali.[15]

India and Maldives have been cooperating to ensure a tranquil maritime environment and to keep the seas in their sphere of influence free from pirates, interlopers and drug runners. A joint surveillance programme to monitor fishing vessels has been initiated between the two countries enhancing cooperation with the Coast Guards so that they increasingly exchange information on the movement of suspicious vessels". Similar continuous surveillance is also sustained in the context of the merchant ships increasing their distance from Somalia in search of 'safer' transport routes and the pirates and they are plying between India and Maldives.

Mumbai, India

Mumbai has long served as a gateway for India to ideas, influence, economic development and trade. It has served as the maritime capital as also the

---

[13] B Raman, 'Violence in Maldives', Paper No 798, at < http://www.saag.com>, n.2. President Gayoom was educated in the Al Azhar University of Cairo and is viewed as politically liberal and modern in his outlook.

[14] B. Raman, "Maldives Unrest: Security Implications for India ", Paper No.1088, South Asia Analysis Group at http://www.saag.com

[15] The Singapore authorities arrested 15 suspected Islamic militants with links to Al-Qaeda and planning to blow up U.S. naval vessels at Singapore. The attack was to be carried against ships transiting the shallow waters by ramming a small vessel packed with explosives. The 'kill zone' was meticulously established at a point where the channel was the narrowest and the fast approaching boat would leave no sea room for the target to avoid collision with the suicide boat.

financial capital. Interestingly, it continues to be the primary hub of financial activity, stock trading, entertainment industry, and a conduit for drug running, gold and silver smuggling and is home to underworld mafia. It has thus emerged as a playground of several criminal gangs[16] and their continuing warfare for dominance.

The interesting feature of these gangs is that a majority is drawn from a poor economic background and was propelled into the world of crime due to economic difficulties. They hailed from outside Mumbai and approximately 30 per cent came from outside the State of Maharashtra and the gangs are not based on region or religion.[17] As regards the organisation structure, there is evidence of a loose confederation of gangsters. Smaller gang may merge into a bigger gang but are left free to engage in any activities of choice so long as it does not clash with the interests of the main gang.

Given the Indian domestic demand for gold, smuggling in precious metals has been a favoured activity by main gangs. In 1987, gold occupied the top position amongst smuggled items, followed by narcotics, electronic watches and silver. However, in 1995, narcotics occupied the number one position followed by gold, electronics, foreign currency and synthetic fabrics.[18] This is so because South East Asia along with South West Asia are the two top opium and heroin producing regions in the world and India, by virtue of its geographic location, is surrounded by the 'Golden Triangle' and the 'Golden Crescent'. India has thus emerged as an important transit route for despatch overseas. Besides, drug trade has flourished in India both as part of legal produce as also a final destination.

Mumbai has also served as an unloading destination for small arms and explosives. In the nineteen seventies and early eighties, Mumbai gangsters primarily used knives and daggers. However, the scene completely changed with the entry of sophisticated weaponry, and currently the underworld is

---

[16] The Dawood Ibrahim Gang, Arun Gawli Gang, Amar Naik Gang, Chota Rajan Gang. For more details see Sumita Sarkar & Arvind Tiwari "Combating Organised Crime :A Case Study of Mumbai City", *Faultlines*, Volume No 12, pp.,143-146.

[17] Ibid., pp.147-148.

[18] Ibid., pp.147-148.

reported to be using the AK series of assault rifles, carbines, 9mm pistols, hand grenades and machine guns, among other weapons.[19] Explosives in large quantity were smuggled to the coast near Bombay and were used in the bomb blasts in Bombay in March 1993. Bombay police recovered RDX from the Vasai coast, the Thane Creek and Mumbai. These had reached there from across the Arabian Sea.

The Indian Film industry is a big money spinner. Headquartered in Mumbai, it is often referred to as *Bollywood*, India's Hollywood. It provides direct employment to approximately 500,000 people and indirect employment to nearly another one million with an annual turnover (bulk transactions takes place in black money) of approximately Rs. 12.50 billion. The underworld has strong business links and interests that shape the financial operations of the industry. Many film artists and other film personalities are known to keep direct contacts with the underworld. This has led to coercion, threats and even physical assault, in which many have died. Similarly, the hotel industry has links and several hotel owners have been coerced to meet the demands of the underworld mafia.

The Mumbai attacks of 2008 represent the use of the maritime medium to launch an attack on the littoral and catalyze the conflict into the hinterland. The Mumbai attacks of November 2008 represent a formidable littoral assault breaching all traditional defenses of India's littoral—even the most powerful regional navy. The terrorists with obvious special operations forces training had mounted a good tactical littoral offensive using *crafts of opportunity* (coop) to reach Mumbai having transferred from their mother vessel to effect complete stealth and surprise. Mumbai for long had been at the recipient point of the clandestine activities of various crime syndicates that have used the external linkages in the sea-smuggling of narcotics, small arms, explosives to be used in the various criminal and insurgent activities in the littorals and the hinterland. The littorals are the staging points for the long chain of links in the smuggling process. The possible conflation between the sustained presence of the crime syndicates and the terror groups provided the enablement of this successful attack with the possible concealment and

---

[19] Ibid.,p.154. The serial bomb blast case in Mumbai in 1993 led to the recovery of: RDX (3.5 tons), Hand grenades (Austria) Argies(459), AK 56 (63), 9mm Pistols (12) Detonators (1150) and Ammunition (49,000).

eventual escape of the other members of the group. Thus Mumbai represents a mix of the underworld, the crime syndicates, the money laundering, the arms and drug smuggling networks as primary points that catalyze internal conflict and use the conduit of the sea for access into the littoral.

Sri Lanka

Ethnic violence in Sri Lanka is now more than two decades old. It has been interspersed with political assassinations, talks on settlement of the dispute, ceasefire and peace initiatives and naval battles between the Sri Lankan Navy and the LTTE. With the end of the war in 2009, the analysis of the conflict reveals a very substantial evidence of how the maritime domain influenced and aided the conflict. Interestingly, what distinguishes the LTTE from the other separatist groups is its ability to exploit the sea to further its cause. It is perhaps for the first time that a non-state actor is conducting maritime operations at such a large scale and has been able to execute a classical sea control in waters off Jaffna in the north east of Sri Lanka. The LTTE was the true non-state actor with state capabilities and was able to own and operate a fleet of deep sea going ships that have facilitated logistic support by way of regular supply of arms, ammunition and other materials. Several reports suggest the conflation between piracy and terrorism in the case of the LTTE by which pirates have been "hired" for raising a sea-based wing of the Al Shabab along the lines of the erstwhile LTTE Sea Tigers. The erstwhile LTTE had an exceptionally well established network for gun running and arms transfer at sea. Its network was vast, extending all the way to Japan. Their arms route normally used to originate in Cambodia; cargo was loaded into small fishing trawlers from the port of Ranong in southern Thailand. Later these arms were transferred to bigger ships, which then transport the consignment to Sri Lanka.

In the post-conflict period, the LTTE has been quite successful in human smuggling operations from Sri Lanka into other havens in countries in Southeast Asia and Australia using the maritime medium. They have continued to use various vessels for this purpose and have been quite successful in their endeavours. Although the ethnic war in the island is over, yet the post-conflict consequences continue to persist with the use of the maritime medium as a means of movement of refugees in the sea.

Chittagong, Bangladesh

Chittagong in Bangladesh is yet another city that has witnessed the transit of militants in the country. Bangladesh has attracted attention due to the alleged presence of Islamic militant groups and the specter of 'militant Islamisation'. Media reports have been widespread with strong indications of Bangladesh as a "hotbed of radical Islam". Reportedly, some 150 men belonging to Taliban and *al-Qaeda* from Afghanistan had entered Bangladesh through Chittagong.[20]

The *Harkat-ul-Jihad-al-Islami* (HuJI) is a Bangladeshi group with a force of about 2000 men of Bangladeshi origin and is closely linked with the *al Qaeda*. HuJI came into existence in 1992 and is believed to be an offshoot of a Pakistani group financially and ideologically supported by bin Laden. Western intelligence officials believe that one Fazlul Rahman of the HUJI signed Al-Qaeda's declaration of holy war on the US on behalf of the *Jihad Movement in Bangladesh*. Reports also suggest that several young Muslim radicals from Malaysia and Indonesia are present in Cox's Bazar and Chittagong and maintain contacts with local Muslim groups. The *madrassas* serve as meeting grounds for exporting terrorism. The presence of *al Qaeda* and now of *Jemaah Islamiah*, a Southeast Asian Islamic militant group, trained in sea-borne guerrilla tactics has fueled fears that Bangladesh could become a haven for militants of all nations.

Amra Sobai Hobo Taliban, Bangla Hobe Afghanistan (We would all be Taliban, and Bangladesh would be Afghanistan).[21] This is a HuJI slogan. It has been argued that what Afghanistan was a couple of years ago, Bangladesh could become to the rest of world. There is a transformation of the traditional nationalism to 'an extremist Islamist nationalism' in Bangladesh and is bound to impact on the regional countries.

Intelligence sources believe that more than two-dozen notorious local underworld gangs are engaged in gunrunning in the port city of Chittagong.

---

[20] Alex Perry " Bangladesh: Al-Qaeda's New Safe Haven?" available online at <http://www.hvk.org/articles/1002/128.html.31990.VINCLUDEFIX>

[21] Praveen Kumar, "Bangladesh: Turning into another Afghanistan?", Article no. 1371, April 17 , 2004, available online at http://www.ipcs.org/article/terrorism/bangladesh-turning-into-another-afghanistan-1371.html

The major groups are: *BDR Selim, Habib Khan, Sunil Dey, Chandan Biswas, Abdul Kuddus* alias *Kana Kuddus, Mafizur Rahman Dulu, Shafiqul Islam Shafiq, Morshed Khan and Iqbal.* They possess over 15,000 illegal arms, including AK-47, AK-56, G-3, M-16 rifles and large stocks of ammunition. Besides, there are several arms manufacturing workshops. Chittagong and Cox's Bazar are a major transit point for arms smuggling.[22] The Bangladesh navy seized 123 foreign made firearms and 146 round of ammunition from the three off shore islands, Sandwip, Moheshkhali and Kutubdia. They also recovered huge number of local made firearms and unearthed 30 local arms manufacturing workshops from Moheshkhali and Kutubdia.

In April 2, 2004, following a tip-off, nine truckloads of arms and ammunition were seized from the port of Chittagong.[23] Reportedly, the haul comprised of two consignments; one consignment originated from the port of Hong Kong and was essentially of Chinese origin and the second was loaded at Singapore and consisted of weapons of both Israeli and US manufacture[24]. The shipment orignated in Hong Kong and was then transported through the Strait of Malacca to be transhipped in the Bay of Bengal to two trawlers, *Kazaddan* and *Amanat*, which ferried the weaponry to a jetty in the port of Chittagong. According to JIR's sources, the shipment involved two key insurgent movements from India's northeast - the United Liberation Front of Assam (ULFA) and the Isak-Muivah faction of the National Socialist Council of Nagaland (NSCN-IM), which since 1997 has been in protracted peace talks with the Indian government, held mostly in Bangkok.

The sea forms the main route for illegal arms coming from various countries. The land borders also provide alternative routes. The LTTE gun

---

[22] See "Terrorists get weapons from the underworld" available online at http://www.matamat.com/fullstory.php?gd=19&cd=2003-09-09

[23] Praveen Kumar,n.22. No reliable list of the seized weapons has yet to be made public. However, the shipment - altogether worth an estimated US$4.5m-$7m - is known to have included around 2,000 automatic and semi-automatic weapons, among them 1,290 Type 56-1/Type 56-2 Kalashnikov-type assault rifles; 150 T-69 rocket propelled grenade (RPG) launchers; quantities of 40mm RPG ammunition; 25,000 hand-grenades; and 1.8m rounds of small-arms ammunition.

[24] Anthony Davis "New Details Emerge on Bangladesh Arms Haul" Jane's Intelligenec Review, September 2004

trade route passes through the Bay of Bengal and Andaman Sea. Arms originating from Cambodia are loaded onto small fishing trawlers in the southern Thai port of Ranong. This was shared between the LTTE and the Bangladeshi groups. These vessels then transfer the consignment to larger vessels for onward passage to Sri Lanka, while small boats transported the consignments to Cox Bazar in Bangladesh. Several vessels engaged in gun running have been captured in the region. In 1996, the Bangladesh authorities seized 600 rifles from a fishing trawler originating in Thailand.[25] In 1997, the Royal Thai Navy seized an arms shipment for the *People's Liberation Army* (Manipur) following a chase in the Andaman Sea off the port of Ranong.

An analysis of incidents over the last eight years in Bangladesh show that at least 75 percent of the incidents were carried out in harbour/ port areas. Piracy is rampant in its seaports and has hit trade since mariners/ ships are reluctant to use Chittagong and Mongla ports. This has forced foreign shipping companies to impose additional charges for discharging cargo in these ports resulting in higher costs for export and import of goods. These ports have been labeled 'vulnerable and insecure' by foreign ships. The Bangladesh authorities are conscious of this tarnished image of their ports but have not made any significant progress in containing this problem.

Some of the most serious pirate attacks have taken place in the territorial waters of Bangladesh. In one incident pirates attacked and killed 14 fishermen; the trawler carrying fish worth US $ 50,000 was hijacked. The survivors reported that the pirates were carrying automatic weapons and ordered the crew to jump overboard. In another incident, pirates attacked a fishing vessel off the coast of Pattakhali and threw 13-crew members overboard. More recently, Bangladesh Police found the bodies of 16 fishermen stuffed in the ice chamber of their boat F.B Kausara. Fish and fishing equipment had been stolen from the boat and the pirates had locked the men in the fish ice chamber and they had died of severe cold and suffocation.

Bangladesh shares a riverine border with India. This makes transborder piracy easier. The hostages are often sent away with instructions to the

---

[25] Muhammad Shahedul Anam Khan, ' Linkage Between Arms Trafficking and the Drug Trade in South Asia' , in *Small Arms Control Old Weapons, New Issues*, Jayanth Dhanapala,(Vermont; Ashgate Publishing Ltd, 1999), pp. 266-267.

families of others to arrange for ransom. The money-prisoners swap usually takes place on the Indian side at Canning, Dakghat or Jharkahali. Bangladesh ratified the 1988 UNCLOS III, but has yet to ratify the 1988 Rome Convention aimed at curbing piracy and armed robbery at sea. Bangladesh had no agreement with India, its maritime neighbour, on anti piracy patrols. It has now been agreed that India and Bangladesh would explore the possibility of conducting joint exercises between their two navies in the near future.

The above profiles reveal that the countries in South Asia are exposed to inter-regional and trans-regional impacts of the use of the maritime medium to smuggle in arms, explosives, trafficking of humans and other contraband that impacts on the land conflicts directly and indirectly. Piracy, arms smuggling are among the dominant sources of insecurity that are evident in the South Asian region, besides the non-resolution of the border and boundary disputes within South Asian countries result in the persistence of the insecurity. In the context of the prevalent insecurities, it is essential to view and analyse how the maritime/coastal security measures could be meaningfully implemented in the region and what measures could find their relevance.

The Context of internal conflicts and maritime / coastal security in South Asia

In the age of globalization and the post-globalization phases of economic development and growth, the "maritime-littoral" have emerged to be hubs of development and transportation linking the seas with the hinterland. In its conceptual definition, the "maritime" refers to the "brown waters" or "green waters" from the coastal shelf. The "littoral" refers to the coastal strip of land 100 km from the shore into the hinterland that's hosts 60 percent of world's population and the next 350km hosts the world's 75 percent of the world's population; cities with population exceeding 1 million are all littoral cities and 50 percent of global cities with populations exceeding 500,000 are all littoral cities (ports)[26] . The global maritime supply chains

---

[26] Vijay Sakhuja, " Asymmetric Warfare and Low Intensity Maritime Operations:Challenges for the Indian Navy", *ORF Occasional Paper* #5 2006 available online at http://www.observerindia.com/cms/export/orfonline/modules/occasionalpaper/attachments/op060831_1163397491234.pdf

are the "principal drivers" of the maritime-based economic interdependence, while they constitute the maritime nations access to sea and trade; the maritime domain also has emerged as an arena of opportunity for various acts of violence at sea and on shore[27].

In its physical and terrain geography the "littoral" connotes a continuum of the territorial maritime boundary and its seamless interface with the sea;

In its social demographic salience, the littoral denotes the matrices of how the density of human demographics and the maritime-territorial geography are configured;

In its political and governance salience, the littoral is the fulcrum of how governance, maritime domain awareness and the operations of the agencies converge determining the security calculus and the development index of the region. Therefore the polyhedral importance of the littorals cannot be underestimated.

Globalization has spawned the growth of ports, the growth of on-shore and offshore "critical maritime infrastructure" that are critical links to the economy of the state constituting vital pillars of the nation's economy and growth. It is these critical assets that are now being targeted by a variety of shore-based non-state actors from within the state and external to the state by a host of Low Intensity Maritime Operation (LIMO) of asymmetric non-state actors viz Pirates, Terrorist Groups and other groups with maritime attack capabilities. Securing the sea and its expanses is a formidable task as the capabilities are disproportionate to the tasks at hand.

The challenges evident in the maritime-littoral domain are not easily explained due to several complex factors that impact on them. It prompted a new definition termed "Chaos in the Littorals" that is defined by the following factors:

Porous territory is characteristic of the littorals in the developing world. The span of territory is long and thickly populated by the sea-faring communities. The stretch of the territory is usually porous owing to the easy

---

[27] Vijay Sakhuja, " Securing India's Littorals", *Journal of Defence Studies,* Vol.3 No.2 April 2009

access to shore by various users of the sea and the freedom of using the coastal waters. The task of securing this territory usually lies with the local communities who have a better territorial and domain awareness[28]. However with the onset of the variety of asymmetric challenges and threats, the porous scope of this territory is being exploited by various actors who have clandestine social and economic agenda of subversion.

Decreasing effect of governance is a concomitant consequence to the porous nature of territory. Until the impact of maritime asymmetric conflicts, the need for constant surveillance and reconnaissance was unknown as the seas were a commonwealth for all its users; benign and malafide. Governance of the maritime-littorals was more informal and voluntary since the scope of threat was more of crime conflation than the orchestrated dimensions of maritime terrorism, but with the onset of the complexities of the varied maritime asymmetric challenges and threats, these complexities have increased.

Cumulative social & civic conflicts over a long time had been festering in the littoral domains. There have been spates of communal, caste and ethnic conflicts and tensions that have often erupted into crisis proportions. These tensions have often affected governance and situations of social chaos have often been prevalent in the littorals.

Continued smuggling and infiltration of light and weapons, narcotics has been a phenomenon of the littoral regions. Smugglers, pirates, terrorists and insurgents have always been able to operate seamlessly in these regions. In the earlier periods, the thriving of smugglers and insurgents had been possible due to the heightened activities of the pirates who have used the littorals and the sea to exploit the maritime trade and shipping. In the present context, one could see new conflations of piracy and terrorism and the linkages between smugglers of humans, weapons and narcotics having close operational links with terrorists and pirates. Piracy and terrorism has been able to thrive on a political economy of smuggling. The 1998 Mumbai blasts and the numerous instances of infiltration have all relied on these illegitimate vehicles and felony.

---

[28] Vijay Sakhuja, *Chaos in the Littorals: An Overview of South Asia in Swati Parashar Maritime Counter Terrorism: A Pan Asian Perspective*, (New Delhi: Observer Research Foundation, 2008)

"Reign of anarchy" armed gangs and the crime syndicates in the littorals have been the persistent trends even with the increasing span of state governance in the regions. Even as the state battles the piracy and maritime terrorism and the groups with maritime capabilities, there remains the "unholy nexus" between the corrupt politicians, the crime syndicates and their activities. Empirical evidence shows that increasing linkages between the criminals and politicians have often been strong with strong economic support to party candidates during elections in return for the "blind eye" towards their nefarious activities. The "reign of anarchy" has been ably supported by the active connivance of several shady political and social elites with highly polemical involvement[29].

Littorals are thus the loci of porous territory; decreasing effect of governance; cumulative social & civic conflicts and the continued smuggling and infiltration of light and weapons, narcotics, armed gangs and the crime syndicates. The often argued factor of "violence at Sea" has always had an inevitable littoral access without which no violence in the sea could be possible. Therefore the contexts of addressing the cumulative violence of piracy, maritime terrorism, insurgency, smuggling that could all be addressed as Maritime Low Intensity Conflicts have their onshore access and established networks that exploits the maritime commons for violent means.

While various conceptual and operational frameworks on counterterrorism have been proposed to combat and contain "violence at sea", there has been no rationale of using these to address the littoral interface in this critical challenge and peril. Critical to the issue of combating and containing "violence at sea" is the imperative for a viable and robust "Maritime Domain Awareness" and the "Awareness of the Craft / Container" –both material and human contents of ships calling to ports and those in continuous transit or those who employ Crafts of Opportunity (CooP) to infiltrate and beach in the coasts. Maintaining sustained domain awareness is complex, given the opacity of the seas, the vastness of the terrain and the immense difficulties of the defenders to spot the intruders. An iron-clad regime of maritime counter-asymmetric operations is a hugely complex task. Such operations would hamper the freedom of the seas as well as the freedom of trade.

---

[29] Peter Lehr, *Violence at Sea: Piracy in the Age of Global Terrorism* (New York: Routledge, 2007)

It is an evident fact that the economic opportunity of trade in the globalization and post-globalization phases in the developing world has produced the polarised sections of littoral populations of the affluent and the desperately poor. Social and Economic human development profiles in the littorals have been either the noveau-rich or the poorest with severe deprivations. It is this huge disparity that has emerged as the levitating point of exploitation by the criminal syndicates and the gangs that have used social and economic discontent to their advantage.

The locus of solution to this problem therefore lies in investing in the littoral populations who are the primary stakeholders of the littoral-maritime commons

The primary argument is that there is the critical need to secure the maritime-littoral from the threats and challenges. It could be better addressed when the contradictions of social and economic disparity and are directly proportionate to the level of social-economic development. Littoral regions lack in Human security and Human development, the development of these capacities could lead to better governance. Better governance is the prerequisite for better securing of the littorals.

The objective of Good Governance is vital with the comprehensive development of Human security that is the resultant of human rights, human dignity and human development. A comprehensive approach to tackle the asymmetric challenges and perils of the maritime-littoral regions could come from investing into Human development and winning their hearts and minds of the littoral populations going a long way to tackle the perilous threats and challenges.

The praxis of building security in the maritime-littorals could emerge from three responses: a) Governance and Security; b) Enhanced Domain Awareness and Responses; and c) Joint Operations.

Governance and Security: The most vital investment should be to address the human development paradigm that goes with good governance providing comprehensive security. Winning the hearts and minds of the poverty stricken coastal communities is highly important as they are the first stakeholders of the littoral maritime domain. Governance and

Development augurs for equitable growth, invests the role of the state in constructive purpose in the public space. This would be the best "human hedge" that would keep the terrorists out and integrate the communities for meaningful, sustainable and appropriate development. Good Governance and social economic development nurtures a vital stake of the citizenry they constitute the vital synergies as primary stakeholders in combating crime and terrorism.

Heavy handed security measures and draconian legislations have no appeal for a discontented populace. Human security from human development is the derivative of good governance yielding comprehensive security. Either countries in South Asia succeed in ushering the due and deserving social and economic development of these communities or it cedes their loyalties to terrorists, criminals and insurgents whose sway on them could be by exploiting their poverty and disenchantment;

Enhanced Domain Awareness and Responses: Asymmetric challenges and threats are better handled with proaction and robust domain awareness—not from constitutionally mandated structures that have no operational and tactical utility. In the learning curve of counter-asymmetric operations, the degree of success in such operations rests in the robust awareness and the effective translation of intelligence into action.[30] The fact is that there could be no actionable intelligence. The cry that there is no actionable intelligence is the most unprofessional admission of lapses and laxity and an escapist argument—No intelligence comes in a platter of accuracy.

Intelligence and its specific domain and theatre milieu do not await the lethargy of bureaucratic perception. Intelligence is tactical and extremely fungible and mutates into newer formidable threats in hyper momentum. Enhanced domain awareness and response is the linking of the sensor and the shooter that demands extreme agility that can come only from 'Jointness' of perception and response; involves all levels of respondents; civilian, military, intelligence and communities—it has to be a mailed fist not an open hand.

---

[30] Rajesh Basur et.al, "The 2008 Mumbai Terrorist Attacks: Strategic Fallout", *RSIS Monograph 17* (Singapore: S.Rajaratnam School of International Studies, 2009)

Joint Operations: In the age of highly coordinated asymmetric operations—"Jointness" is the strength & synergy of the terrorists, insurgents and the organized crime syndicates combining Stealth, Surprise, Speed, Initiative and Manoeuver (S3I&M) along with their state patron; that's how the LeT and the ISI ran the Mumbai operation 26/11. The imperative is to develop counter-intuit approaches in the operational response within the context of a joint operations approach.

Littoral-maritime operations demand a single maritime agency that coordinates the coastal and off shore security. In the case of India it demands the need for a Joint Forces command model evident in the Andaman & Nicobar Island Command with its adaptive linkages with civil machinery.

South Asia thus presents as a complex interdependent region with a security complex that draws in the adjoining regions into its ambit of the several ongoing conflicts. The maritime domain provides the feasible means by which arms, explosives, humans are smuggled across the borders and boundaries. The resolution of the insecurities could emerge from three points: One, the need for better regional cooperation framework to combat the non-traditional and transnational challenges; two, the need for interregional protocols to combat piracy, arms and drugs smuggling; three, the importance to enhance security measures that combat these threats that is combined with human security and human development. In the case of the first issues of regional cooperation framework, the challenges lie with how SAARC and other regional agencies would have to invigorated to specific responses to these challenges and threats, it also involves immense political will to contend these challenges since the sources of these challenges and threats are both within the region and beyond the region sometimes the trans-regional and the global theatres.

These conflicts pit the state actors against the various violent non-state actors that are aggressive to gain control over states and regions. The second challenge has been the need for interregional protocols to combat the various challenges. The drafting and implementing the interregional protocols have also been fraught with complications within South Asia. Although exceptions have been with regard to some cases, one of the major reasons of the lack of the interregional protocols has been the absence of the maritime demarcation among the states in South Asia and that essentially withheld the prospects of interregional understanding to combat these challenges. The importance of individual national security measures are the most logical steps to securing the country boundaries and often South Asian states have shored up their respective national boundaries viz: land and maritime boundaries more effectively than with the regional cooperation.

South Asia would continue to trudge along the paths of maritime insecurity as the states are inherently prone to their own efforts of security rather than to dedicated regional efforts. The crucial linkage between developing human security and human development as the fulcrum to build security especially coastal security has not yet been evolved in the policies of all the South Asian states. There has always been an overwhelming weight given to hard security measures and the failure in the development of viable linkages between physical security, human security and good governance. This failure would have important consequences to South Asia even as it trudges with land conflicts that have vital maritime connections.

Contributors

Brig. K. Srinivasan (Retd) is a graduate of Defence Services Staff College and College of Defence Management, during his active army career of 35 years, participated in 1965 and 1971 wars and in counter insurgency operations in Jammu & Kashmir and has held several important command, instructional and planning assignments. At Centre for Security Analysis (CSA), he guides and supervises the work of research fellows. His area of work includes, conflict resolution & peace building, terrorism, water security, disaster management and role of civil society in conflict situations. He has been an active member of the working group on Disaster Management and Water Security convened by Strategic Studies Network set up by National Defense Univeristy, Washington, DC and Stimson Centre working group on Indus water.

Dr Sudha Ramachandran is an independent researcher/journalist based in Bangalore. She writes on South Asian politics and security issues. She has a doctoral degree from Jawaharlal Nehru University, New Delhi. She was Assistant Editor at Deccan Herald (Bangalore) for five years. Dr Ramachandran has been freelancing since 2001 and contributes articles regularly to publications like Asia Times Online. She has reported on internal conflicts from Kashmir, Sri Lanka, Fiji and Northern Ireland, as well as on India's Maoists. She is a visiting lecturer at the Asian College of Journalism, Chennai and at Kulturstudier's (Oslo) Peace and Conflict program at Puducherry.

Prof P Sahadevan is Professor of South Asian Studies, JNU. Before joining

JNU, Sahadevan was Project Officer at the Rajiv Gandhi Institute for Contemporary Studies, The Rajiv Gandhi Foundation, New Delhi and also a researcher at the Institute for Defence Studies and Analyses (IDSA), New Delhi. While focusing primarily on various aspects of Sri Lanka, Sahadevan has worked on ethnic conflicts and problems of peace in South Asia. In addition, he has strong interest in the areas of terrorism, political violence and civil war; conflict resolution (both theory and South Asian cases); India's foreign policy (with special reference to South Asia), and Indian diaspora.

Dr Geeta Madhavan is an Attorney with specialisation in International Law and a consultant to academic departments that feature International Relations programmes. She is Visiting Faculty of Tamil Nadu Dr. Ambedkar Law University. She holds a PhD with doctoral thesis on Terrorism in International law. Her areas of interest include international security and terrorism and has published several articles on issues of strategic security matters. She is a Founder Member of Centre for Security Analysis. She is an active member of Working Group set up by Strategic Studies Network (SSN) of National Defence University, Washington DC.

Dr.W.Lawrence S.Prabhakar is Associate Professor in the Department of Political Science Madras Christian College, Chennai, India. He is Visiting Professor, Department of Geopolitics, Manipal University, Manipal and Member of the Constituting Committee and Board of Research and Studies of the department Manipal University, Manipal, India. Dr Prabhakar specializes in academic and policy research on the following areas: Nuclear Missile issues in Southern Asia; on Maritime Security issues in the Indian Ocean and the Asia-Pacific Region, Grand Strategy of China and on research in India-United States Strategic Relations; Grand Strategy of India. He is Founder Member of Centre for Security Analysis. He is an active member of Working Group set up by Strategic Studies Network (SSN) of National Defence University, Washington DC.

Appendix

Books Published under the Project "Internal Conflicts and Transnational Consequences"

1. Internal Conflicts in Myanmar: Transnational Consequences

2. Internal Conflicts in Nepal: Transnational Consequences

3. The Naxal Threat: Causes, State Responses and Consequences

4. Conflict in Sri Lanka: Internal and External Consequences

5. Conflicts in North-East: Internal and External Effects

6. Conflict in Jammu and Kashmir: Impact on Polity, Society and Economy

7. Post Conflict Sri Lanka- Rebuilding of the Society

8. Internal Conflicts: Military Perspectives

9. Internal Conflicts: A Four State Analysis

10. Nepal as a Federal State: Lessons from the Indian Experience

11. Consequences of Longterm Conflicts in Northeast India

Other Books

Conflict Resolution and Peace Building

12. Conflict Resolution and Peace Building in Sri Lanka

13. Federalism and Conflict Resolution in Sri Lanka

14. Peace Process in Sri Lanka: Challenges & Opportunities

15. Conflict over Fisheries in the Palk Bay Region

Post 9/11: New Research Agenda?; The US and India: Divergent and Convergent Interests

3. Conflict Prevention and Peace Building

4. Indo-Japan Relations; Independent Police Complaints Commission; Brief on the Seminar on Security Dimensions of Peninsular India

5. Proceedings of the Seminar on Proliferation Security Initiative

6. Proceedings of the Seminar on Women and Legal Security

7. Political Islam: Image and Reality; UK and India on the World Stage

8. Proceedings of the Seminar on Women and Comprehensive Security

9. Global Nuclear Weapon Prospects; India-Pakistan Peace Process Dividends

10. Security Perspectives from Pakistan; Indo-US Relations: Changing Perceptions

11. Sri Lankan Peace Process: Current Status; Sri Lanka Today: Policy Challenges and Dilemmas

12. Religion, Civil Society & Governance

13. Politics of the Nuclear Deal and the US-India Relations

14. India –US Relations; Japan India Partnership in the New Asian Strategic Dynamism

15. Environmental Security; National and International Security in the Context of Globalization and Economic Prosperity; India, East and Southeast Asia: Security Dimensions

16. India-EU Relations

17. India-Japan Strategic Partnership; India-UK Economic and Business Partnership.

18. Right to Information

19. A Sustainable Future: India and Britain Working Together; India and Africa: Issues of Globalization and Development

20. New Initiatives in Nuclear Disarmament; Preventing Nuclear Proliferation and Nuclear Terrorism; Nuclear Fuel Supply Assurances

21. The Economic Cost of the War in Sri Lanka; Peace Process in Sri Lanka; The Sri Lankan Diaspora: The Way Forward

22. Nuclear Deterrence and Disarmament

23. Naxalism: Threat to Internal Security; Ethno-Political Situation in India's Northeast.

24. Japan and Asian Security; India as a Superpower.

25. India's Water Relations with her Neighbours

www.ingramcontent.com/pod-product-compliance
Lightning Source LLC
Chambersburg PA
CBHW031416270326
41929CB00010BA/1473